MW01093768

101 NEVADA COLUMNS

To Mike Taylor, with Thanks
for your interview Help

Rollan Melton
7-26-01

101 NEVADA COLUMNS

ROLLAN MELTON

NEVADA HUMANITIES COMMITTEE

Publication of this book was made possible by a grant from Marilyn's "egg fund" in honor of the author's 70th birthday.

All photographs in this book are used courtesy of the *Reno Gazette-Journal* with the exception of the following:
Elmo Derrico: Elmo Derrico, Page 180.
Don Dondero: Mapes Hotel, Page 228; Clark Gable, Marilyn Monroe, Gloria and Charles Mapes, Page 234.
Moya Olsen Lear: Lillian Olsen, Page 144.
Melton Family: George Bush, Page 20; Rollan Melton, Page 64; Rollan, Rusty and Bronna Melton, Page 69; Rollan and Bronna Melton, Page 71; Marilyn Melton, Page 99; Rollan Melton Sr., Archie Moore, Page 236.
Richard Rowley: Sonny Rowley, Page 168.
University of Nevada, Reno Department of Intercollegiate Athletics: Marion Motley, Page 193.
U.S. Department of the Navy, Naval Historical Center: Sullivan Brothers, Page 164.

Cover photograph: Jeff Ross Photography, Reno, Nevada

ISBN 1-890591-11-4

A Halcyon Imprint of the
NEVADA HUMANITIES COMMITTEE
P.O. Box 8029
Reno, Nevada 89507

To my readers, to whom I am indebted in thousands of ways for opening their minds, hearts and experiences to me.

Contents

Foreword

THE FIRST THING you notice about Rollan Melton is that he *listens*. Talk with Rollie, even in a crowd, and you feel like the only other person in the room.

He smiles, asks a casual question or two, then offers exclusive attention while you talk. Whether you're an old friend, new acquaintance, celebrity or a waitress serving finger foods at a party, Rollie's friendly manner is the same. Even if you've never seen him before—don't know he writes a newspaper column— you get the feeling he's listening. He cares. You discover you want to tell this man your story. Minutes later, you're telling it. All of it.

Some stories find their way into Rollan Melton's column in the *Reno Gazette-Journal*. Every week, hundreds of news tidbits and confidences pour into his office mailbox and into his sympathetic ears. He reads, listens, checks facts and asks for more. Then he sits down at his computer and writes from the heart. Never a scandal-monger, Rollie won't repeat unfounded rumors or vicious accusations. He writes mostly about everyday people and events, introducing us to a revered teacher, a war hero, a successful graduate or a daring female bootblack. From time to time, a celebrity name creeps into the column, but most of his stories focus on the comedies, tragedies and successes of local residents and their families.

Sometimes he mourns a departed friend. At a memorial service for Robert Laxalt, Nevada's literary legend, Rollie's eulogy for the author brought him so many requests for copies that he submitted his words as a column in the *Reno Gazette-Journal*.

On rare occasions he'll write about himself. When Rollie and his wife, Marilyn—along with a few hardy friends—climbed Mount Rose to celebrate his 60th birthday, he told his readers all about it in a column dated July 30, 1991. Published beneath a smiling photo of Meltons at the summit (10,775 feet), that column revealed some of the obstacles that might have prevented such a climb.

Blaming himself for bad habits in his younger days, Rollie lists the consequences resulting from "poor nutrition . . . a sedentary life . . . my growing sloth . . . (and) smoking." After a heart attack at 50, a later bout with lymphatic cancer, two cataract surgeries, a hernia repair and a coronary fibrillation scare, Rollie made up his mind to do something about his health. For starters, he quit smoking.

Eighteen months after signing up for a hospital weight-management program, and after making daily exercise a routine, Rollie had lost 72 pounds and was impressing his cardiologist with his stamina on the treadmill. Along the way, he had told his readers stories about other dieters—including Bertha the Elephant, and a dog named Otto. Rollie was ready to climb Mount Rose.

You'll find 101 such stories in this collection of columns selected from hundreds more that Rollan Melton has written during the 14 years since 1987. The following year, the University of Nevada Press published *Nevadans*, an earlier volume of columns covering the first decade of his column: 1978-87.

What you won't find in Rollie's columns is anything mean-spirited, cruel or sensational. That doesn't mean he's never angry. He can lash out at anyone or anything he considers a threat to his beloved state and city. When he sees injustice, Rollie holds back nothing to express his indignation.

Most of Rollie's columns reflect his innate kindness. That characteristic defines Rollan Melton for people who work with him. During the years when we were coworkers in the *Gazette-Journal* newsroom, I saw that kindness every day: kindness to other staffers, to visitors, to the people he wrote about. The door of his office was always open to anyone who dropped by—usually to ask his advice. Often, he'd plan little luncheon parties to celebrate somebody's big story, or promotion or retirement.

Rollie is especially kind to young reporters. Old ones, too. Soon after I was hired to write for the Lifestyle section, I discovered that Rollie and I had at least one thing in common—July birthdays. My birth year was considerably earlier than his, but he never made me feel like a geriatric case. I was simply a colleague.

Before long, I discovered another common bond. Each of us thought we had invented the early-morning work routine. (How peaceful it was to start writing before phones began to jangle; before pressures of the day could interrupt a train of thought!) If I entered the empty newsroom at 5:30 or 6 a.m.—in the days before Rollie switched to a computer—I'd hear the tappity-tap of his typewriter.

Sometimes we'd meet at the office coffeepot and talk for a few minutes. Now that I've retired, we no longer chat over coffee. But I keep track of Rollie through his column. He keeps on telling stories. Above all, he keeps on listening.

Barbara Land
Nevada Writers Hall of Fame inductee

Author's Note

As WITH MY FIRST column collection, *Nevadans*, the person at the forefront pushing forward this book project was my wife, Marilyn. Truly my better half, she galvanized me into action, pressing me to cull a set of worthy selections from the nearly 2,000 columns that accumulated since *Nevadans* was published in 1988. Then she participated very strongly in recruiting the cast of players for the publishing team that would bring this project to life as a book.

I agreed wholly with Marilyn's assessment that now was the time for a second book of columns. In fact, I believed the passage of 13 years made this book long overdue. I was eager to create a permanent record for Nevadans of this time we live in. And that is part of what a book such as this can contribute.

I tend to look ahead 100 years. Consider readers in 2101, reading about the late 20th and early 21st centuries. These columns covering our neighbors great and humble, their lives and hopes, triumphs, tragedies and comedies, will help Nevadans of the future understand what we were like, how we dressed, spoke and felt, what motivated us, what turned us off. I'm writing for a contemporary audience, but for the history books, too. Newspaper stories are supposed to be disposable, but they also are written for posterity, because journalists write the first draft of history, as the saying goes.

NEVADA HAS CHANGED SINCE *Nevadans* was published. There are a lot more of us, and we are a lot more ethnically diverse. That affords me, the columnist, a lot more opportunity to talk about different cultures, and places around the globe Nevadans have come from. As with all my sources, I seek them out to talk to me and tell me their stories to convey to our fellow Nevadans. I work all the time to have my column adequately reflect the richness of our changing population.

Sometimes we look back on the past as the pioneer days, when newcomers forged a state in the wilderness. But, really, these still are the pioneer days. We're still shaping this land we know as Nevada. But for all our different roots, backgrounds and histories, we join together in a unique place. The hallmark of Nevadans old and new is independence. The drive to do one's own thing as long as it doesn't harm others. The spirit of the West, so to speak. But if there is a new wrinkle to the old embrace of real freedom, it is that a large influx of people of different origins chases away the insular redneckism that can develop in a population that is not racially or ethnically mixed. Diversity helps erase this negative we Nevadans have sometimes been branded with. The more we can chase that away, the better!

My column is intended to give readers a better understanding of who lives here, what we're all about, what we think, how we think, how we arrive at the decision to live in Nevada. Certain themes recur. Over and over, longtime Nevadans hear from more recent arrivals how they couldn't stand it when they first moved here, with the landscape bleak amid a sea of sagebrush. But after three years or five years, we'll hear: "Now I love it." And, "I wouldn't give up being a Nevadan for anything!" By now, the sagebrush has stirred around in them, and they realize there was a reason—perhaps only faintly acknowledged or understood before—why they came here in the first place.

IN 1978, AND IN all the days, weeks, months and years since I wrote my first column, I never thought it would be a good idea for me to be the grand old man of keyhole journalism, to be the Walter Winchell of Nevada. To purvey gossip and hyperbole, sensationalize the news and otherwise present a false image of the place we live, the way a controversy-seeking columnist would romanticize it to be or wish it to be—or would love to attack it as being. Today's media are far too accustomed to trash talking, to accentuating the negative, to sounding the dramatic or discordant notes. I've never wanted any part of it. I like the good guy/girl stories because there are a lot more good stories and good people out there than there are the negative, nay-saying, ne'er-do-wells.

My idea has been that someone ought to hold up a mirror to our true public, and honestly say, "This is how our Nevada really looks like." That has and remains my column's aim. That's why I've shown little interest in writing about celebrities and other names in the news. I've found it much more refreshing to interview someone who does not talk in sound bites—as if a microphone were right in front of his or her face—but who talks real talk.

These are the most exciting, enlightening and wonderful people to interview because they're not artificial. They're real. They're Nevadans.

I learn from everybody I come in contact with. It's a side benefit of being a columnist. And there's no place I'd ever have wanted to be a columnist, than right here.

MARILYN'S REASONING THAT THE time was right for another book of columns also tied into the fact that I faced a personal milestone in July 2001. On the 24th I would turn 70. That's a notable birthday in anyone's life. The notion of retiring at 65 is fading fast in America. But it hasn't fallen away for me—I've never thought about retirement! I intend to work until the day I no longer can. I work because I love to, and can think of no better job than the one I've held the past 23 years.

After I underwent open-heart surgery last year, I was more determined than ever to stabilize my health, and for many reasons, including the fact that I love to write my column. I love to profile Nevadans, talk with them, look in their eyes, and say, "Whadya think? Talk to me, and let me listen." A large part of my self-identity is my column. It keeps me going from deadline to deadline. It's good medicine.

A positive attitude, too, is among the best medicines. After my heart attack in 1982, four years after beginning my column, I didn't believe that I was finished. With the wonders of medical science, and my own resolve to keep going, I have been fortunate to produce some 4,000 columns, which computes to somewhere on the order of 3 million words.

I wrote at the beginning of the previous collection that the Nevadans who have shared their words, wit and wisdom with me had made my column-writing the happiest period of my happy newspaper life. In fact, that decade of penning the column was a period twice as a long as any position I'd held in my newspaper career.

Marilyn declared that I had finally found steady work. That was 13 years ago. Today, I am happy to say that this phase of my career continues—an extended honeymoon with the people I love. Nevadans.

*Acknowledgments*_____

A CONCERTED EFFORT is required to put out a newspaper, and every man or woman who enjoys a byline over a published story is indebted to the small army of people who work behind the scenes or orchestrate the entire operation. I am beholden to the executive editors who've permitted me to put my name to a regular column in the *Reno Gazette-Journal* since 1978, and to the other newsroom editors who've scoured my sentences before they've reached print, and my fellow writers who've supported and inspired and kept me informed, and the newsroom librarians whose research and help have proved invaluable, and the people in the production side—all of whom are too numerous to mention here by name.

I'll always be grateful to those who gave me my start in writing and journalism and nurtured me along the way—teachers, mentors, bosses and friends, from high school on. To name only a few would be to leave out many.

I will cite my longtime administrative assistant, Mickey Wessel, who for years retyped my typewritten columns into the computer and performed other vital secretarial tasks. Mickey retired in 1999—but continues to archive in scrapbooks the clippings of my column, making the effort of assembling a collection of columns immeasurably easier than it would have been poring over 2,000 dim images on microfilm, or digging through musty envelopes or yellowed, ancient stacks of newsprint on dark, dusty shelves somewhere in the nether regions of our newspaper building.

Sandi Sei succeeded Mickey, and fulfills the essential role of helping me maintain a degree of isolation in which to compose my column, amid the constant stream of phone calls, faxes, snail mail, e-mail and drop-in visits to my office from friends, loyal readers or people seeking publicity for some item or other. Sandi

xix

safeguards me from unexpected intrusions.

Mike Sion, author and superlative doctor of manuscripts with an unerring sense of order and continuity, has been an indispensable force as editor in the important business of bringing this book to fruition. I am indebted to the prolific Nevada writer, book author and editor Barbara Land for the nice things she said about me in the foreword. I called upon Mike and Barbara to write the introduction and foreword, respectively, because I trust their expertise and sense of doing the right thing, of calling a spade a spade.

Nancy Peppin has had the task of being this book's designer, and is a very appealing colleague to work with, bringing her vast experience with Nevada books, and adding a great deal to the quality of this book.

Jeannie Rasmussen, *Gazette-Journal* librarian, was exceedingly helpful in the gathering of numerous photographs for this book, with a smile.

*Introduction*_____

"DID YOU SEE Rollie's column this morning?"

If it's Sunday morning in the Truckee Meadows, someone somewhere is probably saying those words. Rollie Melton's column in the *Reno Gazette-Journal*, after all, is an institution. But it is much more than that.

In his foreword to Rollie's first collection of columns, *Nevadans*, Robert Laxalt began with these words: "What author Rollan Melton has managed to craft in this book is a mosaic of the personality, character and attitudes of the true Nevadan—whether by birth or by choice." Eighteen paragraphs later, Laxalt—the Silver State's foremost novelist—concluded: "What he forgot to say was that through his writings, he has become the man who captured the old heart of Nevada before it was gone forever."

Thirteen years later, the fastest-growing state in the Union has more than 2 million residents, about double that of the year Rollie's *Nevadans* was published, 1988, and approximately triple the year he began typing his column: 1978. As for Washoe County, Rollie's territorial beat, our population, too, is twice that of the year he left the hierarchy of Gannett, Inc., to hunker three times a week before his Underwood manual and pound out column inches peopled with the solid citizens and notable, quotable Nevadans whom he so dearly loves.

Everything eventually changes. Ten years ago, Rollie even retired his Underwood and joined the civilized world in front of a computer. But as Herb Caen was to the burgeoning Baghdad by the Bay, so Rollie (what all who know him call him; no need for a last name) remains to the Biggest Little City. Reno and Sparks may have mushroomed in size, subdivisions ceaselessly sprouting and filling in the flat ranchland and crawling up the foothills in all four directions. Starbucks, Barnes & Noble and SUVs occupy terrain once ruled by greasy spoons, feed stores and pickups. But to all the native Nevadans, born-again Nevadans and more recent transplants who've set down secure roots—to all these sagebrush-in-the-soul denizens whom Laxalt referred to as true Nevadans "by birth or by choice"—the four-beat phrase "Rollie's column" is embedded in everyday speech.

"Hey, did you see Rollie's column?" "I saw your name in Rollie's column." Or, "I gotta call Rollie and tell him about this!" There is no better evidence of his unquestionable popularity than these ubiquitous utterances. True journalism is just as the word's root implies—the noting of the daily goings-on of a community. And Rollie's column reflects the true lives of his readers. Not the big headline-grabbing crimes, the flavor-of-the-week political squabbles, the Pressing Issue of the Month that the Deep Thinkers proclaim is facing us. Rather, Rollie's column covers the constant currents in the human sea here in the shadow of the Carson:

• A young female entrepreneur breaking into the shoeshine business—and busting a gender barrier: "Defying a trend that's seen shoeshine operations do less than polished business, (Aileen) Martin has customers lined up four deep at times at Reno Cannon International Airport, waiting for her patented brand of happy talk, humor and a shine you can almost see your reflection in."

• A latter-day, vacant Mapes Hotel, *cause celebre* of preservationists who recalled her glory: "It was a place where Somebodies and Nobodies collided in harmony, where East met real cowboys, without turning up its eastern nose. . . . the Mapes Sky Room was made for lovers, for stargazers, for dancers and showgoers, who could watch the world's best entertainers in the intimate showroom. . . . a sort of social downtown home away from home."

• The hospital aftermath of a Cessna crash that claimed a Nevada woman's life and badly injured others, including her long-time husband, who was running for state treasurer. They had spent the day before on horseback. "It was a picture postcard day, with our cloudless September sky, and a little early temperature nip that hinted the nearness of autumn. . . . They went to a place they loved to ride, on the beach along Big Washoe Lake. Judy was up on See, her favorite animal, and Bob Seale aboard his gelding, Twister.

"They had a day to savor as outdoorsmen. As a team. Being together. Living for the moment. Until tomorrow came."

Rollie is not our poet, but our chronicler. He eschews pretense and pizzazz, opting instead for plain, craftsman-like prose. He has, after all, real printer's ink in his veins. After bouncing around, living with different relatives and attending 18 schools in three states, a 14-year-old "Sonny" wound up with his single mother in Fallon, fell under the mentorship of the high school's football coach and inadvertently started his newspaper career as an apprentice "printer's devil" for the weekly *Fallon Standard*. From there to majoring in journalism at the University of Nevada, a column on the student *Sagebrush*, sports editor and columnist at the old *Reno Evening Gazette*, publisher by 35 and—after the giant Gannett, Inc., bought and merged Reno's sister papers—rising to the corporation's posts of senior vice president and director.

But the early dream of column-writing ultimately prevailed. At 47, Rollie retired from the executive ranks to pound the keyboard again, permanently. And he continues to crank out his columns after weathering the latest in a series of health hazards arising from the beating his innards inevitably took in a life of newspapering, sacrificing his physical wellbeing to the gods of Deadline and, later, Bottom Line.

As Rollie wrote in a column among the 88 in his previous collection, a literal pain in his neck before his 51st birthday turned out to be angina and harbinger of a heart attack. That brought about a self-described "disappearing act" of 16 weeks before Rollie's column again graced the pages of the *Gazette*. Fast-forward 18 years. For months Rollie had hoisted himself from bed to hit his office at the *Gazette* by 3 or 4 a.m., to toil for four or five hours writing the narrative of his autobiography, *Sonny's Story*. Then he'd switch to his regular column chores. Cap that off with a marathon of writing extra columns to run while he would be on vacation in England—and he nearly wrote himself to death. After a 16-hour trip to the British Isles, Rollie's 68-year-old kidneys and heart failed and he was hospitalized in London, then flown home to Reno for an extended stay at Saint Mary's.

Rollie's subsequent "disappearing act" from his newspaper's

pages extended for four months. Then, once a week, his column resumed. And then there was *another* vanishing stunt of four months, for convalescence after open-heart surgery. But as of this writing, the surgery-scarred scribe is back to twice-a-week columns and gearing up to his old schedule of thrice-a-week, his once-bulky body forcibly kept below a weight of 178 pounds, his energy carefully budgeted for the task, his mug shot no longer full-faced, but lean. Yet still smiling.

What the late, beloved Bob Laxalt called "the old heart of Nevada" still beats. And one big reason it continues to thump here in the Truckee Meadows is because Rollie's own ticker still ticks, pumping blood to the venerable old journalist's fingers like the Truckee rushing renewed through its banks after a diminishing drought.

After Bob Laxalt passed on in March of this year, Rollie delivered a eulogy at the memorial service and reprinted it in his column. A few paragraphs earlier I wrote that Rollie opts for "plain, craftsman-like prose." Not always. In giving testament to Laxalt—"the high priest of Nevada authors"—Rollie the note-taker struck resonant chords with such lines as, "The writing office at his and Joyce's home seemed to be an intensive care unit for his Royal manual typewriter's malfunctioning margin releases. For the cantankerous carriage returns."

Who better to place our modern literary giant, Bob Laxalt, in perspective than our indispensable newsprint diarist, Rollie Melton? Who best to lay the legend to rest by concluding, "Robert Laxalt shall remain, to our own final days, the famous man whose presence and legacy blessed us"?

Hey, did you see Rollie's column?

If you missed it, or need to see it again—this collection gives you 101 selections. One hundred and one entries in a chronicle of our collective lives of the past 13 years.

Maybe your name's among them. If not, then certainly someone you know.

Michael Sion

THE COLUMNIST AT LARGE _____

Decades after Tragedy, Ring Returned

AFTER A HALF-CENTURY, my high school class ring is where it should be.

In winter 1949, there were but months left before our senior class would graduate from Churchill County High School. Yet, there was early excitement. Each of us visited Mary Foster's photo studio to get our picture taken in cap and gown.

Graduates-to-be ordered class rings at Dana Coffee's Jewelry Store. But I thought, "What the heck, I've never owned a ring. No need to get one now."

On the morning of Dec. 15, 1949, my dear friend, fellow senior Art Farrel, caught me between class. "A bunch of us are going ice-skating tonight at Rattlesnake Reservoir. Come go with us," he said.

I was working afternoons and evenings at the weekly *Fallon Standard*. So I replied thanks, but no thanks.

"Too bad," Art said. "We'll be going out in Dick Jeakins' 1935 Ford convertible. Swell time. Dick's brother, Bill (also in our senior class), will come along. Sure you can't go?"

"Can't, Art. Got to work. Catch you another time."

That night, as the skating part wound down, Karen Kelly, Dick Jeakins' date, lost her ring. In the blackness, broken only by the students' bonfire, a few skaters hung back in a fruitless search for the ring.

Finally, close to midnight, nine kids piled into Dick's convertible.

Jeakins, now 70 and living in a Reno north valley, has tried unsuccessfully for 50 years to wipe out what happened next. The country dirt road back to town was total ice. He had never driven the road. He didn't know of the hairpin curve ahead. .

The car hit ice and careened left off the road, flipped and landed upside-down in a drainage ditch.

After the terrible impact, Dick Jeakins made a roll call. Everyone answered except Art Farrel; Dick's younger brother, Bill; Edith Swenson, who had graduated from Fallon the prior June; and Byrl Searcy, a young sailor from the Fallon Navy base. The four were dead.

I learned of the tragedy the following morning, knowing that fate had spared me. The grief of losing two from our class, and our close friend Edith, overwhelmed school and community.

Several weeks later, jeweler Dana Coffee called. "Sonny (as I was then known), only one class ring hasn't been claimed. It was ordered by Bill Jeakins. His family apparently doesn't want it. Do you want to buy it?"

I told him yes. "Well, the ring has 'B.J.' engraved inside. We can sand that off and put your initials on it," Coffee said.

"No, Mr. Coffee, please leave it as it is."

It was a fitting memento by which to remember Bill Jeakins. He had transferred to Fallon from Gerlach for his senior year, was slender, blond, freckled and a real nice guy. He had turned 18 just 12 days before the accident.

I wore the ring intended for Bill Jeakins a couple of years at the University of Nevada, then put it aside to wear my Nevada class ring.

But in the ensuing years, through military and newspaper years, I knew precisely where the Fallon ring was.

Three weeks ago at the Churchill County Museum, I was signing my journalism memoir, *Sonny's Story*. A Fallon man asked me to inscribe his copy to him. I understood him to give his name as "Don Jenkins." I asked the spelling. He replied, "J-e-a-k-i-n-s."

"Are you related to the late Bill Jeakins of Fallon?"

"Yes, he was my cousin."

I told him the story of the ring. He promised to tell Bill's brothers, Dick and Ron, the latter who lives in Fernley. Two days later, Ron's wife, Sharon, phoned. "Could we buy the ring from you?"

"It belongs in Bill's family. I'm giving it to you."

4

When Shayne Alford James Jeakins, age 1, of Fernley, grows up, he will have the ring intended for his great uncle, William Edward Jeakins Jr.

Jan. 9, 2000

Ah, Yes, I Remember It Well _____

THIS WEEKEND, I attended my Churchill County High School class reunion (1950), along with alumni from five other classes of the period. Some didn't attend. For instance, Los Angeles artist John Mason.

He wrote in, "It may seem strange, but I am happy to leave that school experience, uncluttered by new realities."

Colleen Barton Chapman, Class of '50, was as handsome as 48 years ago, when I worshiped her from afar. Alas, I had been timid and kept my distance.

At Friday's opening reception, I spied Colleen and edged up to her, awaiting kind words and perhaps a peck on the cheek. "Hi, Colleen! Welcome home to Fallon," I greeted her.

"I'm Rollan Melton."

Colleen's eyes glazed, as though she had collided head-on into a sour memory.

Surely, the 1950 belle of the ball was joking. I stood there, ravenous for recognition. A long time passed (probably a few seconds), and I sensed she was straining to remember.

At last, she looked at me squarely and confessed, "I don't know you. Which high school did you go to?"

Plunging on in quest of remembrance, if not unadulterated acceptance, I kept trying to track down a hospitable, able-memoried soul.

At last, I spied a long-ago buddy. Back in 1947, when we were football teammates, Joe Bell was a hellishly strong lineman. He had a mean streak that began with the opening kickoff and only cooled after the finish.

He reminded me then of a young bull, exploding from a Fallon chute, pulverizing all hapless critters who got in his way.

Anyway, on this Saturday, at an open house at old Oats Park Grammar School, out front in the hot sun stood Joe Bell, smiling underneath his Stetson, talking to past football cronies, including Basil Cislini, John Sharrah, Pete Solaegui, Don Fister and the toughest '47 running back/hombre, Frank "Soup" Souza.

Cool Joe Bell wore dark glasses and tidy Western trousers and boots. I walked over to him, greeted him and told him my name, although I realized that wasn't necessary. Joe had always struck me as having an agile memory for deeds, misdeeds and identities of the souls in his life.

He studied my features, which he hadn't seen in 50 years. His smooth forehead wrinkled in a slick imitation of that beat-up old washboard my mother had used for laundering.

"Oh yeah," said Joe Bell. "Milton, right? Lemme see, did we have Spanish together under teacher Hattie Brown? Or was it English, under Anne Gibbs (Berlin)?" I knew Joe was faking, just spoofing. He must be on the verge of recalling my football exploits.

"Joe, I'll not forget those days, playing for Wes Goodner, and with our teammates, Gene Akins, Freddie Hicks, Don Fister, Windy Howard, Jim Dalbey, Chuck Renfro."

"Yeah," said Cowboy Joe. "I remember. But it's a little hot out here." He took off the Stetson and dabbed at his brow, which looked like a cross between a corrugated roof and that washboard.

I could feel Joe Bell's eyes, roaming 'round historical curves and coming up with zero.

"You were Roland Milton." His voice trailed off, lost in the dust of 50 years.

"I still am Rollan Melton," I said, wearily.

"Joe, where you been living?" I asked, trying to inject life into our comatose exchange, before verbal rigor mortis set in.

He replied, "Carson City. Been there quite a long time."

"Good, Joe. Do you read the newspapers over that way?" I asked.

"Yeah, the *Nevada Appeal* and sometimes the *Gazette-Journal*."

I waited for him to continue, and unfortunately he did.

"Well, Roland, tell me. What have you been doing for a living all these years?"

Sept. 21, 1998

Advice Can Be Silent but Deadly _____

RECENTLY, MY PHOTOGRAPHER FRIEND Don Dondero joined me on a drive to Fort Churchill, where I was to speak to 499 teenagers. They came from around Nevada for the annual Association for Student Councils conference.

It was an august group from 65 Nevada high schools. Each of the 499 is an officer of his or her class or of a student body.

I did advance homework, wanting to give the kids a jazzy pep talk about life beyond high school.

A week earlier, the conference coordinator assured me he would arrange a waist-high lectern on which I could place my speech outline.

Everything, except the tiny office and the restrooms, is outdoors at the outpost where the U.S. Army was billeted after the bloody Pyramid Lake War of 1860.

Given the outdoor venue, I also had requested an amplified microphone. "Certainly," the coordinator had assured me.

Dondero inquired, "Are you ready to dazzle the young multitudes?" I replied that I would try my best.

As students piled from their buses and squatted on an elongated grassy area outside the visitors' hut, I hunted hard for the requested amenities.

The coordinator never came. There was no lectern for my notes, although a security guy offered to fetch a sawed-off box that I could use as a makeshift podium.

The box was about as high as an Army footlocker, and would have been perfect were I still a 3-year-old, standing 2-foot-7.

In earlier years, I had amateur theater acting experience and it has prepared me for the unknown. Was I ready in any event? Yes, of course.

A young man got the microphone in place before I was to

8

be introduced. I had worked up an outline from which to give remarks, writing it just that morning. So, the contents and sequence of delivery were fresh in my mind.

Now, I was set to be introduced by a student.

Then a brisk wind kicked up, whistling hard off the mountains directly west of us. The students, some wearing only walking shorts, shucked off the chill. I overheard one joke about wearing goose bumps atop his goose bumps.

I hoisted my collar snug to my neck. Ignoring the arrival of cold, I stood ready to deliver words that I was fairly sure would keep the listeners awake.

Moments prior to the introduction, a male student waltzed past me and tripped on the wire bringing power to the microphone. Three conscientious young men pounced on the injured cord.

I fidgeted. They fussed and cussed. Finally a boy, who appeared to be in charge, shivered up to me. He delivered the grim word. "Sorry, no sound. Can't figure out how to fix it. You'll have to wing it. Better speak loudly."

The outdoor area where the kids sprawled was shaped vertically. Clearly, I must virtually shout to be heard in the rear.

I stood there confidently facing 499 student officers. Just before I began to speak, I saw Don Dondero way in the back, aiming his telephoto lens.

He was set. So was I. There, amid the chill, the wind, the glorious Nevada rural outdoors, I poured it to 'em. "Welcome to a part of our glorious state that most of you are looking at for the first time. . . ."

I gave the words as much polish as one can muster, when he's cold, is trying to warm an impatient audience and hasn't a lectern or a workable mike to his name.

Things seemed to click. At least, I saw not a single dozing student.

The kids seemed delighted when I cut remarks to four minutes to avoid frostbite. They broke into a spasm of applause as I retreated.

I quickly sought out Dondero, shamelessly soliciting kind words.

"Did it sound all right, Don?"

"Rollan, I've heard you speak many times and believe me, today you were at your most eloquent!"

"Wow! Thanks, Don."

"No problem," Dondero said. "I didn't hear a single word you said. Neither did anyone else."

May 12, 1997

Our Man Almost Reveals All _____

When I am going to be at a head table, or on a stage in front of a lot of people for any length of time, I go sparingly on liquid intake. Further, if I am to be a visible part of a program that takes me up in front of people, I always skedaddle to the men's room at least once. Sometimes twice.

I once learned the hard way that I need to carefully plan, lest nature summon me at an inopportune time. On that occasion, I was seized with the urgent need to go to the bathroom, just before I was introduced as the speaker. I wanted to glare at the gawkers and say, 'Wait 'til I get back from the men's room!"

I then resisted the impulse. Instead, I rushed my delivery, giving my all-time shortest speech, much to the joy of an audience that expected to be bored by length, as well as content.

I finished talking and then almost knocked people down as I sprinted toward relief.

Two weeks ago, my wife, Marilyn, and I were roasted/toasted at a black tie-optional dinner put on by United Cerebral Palsy to raise funds. Understandably, Marilyn got out of the deal with nothing but praise. But the roasters had a jolly time, carving me into itsy-bitsy pieces.

Taking care to properly assault me were John Tyson, Tad Dunbar, David B. Finley and, especially, Cory Farley and Bill Raggio, each of whom appeared bearing a verbal stiletto.

But each roaster was a charmer, compared to what happened to me before the formal program began.

During dinner, Marilyn and I were seated on the Harrah's Convention Center floor at a table for 10. Following the meal, we were to step up on an elevated stage, directly behind our table, hear the toasters/roasters perform, and respond.

Close to the time to go on stage, I made my usual pre-show run to the bathroom. I was wearing a black tuxedo that I've had for a

11

long time, one I believed to be in efficient working order.

I finished and began to pull up the pants zipper. But it wouldn't budge. "Oh lordy, don't fail me now," I told myself. I tugged up ever so gently, so as not to force the zipper off its tracks. All of a sudden, the zipper, still in its down position, left its moorings. I stood, quaking, shaking, sweating and wondering, "What next?"

Picture a guest of honor, with wide-open tux pants, white shirt and undershorts poking out in the breezeless Harrah's air, as if saying, "Melton surrenders without firing a shot."

In my career and life, I've been in some real jams. But this one beat all. I lunged out of the restroom, all hunched over, resembling an outsized bowling ball. I streaked back to the dinner table, sat down in a desperate heap, whispering an explanation to Marilyn. "God, I'm in awful trouble! What can I do?" She answered, "I have no spare tux pants on me just now. I don't know what to tell you." So much for my wife's empathy.

I thought perhaps I could tuck my cloth napkin inside the pants, letting it fall across my groin and thighs. But how wacky! I wore black. The napkin was a very light blue. The contrast would make my situation obvious.

Seated alongside me, overhearing my pleadings, was our daughter-in-law, Mona Meservy Melton. She quickly leaned over to Joy Crowley, who was seated next to her, and told Joy, "The male guest of honor is in a pitiful way. His zipper is kaput."

Joy, unflappable wife of university president Joe, instantly called over a server. "Got any black napkins in the kitchen?" she asked. In a flash, the waiter returned. I tucked the blessed black cloth into the front of my pants. Then Marilyn and I walked bravely up front, I to endure the slings and arrows of my countrymen.

Next day, a close friend, David Ryan, phoned and asked, "How was your coming-out party?" To which I replied, "Fortunately, David, last night I didn't have one."

June 8, 1998

Time in The City an Experience _____

SAN FRANCISCO—I stop here again in Baghdad by the Bay, much too briefly, yet long enough to absorb anew the majesty and the weirdness, including pathetic creatures whom Ronald Reagan decided not to burden institutions with.

The City is having a sunny bath, for it's so hot even the washed, perfumed ladies break a sweat. Authentic "street" ladies are busy hustlers, and it's like Reno's East Fourth, only lots more.

I buy a *Chronicle*, which delivers the cheery news: Hey world, we've made it one more day! In a coffee shop on Powell Street, I read who's doing what to whom. Now, I feel a light tap on the arm.

"Mister, can you give me 35 cents to make a phone call?" I tell him no. He persists. "Can I have your newspaper?" I say no. He says, "OK then, have you finished the sports section?" I say yes and he pursues. "Can you give me the sports?" I must befriend any man who depends more on a newspaper than the Internet.

I surrender the sports, and moments later I hear him chirp to potential buyers: "Read all about it. The *Chron's* sports final. Only 25 cents." He sells the section for a dime.

It has been a half-year of Sundays since I had a haircut, but a shop I know on Eddy Street is gone. Used to be you could get a nice trim from the main man there for $9, and he'd throw in for free his plan to rid the world of all ills.

I stop a fellow on the sidewalk and ask if there's a barber nearby. The guy, who himself hasn't been shorn of any hair in a year, says, "You betcha! Go back yonder to Mason Street, turn right a block and you'll see Moler Barber College.

The 80-year-old owner, Donald A. Forfang, bought the college more than 20 years ago. He's barbered since 1937, includ-

13

ing two years of shearing crowns of fellow Seabees in World War II.

His practiced eyes scan my head and he doesn't need to ask if I'm older than the average bear. He says, "Haircut's $5, but you're a senior so you get our discount down to $4.25. You can pay me in advance."

Mr. Forfang leads me to a chair manned by a young guy in his mid 20s. I sit and am suited up in a protective half-gown, while the neophyte barber starts hacking.

Omnipresent Forfang stays with us awhile. He taps my head. "Notice this man's hair," he tells the student. "The hair's so thin you can barely find it." People flit past me, gawking at me and at the apprentice, who is leaning tentatively at my head. He's eager to convince Forfang that he has absorbed a great deal so far at the college. I feel like a bald circus exhibit.

When all else fails, I interview people. But this young barber is tough. At first, all I can wheedle from him is "yes" and "no." But then there comes the breakthrough.

"How long's the course?"

"Nine months. Twelve if a guy is slow."

"Tell me what were you doing before this college?"

"Construction. Can't depend on steady work. So I quit."

Mr. Fortang again glided to his side and shared concluding advice. The tonsorial deed is done.

"Do you accept a gratuity?" I ask the student.

"'What's that?"

"Well, a tip."

"Yep, I do, mister."

I glance in the mirror. There is now less on top than I had in Army boot camp. Now I can pass for a thickset Yul Brynner.

Mr. Forfang whispers to me, "The kid didn't do bad, being as this is only his second day in college."

Oct. 4, 1999

Goose Tours Church to Attend Mass ___

The Catholic flock was gathering at the entrance of St. Thomas Aquinas Cathedral for Saturday afternoon Mass.

The church organist/choirmaster/composer, Jim Bemis, arrived at 4:15 p.m. to begin preparing his music. But at the copper doors, he saw that a number of early-arriving elderly women were clustered. They seemed afraid to enter.

Bemis hurriedly joined them, then suppressed a chuckle.

A large Canada goose was blocking the entrance. The noisy, feathered sentinel seemed bent on denying their entry.

Mustering what he calls his limited courage, Bemis fetched a copy of the *Reno Gazette-Journal*, opened it to its full width and chased the goose down the steps to Arlington Avenue and Second Street.

Safe at last, or so they believed, the women hurried inside the cathedral. Bemis, bringing up the rear, glanced back to see the determined goose re-climbing the concrete steps. It again posted itself at the door.

Moments later, the organist was upstairs, readying for the service. But then he heard the honk of a goose coming from beneath the choir loft. He glanced below.

There, amid startled gawks, was the brazen goose, behaving as though it owned the hallowed hall. It had waddled up the center aisle, as if proclaiming, "I am a guest. I am here to stay."

The congregation sat, some members laughing, yet nobody knowing what to do.

Bemis got on the loft's intercom and informed Father Charles Shelton, "There is a goose heading toward the altar." Whereupon the priest emerged from the sacristy to assure himself Bemis wasn't playing a joke.

Father Shelton saw the touring goose, which now was almost to the altar.

15

Then the goose saw Father Shelton, clad in white robe. The sizable bird did an about-face and retreated to the third pew. It perched itself next to a couple of bemused/bewildered church-goers.

The service was about to begin.

Father Shelton marched over to the goose and spoke softly to it. The man of God still has not revealed precisely what he said, but Bemis believes it may have had something to do with, "Scram, or you may wind up as Thanksgiving dinner."

Father Shelton then strode north, back down the aisle, toward the entrance. The goose followed. Each marched head-on into the flow of still-arriving worshippers, who had come to pray.

The marchers, confronted with a unique glimpse of a priest-goose parade, quickly parted to permit safe passage of the unusual couple.

As the priest/goose hiked the aisle, musician Bemis couldn't resist. He struck up the organ with, *Go Tell Aunt Rhody the Old Gray Goose Is Dead*.

Now outdoors, the priest spent a minute, wisely dispensing the anti-goose gospel according to Father Shelton.

Then he reentered the sacred cathedral—alone. He walked again to the altar, as the amused congregation smiled collectively.

Following the unusual mix of wonderment and merriment, the feathery visitor was a gone-goose.

Father Shelton returned to the altar, a man who had convinced all he is a worthy communicator with wild geese of the neighborhood.

At this point, he turned to those attending Mass. Prior to starting the service, he delivered an 11-word summarization to listeners:

"If only the rest of the flock were quite so attentive."

Oct. 26, 1997

16

A Peek at the Gentle Side of a Powerful Man

THE FIRST TIME I saw George Foreman was on television back in 1968. He was a king-size Olympic Games boxing champion, being beamed into my Reno home directly from Mexico City.

The classic image was the sort one long remembers: Foreman, having just vanquished his final opponent, paraded around the ring with a tiny American flag clutched in his powerful fist.

A week ago, I watched him in person for the first time, joining more than 6,000 others at the Reno-Sparks Convention Center to see Foreman, former heavyweight champion of the world, bludgeon sadly overmatched Jimmy Ellis, whose skills did not faintly resemble those of the ex-heavyweight champ whose name the journeyman shared.

Had this assault occurred outside a ring, the big guy with the heavy artillery might have been locked away for attempted manslaughter.

Foreman's work shift that Saturday evening was brief—a tad over six minutes—and the pay was superior: just a sliver under $5 million.

As I left the arena, I had no idea that within a few hours I would be visiting with Foreman in person.

When I arrived at Reno Cannon International Airport on Sunday to catch the 7 a.m. American Airlines flight to Dallas, he was among the passengers.

Foreman has become an American cult hero since his spectacular showing a few months ago against heavily favored champion Evander Holyfield. Since then, it seems Foreman is everywhere.

Quoted and noted, he is on television doing a gaggle of commercials, usually about food. His TV talk-show agenda

17

grew so ponderous that Foreman had to cut back on airtime. His greater-than-ever celebrity is surging because Foreman, when one compares him to other contenders and pretenders to the heavyweight crown, is a refreshing contrast.

He doesn't need any cutesy gimmicks to call attention to himself. When you stand 6-foot-3, weigh 260 pounds, are several yards wide and still carry knockout punching power, you don't need a gimmick.

Watching him at Cannon as we waited for the flight, and then visiting with him en route to Dallas, gave me a front-row seat at a Foreman clinic on how to be a classy guy.

As we awaited the boarding call, Foreman, his wife and several of his children held hands and prayed. The perennial swarms of hangers-on who seem always to shadow a top fighter were nowhere in sight. Their absence was refreshing.

Out of the ring, Foreman is the epitome of a gentleman. A brigade of men, women and kids came at him one by one on the ground in Reno and then in the air, asking for his autograph. The big guy patiently signed everything put before him. Foreman also questioned people on spellings of names before personalizing messages. "People appreciate accuracy," he told me.

Minutes after we were aloft, Foreman put his seat back, eased his soft felt hat down over his eyes and took a snooze. But it didn't last long. Awake again, he ate sparingly of the pancakes, passed up the jam and butter, declined sugar and cream with his coffee and explained, "I don't eat half the things I am supposed to adore."

Foreman knows he's got perhaps two more years of boxing competition. He is moving close to his 43rd birthday.

In the meantime, he's enjoying all of the public attention and his ballooning income to the hilt. "It's the good life and I'm savoring it," he declared.

As we landed, I speculated to myself that Foreman and family would be met by a crowd of Texas well-wishers and by the media. But there was not a single soul at the gate.

Foreman helped his wife out of the plane—she currently has a lame leg. He gently led her to a motorized cart he had

18

arranged for, and off they went with the children—a family and a high-quality husband and father.

Dec. 15, 1991

Our Future President a Man of Warmth

IN 1978, A CLOSE NEWSPAPER FRIEND, Jimmy Allison, of Midland, Texas, was gravely ill with leukemia. I wanted to see him for what I feared would be the final time. I phoned him.

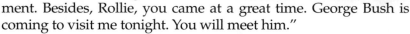

"You bet I'd love to have you come down if you can," Allison told me.

I flew to Houston and reached the hospital on a steamy summer night.

My friend was in precarious straits, but Allison was one who loved each day and lived each like it was just the beginning of a great long life.

"Sure, I got some trouble," he told me, "but I couldn't get better treatment. Besides, Rollie, you came at a great time. George Bush is coming to visit me tonight. You will meet him."

Jimmy Allison was an incorrigible optimist about his own destiny, but the thing that had always excited him most was talking about Bush. He had been bragging to me about his political friend for years, but I had yet to meet the former congressman, United Nations ambassador and CIA leader.

Allison and Bush had become closest friends after the Bush family moved to Midland. Allison was his foremost aide when Bush became a congressman.

My friend was again reviewing some of this history for me when George Bush strode into the room.

Bush shook my hand. "Always nice to make a new Nevada friend," he said warmly. But he wasn't on a politicking mission. He turned immediately back to his friend Allison. Bush took off his coat and tie and sat at the bedside.

It was the conversation of men bonded long before, who had shared the good and the bad. The exchange went on for close to a half-hour and was punctuated by much laughter.

Allison wanted to keep the discussion away from his own predicament, but George Bush, near the end, quietly said, "Well, I wonder about the outlook . . ."

He was at his gentlest as he invited Jimmy Allison to level with him.

I have heard over and over for the past year that Bush is a wimp and an uncaring person. Bush showed at Allison's bedside that such characterizations are untrue.

His friend Allison did level with him.

"It's like this, George. I've got the leukemia that won't back off. If it was chronic, I might get a lot of extra years, but mine is the acute variety. Unless we get some kind of miracle drug, it doesn't look good."

I watched the men intently and Bush was starting to cry. Then Allison broke down. After awhile, Allison again spoke.

"But I've had everything good going for me. I think there's a lot of good left for me down the road."

Bush dabbed at his eyes and I remember him saying, "There's always a great chance when you've got this excellent doctor and hospital care and when you've got Allison spirit."

Jimmy Allison was tiring and I said my goodbye, knowing there probably wouldn't be any other. I walked into the hall while the future American president stayed at Allison's bed for some final words.

In a few moments, the somber Bush joined me in the hall. He was stung by his friend's situation. "You hate this sort of thing," Bush said. "How can you say goodbye the way you really want to?

"I just told him, 'Jimmy, we've come a long way together. There's a lot farther to go. Just remember, I never had a friend I thought so much of.' "

Bush invited me to join him at dinner.

I have always remembered the humanity of the man at that dinner. George Bush didn't talk politics, or probe me with questions about Nevada, or drop names from his public-service past.

Instead, for more than an hour, he talked about his friendship with Jimmy Allison and why the association enriched him.

Three weeks later, our friend died.

Jan. 19, 1989

21

Storm-forced Amtrak Trip Offers New View of Sierra

WHILE RENO AND THE SIERRA NEVADA were being blitzed by unleashed nature, my wife and I rode securely through the snowstorm by the only conveyance that was then budging out of Reno to points west.

This was our maiden Amtrak rail voyage over Donner Summit, and thence to the Bay area, and it was a memorable way to launch our personal Reno-Oakland rail history. Exasperating to a point! But fun indeed!

I'm not recommending such a transportation mode in similar circumstances; yet, when you must get moving, when your car can't hack it, and when the air traffic is smothered on the ground, give Amtrak a whirl.

We were to be in Fairfax, Marin County, north of San Francisco for a Saturday morning wedding—a cherished college friend of our daughter, Emelie, was marrying the young Fairfax mayor. Emelie would be a bridesmaid, so Marilyn and I awoke Friday, gearing for what we believed would be a pleasant drive over our beloved Sierra. Emelie had driven to Marin the previous day, and it had been gorgeous.

I drove to the office before dawn Friday to write my Sunday column. The snow was flying even then—5:30ish—and I called my wife at 7 o'clock, saying I'd have to buy new tire chains for the trip.

Because my mechanical aptitude is akin to that of a pinyon pine, I let newspaper colleague Herb Crockett get the car weather-fit for me.

By 9 a.m. it was clear that anyone who tried to get over Donner Summit in a car that day ought to have a sanity check. Minutes later, another ordinary option—commercial air—was foreclosed. I remembered that the daily westbound Amtrak usually stops in Reno, then moves on about 8:30 a.m.

So I believed Amtrak was long gone. But wait! My secretary, Mickey Wessel, speculated the train might be late on account of big storms to the east. She was so right.

When she called Amtrak at the depot on Commercial Row, however, the small staff there said, "We're booked solid. People are herding in because the train is the only way out, to the west."

Mickey ordered me to "get over there with Marilyn anyway—and stay on standby." I saluted obediently.

So intense was the public's crush on Amtrak on Friday morning that railroad officers wisely used the Sparks stop to add a couple of passenger cars. We bought our tickets—$126, one-way, for the two of us—and the confident ticket man declared, "It usually takes four-and-a-half hours to get to Oakland. Today, it'll be maybe five-and-a-half hours." The guy missed his forecast by a Nevada mile.

The only visible stress time among fellow travelers, who seemed to be mostly Californians, was when we were still milling around the depot, and outside, waiting for Amtrak. Why employees of airline, bus, train—any public conveyance—insist on understating expected arrival and departure times, I can't fathom.

"The Amtrak will be here in 20 minutes; it's berthed briefly in Sparks, now," the young male employee announced. An hour later, he advised the increasingly agitated mob, "Be patient, and we'll have you out of Reno by 11:30." In Europe, trains are on time to the second and, I am advised—maybe only half in jest—that Germans attack conductors if trains are even one-half minute late.

The crowd, watching outside as snow rapidly accumulated, grew a bit testy, especially those older, who don't always have patience on a leash. But the young people were great. To them, what's another half-hour, an afternoon, a whole day?

Amtrak got out of the Biggest Little City at 2:20 p.m.

The Reno-Oakland jaunt is a picturesque milk run under normal conditions—Truckee, Colfax, Roseville, Sacramento, Davis, Martinez, and so forth. As we all know, Friday's unabated weather was the biggest winter storm to hit us since '52.

Our train climbed toward Donner. A small storm-clearing

vehicle chugged ahead of Amtrak, paving our way.

Passengers quickly relaxed and thirsty ones—they were quite a number—ran the bartender ragged in the train's lower-level lounge. An icy draft seeped in on some occupying window seats. Blankets, emblazoned with "Amtrak," sold briskly at $8 a pop.

A substantial number of us in Greater Reno tend to ignore adventures such as Amtrak—Rollan Melton, for instance—until certain events make us choose what often are wonderful options. Then, when we do acquire and savor the new experiences, some of us invariably say, "Why did I wait so long? This was really neat!"

Our trip required 10 1/2 hours, twice the normal running time. Yet it was a joy. The intensity of the blizzard only added beauty and deepened our respect for nature's wonders. The stormy, incomparable view at the top of the Sierra was a marvelous bonus.

In San Francisco, where we stayed the weekend, and now back in Reno, I look back at an incredible experience. Meeting new friends. Savoring the Sierra, which is one of the world's great wonders. Taking in the harvest of majestic Sierra solitude, marveling still at man's indomitable courage and foresight—to lay down such rail track over primitive terrain, so long ago, prospers the lot of us more than a century later.

How blessed we on the east slope of the Sierra Nevada truly are. To have all this is a staggering monument to those who first developed for us the unmatched virtues we too often take for granted.

Feb. 20, 1990

Art, Humor, Good Times Reign at Cowboy Poetry Gathering _____

ELKO—Don't let any intellectual highbrow jostle you away from the truth. So what if all these poets aren't Western Bard? It's no federal offense if literary meter occasionally acquires a creak. The truth is that what's happening at the sixth Cowboy Poetry Gathering is art. Life. Sharing good times.

The 300 officially registered poets from 15 states, Canada and Australia are thrilling this three-day gathering with words, wit and wisdom. By today they will have drawn a record 8,500 witnesses. The event ends tonight.

It's art if it draws a response. The Cowboy Poetry recitations do indeed evoke emotional reaction.

It's life if the soul is reached. Here, it is.

It's sharing good times. Cowboys, their kinsmen and the thousands who come here to savor the human spirit, adore the Gathering. "What they love most," the Gathering's media liaison, Cyd McMullen, says, "is meeting family they never knew they had."

The quality of cowboy poetry again this winter warms the believers who retreat to recitation venues from the snowy chill in Elko air. Humor is king. Witness Colorado hay broker Vess Quinlan:

I've looked over this poet bunch,
And it's easy enough to see
That even the very best of 'em,
Is about the same as me.

Good times now rock around Elko's clock. Venerable Slim Whitman is singin' and pickin' at the Red Lion Inn. The mightiest cowboy festival draw, Canadian singer and rancher Ian Tyson, is a huge hit at Dan Bilboa's Stockmen's Hotel. Happy Dan is being run ragged, trying to wedge in extra chairs. Too bad Americans haven't yet discovered Tyson, a cowboy folk singer, who is as central to Canadian pop culture as the late Elko County rancher Bing Crosby was to the U.S. masses.

Informal cowboy jam sessions end at 7 a.m., and around the cowboy crowd, replete with denim, scarves and jumbo belt buckles, nobody has to say, "Read my lips." Verbal volume at private parties, at the museum, at homes, in lobbies, over a Coors and especially in the lobby of the convention center is at seventh decibel.

Gone are stage jitters too prevalent in 1985 when the first Cowboy Poetry Gathering drew 2,000. Women and men now confidently parade onstage, cuddle up to the standup mike and go for it!

Several poets refuse to be intimidated by so-called physical impairments. For instance, wheelchair-bound Wyman Griffith, a Missourian, made a roaring debut Friday morning.

Two years ago, a falling tree wrecked his spine. Today, his poetry pumps his esteem anew.

Poetry is being spoken in Elko by unregistered reciters, too. Doreen Clifford, of Reno, a retired nurse, chanted this to me at the convention center on Friday morning:

I got used to my arthritis,
To my dentures I'm resigned.
I can manage my bifocals,
But, God, I miss my mind!

By Doreen Clifford, poet? No. Her late mother sent it down from Canada.

Art reigns here! Western artistry is everywhere. Former *Nevada* magazine editor C.J. Hadley, the irrepressible one, has a stunning exhibit of color photographs she took in Australia, showing at the Northeastern Nevada Museum.

Which brings me to the Aussies. Their blue-chip recitations have drawn standing ovations and their strong cattle tradition and literary heritage meld beautifully with us Western American cousins. They wear low-slung cowboy hats and fixed grins.

Thus, the Cowboy Poetry Gathering goes international. What happened is this: Executive director Hal Cannon, event manager Tara Shepperson McCarty and others began brainstorming a global outreach two years ago.

26

Enter an angel in finance and in spirit, George Gund, a San Francisco-based philanthropist and Western spirit. Gund, a trustee of the University of Nevada, Reno Foundation, owns an Elko County ranch, and he reveres the soil, the cowboy and the art and literary worlds.

Last October, Gund and Cannon flew to Australia in Gund's private jet and did final auditions and selections of Aussie poets. Now Gund has flown the talented rovers to Nevada, all expenses paid. His handful of visitors from Down Under bring a global dimension to Elko, and spirit and abundant humor, as well. Witness Thursday night's Aussie poems about a ranch cat that suffered severe constipation, and know what real laughter is!

It is summer Down Under and our cousins can't get over Nevada in January. Early Friday morning, as Australian and American flags formally were hoisted, snowfall beat at shivering hides. It was the first snow three Australians had ever seen.

One Aussie poet showed up at the flag-raising in a short-sleeved shirt. I didn't get her name, but we heard her shout an unpoetic truth as she sprinted toward the warm auditorium:

"I'm getting out of here before it freezes my little tush."

Jan. 27, 1990

27

ON THE SOAPBOX

Police Radio Reminds Us of Dangers Officers Face

As I write this in my office, on the perimeter of the newsroom, I hear again the sounds of an increasingly edgy and endangered city.

It is the police dispatch radio talking to me, reconfirming the trouble we're in. The law-enforcement squawk box chatters around the clock for all in the police family, and in the monitoring media, to hear.

On this morning, the dispatcher on the early shift spews out a report typical of these troubled days:

"Check out suspicious man in downtown alley . . . family fight in northeast . . . approach with extreme caution . . . car seen racing at high speed in residential area . . . apparently inebriated man down on sidewalk, near Mapes Hotel . . . burglary believed in progress . . . check out security alarm, triggered at store . . ."

The chilling monologue numbs the listener each day, reminding us that the sleepy and safe town we knew is now a danger. Who among us would now carelessly leave a door unlatched? Or stand unafraid as our young ones walk among strangers?

But there is something else that the dispatcher's messages remind us of.

The most endangered among us include the ones who wear the badges.

It is the police, and the deputies and the Nevada Highway Patrol and the uniformed people in rural Nevada who are on the front lines, standing guard against the criminal element that would make us all surrender the good we have.

Law-enforcement people have no public-relations

31

hotshots to tell the world of the good they do. They don't earn fancy wages. More often than not, they are dumped on by an unappreciative public.

But they're invariably at our sides when we cry for help!

Accept as truth the peril our police and deputies and highway patrol people walk into every day.

Every statistic rides up on the trend lines around Nevada. More people means more trouble in Reno and in the Yeringtons, Lovelocks and Elkos. Everywhere. You name it: snatched purses, people down with gunshots, women raped, children kidnapped, shoplifters ripping off storekeepers, beatings, knifings, murder.

The cops and deputies and patrol officers walk each day into drug situations, into the hazardous family fight. Walk into places increasingly populated with crazies.

Let us include in the badge family the ones we don't see but who help us. The plain clothed ones. The FBI. The U.S. Treasury men and women.

The undercover people whose assignments probably offer the greatest danger of all. As infiltrators of the drug world, their lives are on the line 24 hours a day.

Such a man was Jimmy Hoff. Working undercover in a drug situation, this young Reno police officer was murdered in 1979.

Narcotics officer Hoff's name has been given to a memorial that stands as a monument to the more than 40 law-enforcement men who have died in the line of duty in Nevada since frontier days. Erected and dedicated in 1988, the memorial bears the names of these victims.

It is a monument that all Nevadans ought to see, a monument to show our children as we urge them to stand by the men and women who wear the badge.

The monument stands at Idlewild Park, a few yards east of the California Building.

A benefit show, featuring entertainers who are donating their services, is to be held at the Pioneer Center for the Performing Arts on Friday, starting at 7 p.m. The proceeds will pay for additional memorial plaques and also go toward a University of Nevada, Reno scholarship to educate those youngsters seeking careers in law enforcement.

The monument now bears the names of 38, including the first Reno officer killed, Charles Augusta Brown, gunned down in 1901. Four names are to be added soon—uniformed men from Nye County whose names, deeds and sacrifices had gone unheralded when the memorial was dedicated in 1988.

Finally, there is something each of us ought to do more of:

Simply say thanks to the uniformed man and woman who support us.

Flowers for the living is a superior idea.

Jan. 16, 1990

Meanness Has Become Epidemic _____

PERSONAL RIGHTS are the gifts Americans cherish and fight to protect. That said, there is such a pervasive meanness now loosened against citizens that it is a perilous epidemic.

Among the freshest crime against the community is the destructive vandalism at the new city park on Summit Ridge in a northwest Reno neighborhood. University of Nevada, Reno development officer Melanie Perish's reaction best describes whoever did this reprehensible act:

"Some people are hardwired for evil."

How does a society deal with such thugs to best discourage them from ever again viciously roughing innocent victims?

Lectures frequently misfire. Mollycoddling is a joke. Suspended sentences tell offenders it is just ducky to loose poisonous acts on the populace. Light sentences make the guilty laugh all the way to, and through, their too-brief, too-cushy confinement.

I hope you don't think me daft for making a simple suggestion, one that probably would tell creators of bad things against good people that we've had our fill. That so far, society's correctional methods aren't getting the hoped-for results.

The use of my idea does not necessarily lead to incarceration, which in our cities, state and nation so frequently consists of free room, board, television, library privileges, non-work, mail service and, sometimes, conjugal visits.

Maybe I'm guilty of talking down to you here, but I remind you that those amenities, and many others, are at the total expense of We the People.

I am convinced that my suggestion of punishment could persuade evildoers to think hard and pause long, thus saving citizens' bodies, homes, personal treasures—such as our community parks.

I hope most of you agree that my suggestion also could

shrink jail and prison populations, and the cost of administering lockup places. The fewer jailbirds to house, wash, cook for, clothe and launder for, the less citizens' taxes would be needed.

Lessened expenses brought about by reduced confinements could enable us to better finance many other paramount needs, none more vital than the first-class educational system we owe all Nevadans. Plus such elements as libraries, nifty cultural efforts, a sounder infrastructure.

If my very fundamental innovation ever came to pass, the American Civil Liberties Union would have a fit, and have its noses all out of joint. The punishment option I am about to share with you would spur the ACLU to instantly decry "too-harsh punishment."

In so pleading, critics of such punishment could win headlines and expensive legal delays, something many lawyers love.

I am not just thinking that applying my notion of workable punishment should be used exclusively against those who destroy the Summit Ridge parks of our city and land.

What I have in mind could also be a helpful deterrent in instances dealing with convicted rapists, murderers, thieves, arsonists, extortionists, child abusers, molesters and those whose weaponry wantonly kills cows and horses.

What we are doing to discourage crime isn't producing a heck of a lot of results. My idea: Arrest suspects. Give them fair trials. If they are guilty, let the strongest whip-hand we can commission apply what works in Singapore:

Cane 'em.

Dec. 6, 1999

We're Prisoner to the Mean in Our Streets

THIS COLUMN usually visits with readers about the bright, positive, sane and safe slice of Nevada life. But not this time.

Larry Johnson, Sparks policeman. Lost forever.

Donald L. Cameron, thug-felon-murderer. Dead, too.

These days, punishment is rarely swift. But police guns
took Cameron out, sparing society a trial, conviction and the
long comfort of Death Row.

What happened to Larry Johnson and his killer is not new
to Reno. From the beginning, Lake's Crossing (Reno) was
what it is today. Man's best and worst.

Early newspapers told of a brew of kindness and mischief.
People found this a good place to settle, but often contended
with holdup men, rustlers, liars, murderers.

In my first 28 years here (1950-78), what made Reno-
Sparks great and safe was that everyone had space to walk,
visit, work, play—to live happily.

Neighbors were friends. They borrowed sugar and paid
it back. They baby-sat kids next door and forged warm friendships on mutual trust.

Life was intimate. Reno-Sparks had little grocery stores
whose Mom & Pop owners closed, come dark. You came to
tidy downtown and its neat shops, and knew almost every
stroller.

Yes, there was crime, but usually prompt reckoning. Two
Reno policemen were murdered in 1947. The killer went to
the gas chamber soon after.

Today, we are a complicated, urban city—overcrowded,
more diverse, less innocent. All of us are on guard. We worry
about family, friends, personal safety.

We lament, "Who is in this room whom I know? Nobody!"

People don't make friends fast when drive-by slugs part

their hair or brains.

People fear going into parking garages, elevators, city parks. The threat of burglary is omnipresent.

In Reno-Sparks, a prosperous business to own is a security firm. May the Lord have mercy on you if you're old and stroll alone, or wear lawman's blue or gray, drive a cab nights, or if you are gay.

Ours is a scared-stiff place.

Can you think of any parental worry greater than having your kid working nights at 7-Eleven?

Of visiting the Washoe County Courthouse, now wired to detect knife, gun, bomb?

Of being a teacher, who must deal with young school renegades, some armed? All the while fearing that your principal might be too frightened to back you up?

In truth, we, the innocent, are prisoners in our own environment.

The Big Change commenced in 1978 when the MGM Grand opened. Casinos begat casinos. New people poured in, and we were in denial, asserting, "It's OK. We'll never be Baby LA."

But we misjudged. Now there is sugar in our tanks, mean in our streets, and Mom & Pop are forever replaced by 24-hour convenience stores—frequented by wary nighttime shoppers and, sometimes, bandits.

When too many people move to the confined Truckee Meadows, when 5 million visitors a year pop in to take a look, when thugs infiltrate our turf, when copycat rebels imitate evil role models, when stress, anger and fear overtake us, as they have, there is plenty of worry to go around.

When these elements intrude simultaneously, even the most positive of us needs to admit we are, indeed, imperiled.

Pogo was right. The enemy is now met, and he is us. Because there are too many of us.

Is there a solution?

Examine all of the formerly serene places, now over-full urban areas. None is totally safe. Few are fully sane. Those cities cry for a way out. Few find solutions.

This summer, as a giant new casino opens on the heels of

other expansions, the community will confront a vast new people tide, and have more problems to contend with.

Or, as with brave, good policemen such as Larry Johnson, perhaps to die from.

May 25, 1995

The Values of Thanksgiving Are Incorruptible

THANKSGIVING, the most hospitable holiday, always seems to sprint to that distinction in a turkey-trot runaway.

It is a cherished carryover of what used to be. Call it the enduring example of golden values, or of truly good old days, or even of *Pilgrim's Progress*.

Thanksgiving is that one tradition that soars beyond the greedy grasp of crass commercialists.

Christmas long ago became a marathon sales event. We are smothered by the mercantile beats of yulogists, even before the roasted turkeys are placed before us, and there is a relentless sales march then, right through the New Year's white sales.

Those other traditions on our calendar have not escaped the cash register's bang. We are beseeched to smother Mother with floral rewards on her day and the least we are commanded to offer Dad on Father's Day is socks, or the down-payment on a retirement hammock.

We feel akin to a Benedict Arnold if we neglect to shower newly bought shamrocks all around on St. Patrick's Day.

As to Valentine's, a honey forgotten is one scorned honey too many.

We are now confronted with the elongated Presidents Birthday weekend, then the follow-up stories about how many tourist visitors were lured in.

The contemporary commercial march even includes the hustling of Old Glory flag sales on the sacred Fourth of July, not to mention Armed Forces Day and, of course, Flag Day.

But let us return to reasons to be thankful for Thanksgiving.

Time magazine put it aptly last year:

"Flower-power florists must lament a national holiday in which they are doomed to play a minor role. For if one cares to send the very best, one flies home for Thanksgiving."

Thanksgiving is such a perfect time to covet personal reasons for gratitude. We can formally do so at church, where unlike the Easter and Christmas services, we won't get boxed around the ears for not showing up on all those other Sundays.

Thanksgiving is private. Personal. A family pageant. It still offers the basic meal that has evolved from the 17th century, a feast that continues to emerge from conventional ovens, rather than the microwave.

Of contemporary presidents, only Franklin D. Roosevelt successfully tampered with Thanksgiving. In 1939, he orchestrated the move of the holiday from its traditional time—the last Thursday of November—to the fourth Thursday. It remains there to this day for the reason FDR intended—to give businesses a longer sales season, leading to Christmas.

But Thanksgiving endures as the holiday still untainted by commercialism.

It is a day when we don't loiter in the malls, because they are closed. Nor do we hustle to the banks, which also are shuttered. Traffic is mercifully lighter and we don't bother checking the mail, because our postal friends get a day with family, too.

Thanksgiving Day revelers have never rioted in downtown Reno, and won't. Across the land, and Nevada, jail bookings are light and sometimes almost none on this gentle day.

On Thanksgiving Day, not a single street-corner bell-clanger is heard to shill for our best holiday. Thankfully.

Thanksgiving: a time when most of us dine in the sanctity of our own homes, surrounded by the most important people we shall ever know. A time when there is no hackneyed drumming of little hooves upon our rooftops.

Never on this festive occasion will we be buried in Thanksgiving Day gift wrappings.

As sure as our God made little red cranberries, the beauty of Thanksgiving Day will prevail.

For this is our private, personal holiday. And it is not for sale.

Nov. 22, 1990

Americans Have Gift That Requires Constant Renewal

WHAT AN EXTRAORDINARY GIFT to be born American, or to become naturalized, or to be able to visit the United States on a green card!

How blessed that these words come to you uncensored. That all writers, lyricists, critics of government and creators of dissenting messages can sound off without landing behind bars.

How sweet, every day, to savor Nevada as free people. At liberty to find the joy, the rewards and all the opportunity one can lawfully pursue. As John Gunther said, ours is a nation deliberately founded upon a good idea.

When we think about the luxuries we have as free people, the miracle is all the more a storybook dream, akin to a fiction cooked up a relatively short time ago. Being free is now so routine that it is easy to take for granted. It is easy to forget that people risked their lives, gave their lives and surrendered what they owned.

It is invariably from those born in other countries that I get the strongest sense of what it means to be an American:

"You don't really know how fortunate you are to be American."

"How blessed to be free to go to the church you want, rather than to the mandated one."

"I had heard all my life what America was like. It was unbelievable. But now I am here. Now I believe."

Living as Americans is an unending tailgate party, a celebration that continues day after day. A journey that is a joy to behold! Governing ourselves, for better and for worse. America still is the final destination of modern pilgrims, arriving from places where there was the punishment one gets when not free to decide one's own destiny.

For these many years, I have had the joy of witnessing democracy from the front-row seat one gets in journalism. It has been a

41

daily joyride, with no day like any other. But for all the events seen, the naturalization ceremonies remain the most poignant, inspirational and satisfying. At such events, one sees firsthand the magic that is our country.

Always there are the galleries filled with families, bursting with pride. Always there are the honored immigrants, who yearn to walk through the opportunity doors just beyond the courtroom. Always there is the presiding jurist, more than an officiating leader in black. Foremost, the judge's presence reminds Americans, new and old, that without law and the compulsion to live within its boundaries, we shall be lost.

The beauty of the naturalization ceremony is that diversity is celebrated. The faces of the new Americans are all of the human colors. English is spoken, but so is a myriad of other tongues. Most of all, hope and love are spoken.

For each of us, it is urgent that freedom be celebrated and appreciated on all days. Not simply on the Fourth of July.

The danger I see more and more is that society's patriotic muscle is turning to flab. Increasingly, we meet young people, fresh out of the classroom, who cannot recite our country's basic founding history. It also is discouragingly commonplace to meet adults who know not the difference of the Declaration of Independence, the Magna Charta or the Bill of Rights.

The greatest rising peril is not the crazy leader from the Third World. Or the Rising Sun's powerful economic mechanism.

Our largest enemy is our own apathy, our worrisome belief that someone else always will be around to fix what is broken. In fact, if we as individuals can't believe we have the power to do the fixing, then we shall be in the greatest trouble since we became a nation.

Self-governance, along with continuing individual efforts to maintain freedoms, has to be every person's job. Every day. When we so act, we keep the extraordinary gift of being free.

July 4, 1991

Two Cities on the Truckee: a Study in Contrasts

A TALE of two cities.

Reno, with its downtown resembling something that didn't get washed behind the ears, its flat gaming economy, its one-industry domination, reminds me of a weary old prizefighter.

Reno shoppers pass a downtown derelict, 1994.

Once proud, confident, resourceful and competitive, the city now seems bereft of the speed, power, flexibility and the will and courage to win.

The younger can-do Reno that a few of us remember is buried in the wake of ideas that can't get airborne, of too little teamwork, or too much coveting of "me" instead of "we."

Reno has lost movement, isn't up on its toes and is instead the victim of municipal rope-a-dope. On the ropes, you lose punching leverage, get body burns and, ultimately, an Ali springs in to punch you out.

In Reno, persuading the city and business leadership that quaint ways aren't working has been as easy as growing roses in the Sahara sands. Now, as visitors go elsewhere, as supposedly fail-safe casino operations lock their doors, now at last the warning flags are seen.

Why must it require peril to awaken us?

43

Reno: The people who had the power to create a downtown mall screamed when the idea came up. The idea was flogged to death.

Reno: The city a lot of us remember much as a favorite relative who died—the one that featured neat places to shop and to poke around in—is gone.

Reno: Today, tourists ask, "Got any downtown places where we can shop?" We reply, "Hardly any."

People today travel with many destination rewards in mind. You can be dumb and still know that. Gambling alone is no longer enough to entice them, and/or to cause them to return.

Reno: Is there another American city with a beautiful river running through it that has failed to develop and show off the river's attractiveness? I believe we are the only one.

Then consider neighboring Sparks, three miles distant, but in another world as far as attitude and results.

Sparks: So vigorous and exciting now, in looks and spirit.

A city moving smartly toward the new century. A business and municipal place that now exploits the virtues of a downtown mall, of flowers, of gorgeous young trees, of places for strollers, of benches to comfort visitors.

Sparks, with the commonsense to engage superlative architectural partners Don Clark and Larry Henry. Their Victorian Square landscaping and structural results suggest again that the cities that respect and accommodate people's love of beauty and comfort will prosper.

Let themselves be shaped by inertia and an absence of meritorious objectives, and leadership will languish.

Cities with the overall savvy and commitment of Sparks Mayor James Spoo will outpunch, outthink and outwit those led by a mayor caught up either in bouts with an ex-wife, or with China trips, or both.

Sparks drew more than 110,000 people to Victorian Square's summer events. The reasons to throng there included sunshine, shops, grass, trees, fun events, music, flowers, singing and laughter.

The lovely new Sparks amphitheater is a phenomenal success. Such an idea would have been flogged dead by downtown Reno interests.

Where will present and future Nevadans and visitors ice-skate? In Sparks' arena.

Sparks, and an admiring northern Nevada, can boast also of the expansion of John Ascuaga's Nugget. Here we have a hotel-casino owner who has demonstrated that as Sparks goes, so goes his corporate destiny.

We have proof here, again, of the merits of sensible architecture. Peter Wilday's structural creations and his interior design are outstanding.

The Nugget has an honest-to-God hotel lobby! A real beauty! The place that Ascuaga built has a new convention area that offers much space, and something else Reno casinos haven't permitted—spacious windows. Look outside. See the Sierra. See Nevada.

A Reno advertising executive once hoked up a campaign suggesting Sparks be renamed East Reno. It was quickly drowned by proud Sparks.

But the way things are going in this tale of two cities, perhaps Reno some day will see the wisdom of renaming itself. How about West Sparks?

Finally, if downtown Sparks was located a mile or so south, along the banks of the Truckee River, and had the leadership of James Spoo, Ascuaga and Company, it truly might be economic twilight for Reno.

Come to think of it, if we don't get our act together, struggling Reno may be counted out on its feet, in any event.

Oct. 10, 1989

Will We Learn the Lessons Floods Teach?

MY EDITORS didn't need to look beyond me to find the local media person with the longest memory about Reno and Washoe County floods.

I have been a sandbagger on two occasions, and twice have written or edited *Gazette-Journal* flood coverage. After each such catastrophe, I was confident the new flood wouldn't slug us as badly as the last.

But my vision has been flawed.

Sandbags in Reno, 1955.

It has been foolish to understate what a mauling that unharnessed Mother Nature can inflict. So often, that "next big one" has left me eating my words.

My first brush with the rampaging Truckee River occurred in 1950. It was November, and the familiar scenario was in place to deal Big Trouble.

Heavy early snowfall in the Sierra Nevada, then warming temperatures, followed by unrelenting rain.

I was a 19-year-old freshman at the University of Nevada when the '50 call for volunteers was issued. Riverside Drive was swamped by the rampaging river by the time a squad of us showed up from Hartman Hall men's dormitory to join other volunteers.

As young and well-conditioned as I then was, I quickly discovered how exhausting sandbagging can be. We were no match for the churning water.

The raging torrent swamped the Christian Science church and houses along Riverside Drive. Gradually, we were forced to retreat, to north of First Street. Finally, our weary flood fighters were replaced by fresh sandbag troops.

During the 1950 flood, Reno's foremost newspaper reporter-writer nearly was killed. Churning waters almost sucked Frank McCulloch into a manhole on First Street near the Center Street bridge.

By chance, I was home on Christmas leave from the Army when the 1955 flood over- whelmed the city. I volunteered as a sandbagger, this time downtown on First Street. Again, as five years before, the flood divided the city north and south, because there were fewer bridges than to- day. For a time, all bridges were closed.

The Mapes Hotel front is protected against floodwaters.

Today, the Mapes and Riverside hotels are silent sentinels. However, in 1950 and '55, they were the entertainment toasts of the town. But at flood time, each was swamped. So were other businesses on the Truckee's bank, including Home Furniture, Herz Jewelers, Paterson's Men's Store, Tait's Shoes, Spina Shoe Repair Shop, the Majestic Theater and the Reno YMCA.

In both '50 and '55, flooding reached Second Street on the north side of the river, and Court Street to the south. The sights and sounds were like those existing during today's horrific flood:

Men and women and youngsters battling alongside each other, trying to harness unruly waters.

The 1963 Reno flood was familiar history flashing before our eyes. The bad-mix formula was again heavy early snow, followed by rain. The unforgettable sight then was the under-construction First National Bank headquarters building at First and Virginia streets. Waters rose so quickly that surprised workers had to scramble to safety.

Not emphasized in news coverage of recent days was the close call Reno experienced in 1964. Bridges were wiped out, a few homes were smacked and, tragically, a young boy dove from the Arlington Avenue Bridge into the violent Truckee waters, trying to save his little dog. The boy was killed.

In the 47 years since 1950, I've missed one flood. That was the glancing water blow of 1986. I was away at a newspaper convention when the Truckee Meadows was socked.

Upstream storage helped minimize the '86 damage.

But in the great flood this time, upstream storage, which didn't exist in '50 and '55, failed to minimize flood peril because upstream reservoirs were already close to full when torrential rain demolished the early snow pack.

From such history, we know that future floods will occur.

This year's tragic reprise reminds us not to underestimate the Truckee's potential to do us major harm. This month's flood also should reemphasize the folly of designing and building structures in a way that makes them an easy target.

The new Washoe County Courthouse annex is today's classic example. Its basement is now swamped by floodwater.

Jan. 5, 1997

Kitty Kelley Earns Herself Hatchet Award

KITTY KELLEY has tried diligently to slice the Reagans into little slivers of whatever is left after you are shoved through a killing machine. Thus, the queen of barnyard-keyhole journalism qualifies for this year's Hatchet Award.

It is given occasionally to those who set upon their fellow man with malice, with reckless and relentless pursuit and with intent to do mental and bodily harm.

The Reagans will be all right. They have been in this arena a lot of times. As they say in Christian Science, "Rise Above It." Ronnie and Nancy are always aloft, not because they are saints. They are human and flawed, just as are we all. They elected to reside in glass houses in Sacramento, Washington, D.C., and, now, Los Angeles.

When you are Joe R. Smith, high school graduate, doing a hard job for too little, paying taxes regularly, praying, whether in trouble or not; when you're Alice Riley, raising kids alone, being mother, working two jobs, trying to get more education; or when you are Sybil Potter, bank teller, just starting on low pay, faced with high rent, high bills, but doing it all with a smile and a hunch that you'll make it—when you are Smith, Riley and Potter, and all those other wonderful Americans, you don't get written up in books. In Kitty Kelley's book, or in anyone's book.

The guy with the hard job; the teller; the single mom; the decent people who are America—none usually gets any ink. Or airtime. Unless they become a statistic, get into trouble or rescue a drowning man—and the press somehow gets the heroic story.

All these anonymous, faceless, hardworking, taxpaying stiffs—a lot of whom vote and faithfully face up to their bill collectors, go out of their way to do civic voluntarism, care for their frail parents, be decent, beautiful, funny and humble people—they ARE the USA.

49

So are the Reagans USA.

But Nancy and Ronnie Reagan are grist for Kelley mills. So be it! But is it right, even in a country where the First Amendment is the most essential of the freedoms? Is it right that a Kitty Kelley perform on her unfair, unlevel playing field?

No, it isn't fair! No more fair than it is to kick a downed player, a non-player, or to avoid the other guy's side of a story, or to deny any American an opportunity, because he or she is Jewish, black, over 50, too young to vote, uneducated, homeless, hospitalized or a victim of parental neglect.

But in America—and in the media—there are Kitty Kelleys. They have different names and axes to grind. They aren't numerous. But it takes just one Kelley Hatchet Award contender to suggest widespread malfeasance.

One true stinker and all of us in the media, writers of books, massagers of public opinion, get tarred with the Kelley-colored brush.

OK. It goes with being in journalism. We get rhinoceros skin. We try to be fair and not to worry about the Kelleys.

Miss Kelley is a poor reporter. She's a worse writer, an impersonator of a true researcher. Miss Kelley gets an F-minus. Miss Kelley, big name just now! I don't know her personally. I don't recommend that any of you associate with her, or hear her dirty the talk shows with claptrap about how many sources she heard from or how diligently she sought balance. I hope you shall not be subject to her agent's drum-beating and her publisher's appeal that "this is the book of the year, if not of the century."

The verdict already is in. Conclusions stack higher.

Kelley, a bitch, is getting richer by the minute.

However, Americans, 99.9 percent of them favoring a level playing field, just voted Kitty Kelley as the bum who has delivered the bummest rap.

April 11, 1991

50

Huge Athletic Salaries Show Our Sickness

JEFF HORTON jumped overboard and paddled to the University of Nevada, Las Vegas, to earn $30,000 above what the University of Nevada, Reno paid him to muddle through a 7-4 football rookie coaching season.

Chris Ault quickly reassumed his twin duty as athletic director and coach. People have since anointed him so lavishly that one can envision the savior-coach riding into Mackay Stadium in a chariot. Is it a scene for *Sheep Dip*, or next year's home opener?

Ault's return to football power is pure personal gain: His psychic income is soaring; his new five-year contract will be the longest in the school's century-plus history. His 1993 pay of $91,000 kept him off food stamps. Now, poverty will be further postponed, for with booster inducements, he'll earn $200,000. That is far more than university president Joe Crowley or Gov. Bob Miller earn.

All this is a fresh example of the skewed priorities and values of a society that exalts rock stars, exotic Madonnas, superstar jocks and some coaches.

But while genuflecting to celebrities, the public withholds merit pay and applause for our noblest heroes—scholars, healers, teachers, scientists, authors, artists, architects, clergy, and people who bandage the social wreckage.

Ault's income will be four times greater than many of his faculty colleagues, some of whom are among the nation's best. Further, among campus deans, vice presidents and department leaders, only Ault needs not tell his fund-raising strategies in advance to the university's vice president for development.

However, as university athletics rise in both image and cost, paramount concerns fester out of the apathetic public's mind.

They are problems that ought to be regularly played on Page One, on TV nightly news, discussed in business boardrooms and

51

by students, their families, alumni and an aroused general constituency.

Returning to a stable method of raising state revenues, a stability abandoned in 1982, would help the institution sweep onward and upward.

But now, it is a campus bloodied at the 1993 legislative session. Mandated money cuts left deep wounds, and powerless students are damaged most.

UNR is short 55 urgently needed faculty; some classes are vastly overcrowded, thwarting quality teaching, and putting off some graduations by semesters, or years. With courses down, learning plays third fiddle.

Laboratory equipment is aged and grown cranky; students complain desperately about lack of advisement; if the library system was released today from the budgetary asylum, it would require years to buy the books needed *now*.

The gravest physical concern is the computer system, funding for which lawmakers botched. On campus, the system is pathetically overloaded, and frustrated users struggle to get on the Internet information superhighway.

Until legislators act, neither state nor campus can compete with adjacent states, which are years ahead us. A campus source says, "Without adequate computer infrastructure, our economic development roadblocks will make the Indian casino gaming threat seem minuscule by comparison."

Even as Coach Ault urgently pursues coaching and player talent, there is campus-wide agony over building and equipment maintenance funding cuts—they invite rust, rot and ruin. Roofs leak. Furnaces falter.

Faculty and staff salaries stagnate. Hearing of huge athletic salaries, demoralized faculty and their deans roll their eyes.

Universities were founded in the Middle Ages to develop minds. That objective should never be diminished by athletics. Or by anything.

Nov. 29, 1993

'93 Graduates Get Pointers for Real Life

FALLON—When I returned to my hometown to speak to Churchill County High School's 1993 graduates, I gave them these 20 pointers:

1. After you get your diploma, you simply must take off the cap and gown. You'll look pretty silly wearing them the rest of your life.

2. I know you're graduating. But don't tell your teachers you can't stand them. They may have a colleague at a higher education level who will grade you next.

3. Don't dash away from here with school mementos. The classrooms and furniture are too expensive to replace.

4. If you go off to get more education, avoid rooming with 10 or more students at once. Studying in a regiment can be distracting.

5. I admire your fiery ambition. However, you need more education and job experience before being a CEO. Lack of patience kills many dreams.

6. Don't feel obliged to marry the first person you date after graduation. Settling on whom to wed probably will be the most important decision of your life. Don't rush.

7. Pick your line of work with care. Writing poetry is OK. But doing it for a living can be perilous, unless you don't need food or rent money.

8. Life beyond high school ought to be fun. But carry a seatbelt, just in case.

9. If you win the California Lottery, you'll acquire many temporary friends. But a safer bet will be more education and job experience.

10. Ignorant people think it's nice to be important. It's much more important to be nice.

11. I graduated from Churchill County High School 43 years

ago. If I could live those years over, I would read many more books. Learn from my failure.

12. Some grow old too soon by treating their body as if they have a spare in the trunk. You have only one. Take good care of it.

13. Be curious. Everything and everyone is a book. Learn to read them. Question. Talk less. Listen more.

14. One of your most precious assets is your youthful idealism. Treasure it. Keep it.

15. One of Nevada's and America's most dangerous adversaries is apathy. You can help change that. Get off the sidelines. Get involved.

16. Relationships make us grow. Multiply the number of people you know.

17. Whether you fry fast-food hamburgers or go on to school, if you focus on personal improvement, you will win.

18. Some people spend life chasing rainbows, never realizing that the rainbows are home. Cherish your family—it is the embodiment of what you are, of what you can become.

19. Do you wonder where miracles are? Look inside you. The miracles are there.

20. The final point was given me by Reno architect Ray Hellmann in an interview just before graduation last year. His point applies to you and graduates everywhere and always. Hellmann said: "We face great issues. But the greatest issue is YOU! The issue is what YOU decide to do with YOUR life!"

June 20, 1993

A Few Trenchant Opinions from Daily Headlines

PEOPLE frequently ask me if I ever have an opinion of my own. "You usually quote others. Don't you have your own ideas?"

Or they say, "Your column is fairly positive. Do you at times think negatively, too?"

I do have opinions.

I do think negatively. Yet, I don't regularly burden readers, who have too many negatives bombarding them as it is.

However, as to personal opinions, let me share some as I react to recent *Reno Gazette-Journal* headlines:

1. "Russia, China end hostility."

Famous non-last words.

2. "Many local voters baffled."

Also puzzled, perplexed, mystified, vexed, dumbstruck.

3. "Local governments often face funding problems."

What Nevada needs is a healthy cigar and some new news.

4. "Teen muggers face year in wilderness isolation."

Far, far away won't be nearly far enough.

5. "Two Reno bridges make list of state's problem sites."

Had the writer interviewed University of Nevada, Reno professor Bruce M. Douglas, one of the nation's top experts on infrastructure, Douglas would have told us that the local and national situation is even more desperate than we know.

6. "Nevada's tight money leaves university funding in doubt."

There isn't a sitting legislator with guts enough to publicly call for enough new taxes to create a top education system.

7. "Push needed if building is to bear (Bruce) Thompson's name."

The naming is up to U.S. Sen. Harry Reid. However, only direct intervention from heaven can prompt Reid to support Reno's revered Thompson (1912-92).

8. "Reno Little Theater launches 60th season."

It's disgraceful that our alleged culturally literate city gives this enduring gem such pitiful support.

9. "Country music's women fight for independence."

So do most women.

10. "Picture Liz Taylor selling Avon."

One of the world's most overweight, overrated hucksters is shilling anew.

11. "Football Pack escape's Lumberjacks' ax."

At present, this Nevada team is in about the same condition as our bridges. (See headline No. 5.)

12. "Coach Ault: 'We've still got a lot of work to do.' "

This football season, we will find out if God truly is on our side.

13. "The bottom line was we found a way to win."

Jeff Horton, UNLV football coach, continues the cliché-speak he mastered as a disciple of Coach Ault.

14. "Florida 70, New Mexico State 21."

The New Mexican who scheduled this game ought to be publicly caned.

15. "Jason Kidd (basketball star) signs for $60 million."

Eventually, greed will kill most professional sports.

16. "Casinos say dinner shows are losing proposition."

More of the public-be-damned pap.

17. "Candidates flood airways."

I haven't heard this much screaming since the hogs ate grandma.

18. "Nugget opens new garage."

John Ascuaga now has the finest Nevada garage since we won statehood back yonder in '64.

19. "Vegas teen dies of AIDS."

Most people don't know that Nevadans die almost every day of this terrible illness. AIDS is being hidden from the public by relatives, just as cancer once was. But AIDS ultimately will threaten all humankind. Denying its existence will help perpetuate it as the eventual Public

Health Enemy No. 1.
    20. "RSCVA woos air executives."
    Thanks, RSCVA, for at last getting off the dime.

Sept. 5, 1994

COLUMNIST CONFIDENTIAL _____

Columnist's Decade Exciting, Rewarding

THE ROLLAN MELTON COLUMN is written first and almost always about my readers. In most of the 750-word pieces, I subordinate myself, for most readers deserve to be spared the writer's presence and ego.

But today I make an exception. On Oct. 8, 1978, the first of what soon will be 2,000 Melton columns toddled creakily out of this Underwood. My debut as a columnist originally was to have been Oct. 1, but I had procrastinated a full week, trying to get up enough confidence to show my stuff to the world.

I hadn't written for the public print for 19 years, going back to my Reno sports editor days. In the years 1959-78, the news sources I had relied on, mostly in sports, had drifted away. So, it was urgent that I rebuild a broad mass of sources.

I was a 47-year-old babe in the writing woods in 1978, rusty as sin and much too slow. I disappointed people early, and I worried about that. The first column was a few limited-interest items and was awful. *Mason Valley News* publisher Walter Cox, the sage of Yerington, expressed some readers' torment when he wrote me, "Each of your columns is better then the next."

In my first week as columnist, I had an absolutely clean desk, but it has never been tidy since. As I look back on this, the 10th anniversary, I realize I have had this job twice as long as any of my others. Thank God I found steady work.

Writing the column is the most exciting, rewarding and, at times, frustrating job I've had in my 47-year newspaper career. But I am excited about the joys that unfold each day, for I have learned of the unending talents and potential of Nevadans. To interview them and to write about them is tantamount to a post-graduate scholarship to study life.

I try to keep the content evolving as the audience changes. What the column needs is fresh topics and inclusion of people

61

I've not yet gotten to. I'm working on these objectives.

I'd like to log 50 years as its author—which would make me 97 upon retirement.

Some people who remember my long administrative span with newspapers see my byline now and ask how it feels to be retired. I answer, "Fine." I seldom tell them that writing three, and occasionally four, of these babies each week is full time, and then some.

What takes the most time is the researching, especially of item columns—those that include four to 10 vignettes.

I prefer writing single-subject pieces, but sources and readers keep asking for item columns. I am trapped, so I do them.

Here are answers to some of the questions most often asked:

Sunday's column is written on Thursday, Monday's on Friday, and Thursday's piece usually on Tuesday. I rarely write spares for emergencies.

The column that has drawn the most comment was the one about my late mother, published last Mother's Day.

What are my personal favorites? That is the most difficult question, but I suppose they are columns about Nevadans who aren't necessarily public figures but who are the real heroes by dint of their honesty, creativity and caring.

Frustrations? People dying on me before I can write something that makes them smell the flowers. Why can't they cooperate by staying longer?

If I had six columns a week, I could make a dent in this growing pile of "must-do" subjects. I have a Frankenstein's monster on my hands. I cajole, plead and twist arms to acquire worthy material. But I can condense just so much. At my frequency, there is hardly a way I will soon get all those stories into print.

Sometimes, I wish news would cease for months so I can catch up. News keeps occurring. Relentlessly. People call and they're nice when impatiently they ask, "That column you were going to do last year. When will we see it?" "Later," I mumble.

Virtually everything you see in my space appears as it was originally composed. We are history done in a hurry.

I get the most feedback when I make an error. I try to correct each error soon, and in a prominent position.

I have critics and value them, but none is as tough on me as

I am on me. I do reread my published work and often wish I could do it over again.

I prize highly the people who never get public credit for helping me. They include my court of last resort—the young editors who take a final look at my words before we go to press— and the *Gazette-Journal's* composing room people, tremendous allies, who save my hide again and again.

These 10 years have been the highest quality period of my life. The nicest part is all of you out there.

Bless you. Thank you.

Oct. 9, 1988

Dragged, Muttering, into the Computer Age

THE SUMMER BEFORE the start of my senior year of high school, I was a grassy-green cub reporter on the weekly *Fallon Standard*. I regularly banged out local sports stories on a Royal upright type-writer, going at what I then proudly knew was blazing speed.

I was up to 30 to 35 words per minute, a self-de-fined "hunt-and-peck" artisan. I felt no compul-

Sport editor Melton at his Underwood, 1958.

sion to learn the touch-typing system, because I was as quick with those Royal keys as I would ever get. Or so I calculated. But my friend, mentor and role model had a superior idea. He was Kenneth A. Ingram, and I blatantly ignored his suggestion that I enroll in a basic typing class as my final prep year dawned.

I had it in my mind that my youth contained more wisdom than did Ingram's experience. But the veteran newspaper leader, to my chagrin, put a flanking move on me. Going behind my back to school officials, he convinced them to compel me to take Typing I. So I was hauled into Paul "Buck" Jensen's class.

It was humiliating, for here I was, a so-called high-and-mighty senior, sitting alongside punk freshmen. Furthermore, typing was an elective I didn't need in order to graduate. Worse, I was the only boy in the room.

I pouted amid my *Standard* newspaper chores, doing my best to ignore the well-meaning Ken Ingram.

But he shadowed me at work, insisting that I not revert to the hunt-peck routine. And wouldn't you know it—within four weeks I was zipping along at about 50 words a minute as a touch-typist.

There hardly has been a day in the ensuing 42 years that I haven't used a manual machine. I roar at a 90- to 100-word-a-minute clip. All my composition, including nearly 13 years of writing this column, has been on my Underwood. I have never used an electric typewriter.

But effective this day, I am taken captive by the current technology. As you read this, you are present at the creation. At least my boss, Lifestyle editor Catherine Mayhew, alleges it is creation. "You will be a more creative writer now that you are on a terminal," Mayhew soothes me.

Now, however, I am pouting. After 42 years of trying to be civil to the Ingrams and Mayhews of the world, I am certain I could do better punching keys with my elbows than with these confused fingers. I may not be polite to Mayhew for hours. Unless she orders good manners. Which she may.

I am the last of our full-time writers to go to the computer. Until now, my secretary, Mickey Wessel, input my typewritten copy into the computer.

So I commence reversion to "cub" level after more than four decades. My typing speed today is maybe 15 to 20 words a minute. God, even my mind operates faster than that! I also am caught up in nomenclature simple to little school kids:

Cursor, sign-on, password, SEND, STORE, delete, insert, erase—to name a few.

Perhaps this "new world stuff" will be for the better. People decades my junior tell me to relax. "It's a snap, once you get the hang of it."

Had I stayed with my Underwood, it could have fallen apart before I do.

Another advantage: Children occasionally tour the newspaper. Until now, they've been drawn to my office by a sound foreign to them: the clatter-chatter of the Underwood.

They used to stare at the manual and columnist as if confronted by museum pieces. Now they have only to focus on me.

One day, if I work diligently, I may come to praise editor Mayhew for hurling me into the modern world.

Colleagues assure me that I shall soon proclaim, "I should not have waited so long!"

For this luxury, I can hardly wait!

Aug. 8, 1991

One Slip of Pen, Lifetime of Confusion

AFTER MY BIRTH, 66 years ago today, my father, Rollan Melton, insisted I also be a Rollan. My mother opposed this, knowing that his name was invariably misspelled and mispronounced. He prevailed.

As a boy, I seldom listened to my elders and their family stories. Except when grandmother told me, "I was pregnant with your dad when I saw the name Roland in a romance magazine. I liked it. When he was born, I told a nurse that's what we wanted our baby's name to be." Grandmother should have spelled it for them.

On his birth certificate, my father's name came out R-o-l-l-a-n, instead of R-o-l-a-n-d. My father seldom used his name, due to the spelling problems. To the end of his life, he was called by his nickname, "Bunk."

Anyways, he wished that his given name live on. It passed to me. The Internet indicates I am unique, the only Rollan Melton currently residing in the United States of America.

From infancy to age 6, I was called "Sonny," allegedly because of a cordial personality. I didn't know I had a real first name until 1937, when mother took me to school to start first grade. She spelled my name for the teacher: "R-o-l-l-a-n."

Difficulties multiplied as both first and last names were systematically misspelled on report cards and records. The second-grade teacher wrote "Rolan." In third grade, I was "Ronald." By age 12, I had acquired a double-errored identity: "Roland Milton."

I never got my name in public print until I was 14 and won a swim race. The *Times-News* in Twin Falls, Idaho, reported that first place went to one "Ralyn Nilton." Notwithstanding the spelling, I lugged that tattered clipping in my billfold until it disintegrated.

When I entered high school in Fallon, I dropped my nickname, electing to come out of the Sonny closet and become a Rollan Melton.

67

My name showed up twice in my first-year *Lahontan* annual. Shown alongside pretty Jacqueline Pyke, I was called "Ronald Milton" in the caption of the freshman class picture. In the "C" squad basketball team photo, I am immortalized as "Rolyn Milton." Thereafter, Rollan Melton was accurately spelled in the *Lahontan*, for I was a staff member of the yearbook.

Early in life I gently corrected people who twisted my names beyond recognition. But eventually I regarded misspellings with amusement, marveling at misspellers' creativities.

I kept a file of wrong spellings, many done by teachers and university educators; also from readers who've seen my name on this column for years. The list keeps getting longer. To date, it includes such creations as:

"Rolando," "Renaldo," "Relgan," "Roland," "Rolland," "Rol," "Roly," "Roly-Poly," "Milton," "Malton," "Meltone," "Rollum," "Rollie," "Mel" and "Melville," with apologies to Herman: How dare they confuse me with the great literary creator of the white whale?

Letters have arrived addressed to "Raleigh Melton," stirring within Sir Rollie's kindly breast an urge to fling a cape atop ye ole puddle, so lady fair's toes escape a soak.

Once, honoring my upbringing in Fallon Hearts of Gold country, a roving caricaturist, "Pancho," drew my face and added a cantaloupe stomach. He entitled the portrait, "Melon-Belly Melton."

For many people, pronunciation of my name has been a stern test. Easy-way-out variations include "Ron," "Roland," "Ronald" and, "Hey You."

The true pronunciation is Rawl-Un.

Actually, I respond cheerfully to most any name, especially to Rollie.

I love my given name. As I mentioned above, the Internet declares that, name-wise, I am unique.

If I'm wrong, surely other Rollan Meltons will advise me of the error of my ways. If so, I know they'll spell our name accurately.

July 24, 1997

Abuse Lingers Long after Dad's Days of Fury

I AM 62 YEARS OLD. But when I learn another woman has been beaten or killed by a man, my mind races back, and I am a little boy again.

It is the saddest of memories—a man attacking an innocent woman, again and again. He was strong. She was weak. She was his victim.

He was my father. She was my mother, and what he did to her scarred her body and beat up her sense of esteem.

What happened decades ago has shaped me and helped me to be acutely attuned to what women are up against.

I learned so early that verbal and physical abuse could wreck a woman's life.

Rusty with Bronna, left, and Sonny, 1937.

1935: I am 4, and on a night I will see to my last day, I crouch with my little sister. Both of us are scared to death.

We are in our little house in Boise, Idaho, the city where we were born.

Our mother had told us a few days before, "Your daddy don't live here anymore, Sonny and Bronna. He's still your daddy. But I had to divorce him."

Years later, when I was old enough to understand, I was told what father's problem was. I understood, I guess. But I never accepted.

69

Our father had been a drunk since he was 19. Though a little boy, I understood that he was two men.

I loved one of them. But even then, I learned to fear the one who could become corrupted by alcohol, the one who frightened us so, and who tortured our mother.

He would shove her, cuss her, yelling how she made his life unbearable. I could never understand how he could loathe the mother we loved.

Our mother seemed always to have black-and-blue marks on her arms, and she cried until her eyes were red.

At last, she was sick to death of his abuse and got up the courage to get money from her mother and go to court.

The attack occurred one night, not long after she had told us, "Your daddy don't live here anymore."

It was night and I awoke and heard him yelling at her through the door. "Just let us in. Just want to talk for awhile," I heard him say.

Poor mother was persuaded to obey. She must have believed he wouldn't hurt her again. After all, they were no longer husband and wife.

It was a classic misjudgment by a trusting woman.

Mother let my father in, and the beating began. There was a man with him, and I remember his name, though it has been 58 years.

Jess Hug, like my father, was a baker. He had always seemed to be a nice man when I would go to the Holsom bakery, where my father and Hug worked. But on this night, Hug was drunk. So was father.

Bronna and I cowered behind the cook stove, then crawled in back of a bed, staying together. Afraid.

We could hear mother scream, and hear his blows destroying her.

I see in my mind's eye mother trying to shield herself, and I can see her knocked to the floor, and struggling up.

I can hear Jess Hug, the spectator at an assault, laugh and encourage our father.

I still hear her cries for mercy, and I see her beaten down and defeated.

A night to remember. A time that is impossible to forget.

June 23, 1994

A Story of One Mother Who Wouldn't Quit

WHAT AN AWFUL FIX Rusty was in!

Trapped in the midst of the Great Depression with her two little children. A sixth-grade education fitted her for the lowest menial tasks. Jobs were pitifully few.

She had divorced her gambling, drinking man and now faced the tough world alone. There wasn't any child support. Her people couldn't help much because everyone was strapped.

She had seen as a child the havoc a drifting father could inflict. Rusty, born Beulah Williamson, in Iowa, had flaming red hair, and a father who abandoned the mother, Rusty and two

Brownie and Sonny, 1937.

other children. Rusty's mother, uneducated and unskilled, had carried on alone. The family's history was being repeated in the 1930s.

Rusty mustered strength to do what must be done. She talked most about somehow raising her children, nicknamed Brownie and Sonny.

In the 1930s, they lived in a parade of rundown places, a step ahead of anxious landlords.

First, Rusty went to her hands and knees, scrubbing the mansions along Warm Springs Avenue in Boise, Idaho, getting 10 cents an hour, hating "the stingy rich." She learned to tend bar and to wait on tables and sent the kids scurrying through alleys, scrounging for soft-drink bottles that would yield deposits.

By 1937, Rusty, Sonny and Brownie were living in a converted chicken coop, rented for $5 a month. To her little ones, it was seventh heaven. There were pastures to roam and chickens to chase. The place could be exciting, as on the night police came to scold Rusty, who had waited until dark, scooted through a barbed-wire fence and milked a neighbor's goat to get milk for the kids. Creative and unlawful.

After the United States went to war in 1941, Rusty got a waitress job at Gowen Air Field, Boise, where the hard life was sweetened once in awhile: Shaking actor Jimmy Stewart's hand and rescuing Clark Gable's cigarette butts for posterity after he had eaten and flashed her a major-league smile.

She always kept Brownie with her, but times were so lean, the boy was sent to live with a succession of relatives and other families. He staggered through eighth grade, counting 18 elementary schools in his life.

But the three were reunited in the mid 1940s. Rusty found waitress work in a little rural Nevada town. By this time, the kids were in high school. Like their mother, they weren't afraid to work. Brownie had various schoolgirl odd jobs and her brother found an apprentice job.

Rusty worked at a string of restaurants, at $5 a shift, doing occasional back-to-back shifts to beef up income. The main thing was that her children became the first in family history to get high school diplomas.

The mother's health was starting to wither as the pace— and her parade of illnesses—ganged up on her. She worked on, telling the kids something she never thought she could say: "Maybe you can go to college if you can pay your way."

She knew that with education, many more things are possible.

The daughter passed up college to marry. The son, helped by townspeople, won a full-ride academic scholarship to the University of Nevada, largely because a young, courageous mother had not an ounce of quitter in her.

Years ago, Rusty moved to California to spend the balance of her life. In 1985, daughter Bronna died, and that started Rusty's final decline.

At the hospital, just before Christmas 1986, the son held her hand a final time and, though barely short of her 75th birthday, she showed that mothers never stop worrying about their children. Her last words to him were, "Sonny, please be extra careful driving home over the Sierra."

He left, remembering then and always, the classified ad she had placed in the Nevada weekly newspaper after he graduated from high school:

"Thank you, Fallon, for the beautiful things you have done for my son, Rollan Melton."

May 9, 1988

QUOTABLE NEVADANS _____

A Sense of Humor in the State Bar _____

NEVADA BAR ASSOCIATION president Margo Piscevich has long believed in the axiom, "If we learn to laugh at ourselves, we'll forever be amused."

The Reno lawyer, in her 24th year of law practice, has kept a journal on courtroom quips, famous last words and how laughter often invades legal inner sanctum.

She says, "When I am asked what is most important in surviving in the law profession, I answer, 'You must be able to laugh at yourself.' "

Here are a few of her recollections of courtroom humor:

• Retired Washoe District Court Judge John Barrett asked a panel of prospective jurors if anyone knew the lawyers. One man was acquainted with Piscevich, who earlier had represented his ex-wife against him in divorce court.

Barrett asked the man if he could treat Piscevich and her client impartially.

"Oh, yes, your honor, I found her to be more reasonable than my ex-wife!"

• This year, Piscevich was the defense lawyer in a case tried in Washoe District Court. A young woman and her 3-year-old son entered the gallery. The boy didn't utter a sound. Upon adjournment, Piscevich asked, "How did you get your son to stay so quiet and still?"

The mother replied, "Before we went in, I told him the courtroom was like church, and he must be absolutely quiet. The judge (Mark Handelsman) entered, wearing a long, black robe, and he seated himself in a big chair in front of a marble background.

My son whispered to me, 'Is that God?' "

• There was a politically correct jury in California, which upon returning a verdict in a murder trial, declared, "We find the defendant not quite guilty."

• In a rural Nevada courtroom, the district attorney was questioning the witness, a cowboy. He was cooperative, but directed all his answers to the prosecutor, who finally suggested, "Speak directly to the jury."

The witness looked squarely at the jurors and said, "Howdy."

• Piscevich was once in the courtroom of Washoe District Court Judge Grant Bowen, waiting for the uncontested calendar. After Bowen handed a sentence of two consecutive 30-year terms, the convicted man, in his late 60s, said, "Your honor, I don't think I can serve this sentence."

Judge Bowen peered at him over his omnipresent eyeglasses and replied, "Just do the best you can."

• It was a Reno fender-bender case and the defense attorney said to the witness, a young woman, "What gear were you in at the moment of impact?"

She replied, "Gucci sweats and Reeboks."

• "What do you do?" a potential juror was asked by a lawyer. His reply, "I've never had a job and I've never been fired."

• There was the potential juror who asked to tell about his job.

"Very boring."

"Even more boring than this proceeding?"

"No, not this boring."

• There was the prospective juror, a conservative rancher, who felt that candor was the best approach. "What do you do in your spare time?" he was asked.

"I smoke marijuana."

• A lawyer halted his long cross-examination of a witness, exclaiming, "Your honor, one of the jurors is asleep."

"Well, you put him to sleep. Now wake him up."

Margo Piscevich's summation for fellow lawyers:

"Humor gives perspective, a reality check with a chuckle. Humor helps make the legal profession human. Don't leave home without it."

Nov. 21, 1994

Manoukian Quotes Worth Repeating ___

FOR YEARS, I'VE COLLECTED the one-liners of Don Manoukian, the incomparable Reno developer, Realtor, jolly good fellow, former pro football star and wrestler— and much more.

The late San Francisco columnist Herb Caen once wrote, "Don Manoukian makes Don Rickles sound like Oral Roberts."

With that, here are Manoukianisms:

• "My brother-in-law, Roy Powers, says when I drop in for dinner he has to get an emergency loan for food."

• "When I'm ravenously hungry before dinner, I warm up with Granola bars. Sort of anorexia in reverse."

• "Once I was invited to pose nude for a *Playgirl* magazine centerfold. But I had to decline. My hands were too small."

• "The fans really create a pro wrestler's image. If you're short, stocky and a little hairy—well, I'm no matinee idol, you know."

• "The smog is so thick in Los Angeles, it looks like the card room at the Reno Elks Lodge."

• Los Angeles is the only area I know of that the Indians don't want back."

• "It's well known in pro wrestling that the promoters always split it down the middle. They take 70 percent, and give the rest to the gladiators."

• "The power company will continue the longest-running comedy in Nevada, called, 'One guy in the hole digging, while four guys look down and watch, as their five pickups block traffic.' "

• "The gals with the tight sweaters and short skirts will not let up. They already have 90 percent of the world's wealth and 100 percent of what man has pursued since Adam and Eve. That's why they have 90 percent of the wealth."

• "Conservationists are consulting engineers in drag, creating business for themselves."

• "What will the future bring? We will still be electing C students who are guided and advised by D students."

• "Business is fantastic! It's exciting! Something to rave about! Just terrific! If things get much better, pretty soon I'll be breaking even."

• "Sure, I graduated from Stanford. If you ever get into the university, you graduate. The people there are so vain, they won't admit they've made a mistake."

• "I was on Stanford's all-Armenian team for three straight years. I always thought America was discovered by Christopher Columbusian."

• "Back in my professional-athlete days, I used to travel with Leo Nomellini, the 49ers tackle. Leo had a habit of pounding on the dashboard. In six months, he wore out three cars and 50 radios."

• "Fellow athletes sometimes poked fun. Like Ron Mix of the San Diego Chargers, who said I could do everything with a football except sign it."

• "I need to make one thing perfectly clear. Everything I say is completely unrehearsed."

• "My Stanford teammate and friend, Jim Plunkett, got so rich he took to serving top sirloin in his tacos, instead of hamburger."

• "Years ago, when I was on a long wrestling tour in Japan, I learned they are the world's greatest copiers. I ordered three-dozen shirts, and gave them one of mine to get the size right. I was going to throw it away anyway because it had a cigarette burn on one sleeve. When I got the shirts back, they were all perfect—36 shirts, 36 burns in the sleeves."

Aug. 23, 1999

80

Wise Words to Grads as They Move on _____

HERE IS RENO Rotary Club members' advice to 1992 Nevada high school graduates:
- "You can make the world better by making a better you."
Richard Abbott, 48, Sierra Nevada Job Corps director
- "Education is most important! Look to yourselves, not government, for solutions."
Oliver Aymar, 77, retired Reno businessman
- "Remain family oriented, for it is family that perpetuates what and who we are."
John Bancroft, 59, Reno retired inventor and developer
- "Help keep our national defense strong. We don't know who America's next enemy will be. We need to work to improve other countries' standards of living. It is getting to be more of a have-nots' world, and that's dangerous."
Clarence Becker, 73, U.S. Air Force, Ret., Reno
- "Think of yourself as an artist, your life as the creation of art. Every moment is a creative moment and each moment a new opportunity. Whatever you try to create for another always will come back to you. That includes both loving, helpful or healing actions, and negative, destructive ones."
Peggy Berkaana, 45, executive director of Reno American Red Cross, in her letter to daughter, Veronica, who graduates from high school with an $80,000 Navy ROTC academic scholarship
- "Don't rush to college if you aren't ready. You may get more out of higher education when you're older."
Lisa Billow, 31, Yerington veterinarian
- "Continue to work on your relationships with people. It can be the most important thing in life, making you continue to grow."
Robert Blanz, 60, president of Nevada Bell
- "Avoid the bad habit of expecting others to do it for you. We must be responsible for things we get ourselves into."

Dr. Treat Cafferata, 54, Reno physician and surgeon
 • "This is no longer a WASP nation. Make yourself increasingly aware of the diverse background of fellow citizens. Be sensitive to the differences. If we don't do a good job of getting into the tent of democracy, it is going to be torn down."
Washoe District Judge Lew Carnahan, 46, Reno
 • "America is the world's greatest country. Don't screw it up!"
Johnny Cassinari, 71, a retired musician and Johnny's Little Italy restaurateur
 • "Whether you're flipping hamburgers or running a company, give it everything you've got!"
Chuck Clipper, 75, U.S. Marine Corps, Ret.; retired executive director of United Way of Northern Nevada and the Sierra
 • "Be citizens! This means getting beyond yourself and beyond complaining. Get involved!"
Joe Crowley, 58, president of the University of Nevada, Reno
 • "Do your best to help others, and you yourself will be rewarded."
Henry de Wyk, 50, chief executive of the YMCA of the Sierra
 • "Don't let barriers stop you from attaining goals. Rely heavily on yourself and on your instincts."
Geno Del Carlo, 46, Valley Bank executive
 • "Our country's got big, big problems. Let's get on with solutions. It's time to cut out the dancing."
Bruce M. Douglas, 55, University of Nevada, Reno professor of civil engineering and earthquake research
 • "You either can be player or follower. We need honest, committed players, rolling up sleeves to solve economic, environmental and sociological problems. As an individual, you can make a difference."
Bryce Griffith, 50, Reno corporate health-care executive

June 14, 1992

A Grandfather's Words of Wisdom to His Grandson _____

AFTER THE DEATH of Elmer Briscoe (1913-91), Reno's police chief from 1960-71, I was visiting his wife, Margie, and daughters Barbara, Judy and Nancy.

We spoke of how he had been reared by his mother after his police-officer father was killed in the line of duty; they mentioned that Elmer had grown up poor, but with a loving and supportive mother.

We talked about the young Briscoe's great work ethic, of how he educated himself, of how he encouraged young people to educate themselves so they could better their lives.

Margie Briscoe and her daughters gave me a letter the old chief wrote nearly nine years ago to his grandson David. The letter was composed on the boy's 13th birthday.

A fortnight ago, that boy, David Elmer Ross, of Reno, turned 21.

I share what police chief Briscoe wrote to the youngster, because the message is applicable to every boy and girl, particularly as they head into the teen years:

"You are no longer a child, and in a few short years you will be a man.

"The man you will become depends on the teen-ager you will be, so this is probably one of the most important landmark birthdays of your life.

"There is a 'Y' in the road, and you will have to decide now which of those roads you will take.

"One road is paved, but goes nowhere. The other is rougher, and a little longer, but it will take you wherever you choose. You can become whatever you wish.

"When you set your sights high, you will get there. As I said, the road will become a bit rougher. But its distance is not much longer. The time and effort you exert to get there will be worth it, and you will never regret your choice.

"Living is like running a marathon race. Sometimes, the farther you run, the more difficult the race. But if you slow down, or drop out, you won't win—and you know it is important to win.

"It is important that a runner train and practice, because if he doesn't, he cannot win.

"Most of us want to get to the top. Some will, some won't. Only those who work extra hard can reach it. They will be the champions in whatever field they choose.

"They will be the leaders of tomorrow. They will be respected by the others, and the others will support them in accomplishing even higher goals.

"It is possible for you to be the president. A U.S. senator. A great scientist. A famous doctor. A leading lawyer. An engineer.

"But first, David, you must take the right road. The road that leads to what now may appear to be unattainable.

"There are kids you now go to school with who will get there. So ask yourself, 'Why can't I?'

"You have your chance and you don't want to let it slip through your hands. Grab hold and hang on tight.

"In taking the longer, rougher road, be careful of stumbling over roadblocks—alcohol, drugs, disrespect, bad company, laziness, lack of ambition, prejudice and dishonor.

"Grandson David, this letter may not have made sense to me if my grandfather had written it to me when I was your age. But it would have when I was 20 and 40 and older. I believe it can be meaningful to you now and always.

"Remember, David, some men will die in the White House. Some will die in prison. The latter probably never got sound advice. Or did not listen if they did.

"Thanks for listening, dear David."
—Love, Papa

Nov. 7, 1991

Native Reno Doctor Shares His Thoughts

EACH MOMENT of my newspaper columnist existence is a joy, a kind of postgraduate scholarship to life. I meet fascinating people who invariably educate me.

Take last Wednesday, for instance, when I again visited with a great Nevadan, Dr. Louis Ernest Lombardi, born in Reno 80 years ago. He is a premier general-practice physician and surgeon, a guy who grew up in the house where he was born, at Fifth and Vine streets, a man who has been to war, who served longer as University of Nevada System regent than any other, a man unspoiled by his successes.

Dr. Lombardi has rubbed elbows and traded humor and swapped golf tales with the famous; he delivered more than 4,000 babies in a medical career that began in Reno in 1934 and continues on a limited basis today.

To scratch and earn his way through the University of Nevada, his studies at Stanford University and through medical school, he worked variously as news hawk on Reno streets, sales boy, theater usher, gas-station attendant, janitor and delivery boy.

He is a quiet, attentive listener, a man who grew proud of his Swiss heritage; he has been for a long while an overachiever as a golfer; he is not an eloquent public speaker, yet you will not often hear a better one. He has that wonderful knack of understating his own role in making Nevada a better place.

He was in a reflective mood four days ago. I asked him to speak on any topic, and out came his feelings: He shared his philosophy; he spoke of the great athletes seen and admired; he spoke of the American fighting man's valor; of the courage he

85

has seen in women in childbirth; and of the humor and wisdom of his friends and golfing partners. He remembered the virtues of his own unsung parents, Lena Yori and Samuel Lombardi, who were the first of his many role models.

Here follow his comments on a number of topics:

• SCHOOL DROPOUTS: "It breaks my heart to see kids leave school. I've seen so much potential go unrealized. If only we can convince them that quitting is folly."

• EDUCATION: "The more you get, the more you can solve a multitude of problems, and maximize your opportunities. In the 30 years I was a regent, I saw many thousands lift themselves with learning."

• ROLE MODELS: "It is essential throughout life that we have people we can look up to, whose qualities we try to emulate. It is impossible for me to list all my chief mentors. But the one in education I must list is Silas Ross Sr., with whom I served as regent."

• INJURIES: "I was Wolf Pack team doctor almost 25 years. Athletic injuries are child's play compared to what people do to themselves in cars, on cycles and skateboards, or by falling down the stairs."

• THE BEGINNING: "Our family doctor would come to our house; he would give us all-day suckers; he carried that little bag and he always wanted to help us; I decided at age 7 that I wanted to become what he was."

• WAR: "I ran World War II combat field hospitals in the South Pacific. I arrived on Iwo Jima the day after the historic flag-raising. War is total hell, the wounds so terrible, the aftermath so irrevocable. How I pray there will be no more for us."

• VALOR: "I was a Navy doctor, but I never saw such courage as our Marines possessed. They couldn't have averaged more than 19 years old in 1943 and 1944. Kids like this kept us free."

• WAR'S END: "After Iwo Jima, we commenced training for the invasion of Japan. They told us to get ready to die. It was estimated a million of us would be killed. Then we dropped the two bombs. If you had seen what the enemy did to our boys, you would have dropped them, too."

• NEVADA BUDDIES: "No matter which combat area I reached, I always sought out Nevadans. Their friendship meant I was home, in a way. One day on Guam, I counted 22 Nevadans in my tent."

• Loss of Spouse: "I was married to my classmate, Alice Lunsford, 31 years, until her death in 1966. Widowhood can be unbearably lonely. I advise staying with your friends, making new ones. Depression can be a harmful adversary."

• His Wife: "Mary Louise and I will be married 21 years come June. She is a great person—my great friend."

• Patients: "I never got materially rich, nor tried. I hate to collect my patients' money.

"I hope to be remembered as a doctor who loved his work. I want my patients to have a good opinion of me. Seeing my patients get well has given me the greatest thrill of my life. The rewards of watching as health is restored is more than I can describe."

Jan. 3, 1988

90-Year-Old Poet Has Deft Observations on Life

CONGRATULATIONS and all the best to one of Nevada's outstanding writers, Thelma "Brownie" Ireland, upon reaching her 90th birthday.

Here is a true mighty mite of the Silver State. Small in stature, she is a literary heavyweight, having crafted thousands of poems, beginning during the years of World War I.

Her style is deft, lyric, rhythmic.

The Reno woman was reared and educated in Nebraska, where she first took up the writing pen. She moved to White Pine County in 1922, building a reputation as an excellent classroom teacher in McGill.

In 1924, she married William N. Ireland of the Kennecott Copper Corp., and they had two children, Patricia Clare Helmick, now of Moraga, Calif., and Bill, of Las Vegas, who had a career as University of Nevada athlete, high school coach at Fernley and Lake Tahoe and football coach and athletic director at UNLV.

Her husband died in 1962 and she moved to Reno in 1975.

Brownie Ireland's love of life has been set down in poetry since her girlhood. As her keen friend, Agnes Nelson, freelance writer from Sparks, says, "Where others see ugliness, Brownie sees beauty."

She began regularly selling her poetry while her children were youngsters, and the family would hear Mother's words being read on such long-ago radio shows as *Don McNeill's Breakfast Club* and *Fibber McGee and Molly*.

A widely traveled person whose work has appeared in *Ladies Home Journal, Better Homes and Gardens* and *Sunset*, Ireland was among the founding members of the Nevada Poetry Society, in 1976.

Her number of poems exceeds 3,000.

Here are samples:

BEST RECIPE:

"Cosmetics get the man, it is said, and in its guile enfolds him. It's true, face powder wins a man, but baking powder holds him."

DEFENSE:

"A new boy came to school today. He stuttered when he spoke. Some children snickered ruthlessly, although it was no joke. He bit his lip but stammered on. The tears began to smart. Then he became belligerent to hide a broken heart."

A GHOST TOWN:

"A heap of scattered ruins that once held wealth galore, a street of vacant buildings, a schoolhouse and a store. An old deserted smelter where blocks of gold were cast, that left behind black slag dumps in mourning for the past. They call it just a ghost town, remnant of greed and schemes. To me, it stands an emblem of courage, faith and dreams."

DOUBLE TROUBLE:

"Some days you're kind and patient, dear, some days you're cross and cruel. Some days you're wise, intelligent, some days you act a fool. Although I really love you, dear, it's very plain to see, that I could never marry you—it would be bigamy."

SUNDAY SERVICE:

"He ruffles through his hymnbook. He fumbles with his tie. He laces up his oxfords. He overworks a sigh. He goes through all his pockets, engrossed in deep research. There's no one quite so busy as a little boy in church."

CORONATION:

"Blue fingers on the mountain with jagged, storm-stabbed scars, reach up into the twilight to catch the coming stars. And as the night grows deeper and spreads throughout the land, the black and distant mountains wear diamonds on each hand."

SON OF THE PINES:

"A pine grove hulas to the wind and sings. Hark! Can you hear it? How can its song sound like the sea when it has not been near it?"

MOUNTAIN STORM:

"White feathers float and fill the air, released by thunder's jolting. Is there a cockfight in the sky, or are the down clouds molting?"

July 21, 1989

HUSBANDS AND WIVES

Promises of Tomorrow Fell out of the Sky, too

SO MANY THOUGHTS after the plane crash.

The hurts, again ganging up on Sue Wagner.

The death of a lovely friend, Judith Seale.

The grievous wounds of Bob Seale and Wagner.

There in Washoe Medical Center's Emergency/Trauma section, friends continued to jam in, as the news got out.

Plane crash on Labor Day in Fallon.

At the hospital, the visitors had public names.

Raggio. Miller. Crowley. Jan Evans. Townsend. Bryan Nelson.

Judith Seale

But noteworthiness wasn't on parade.

There were crying jags, and hugs that propped each other up, and there were no Democrats, and no Republicans. Labels vanished. Camaraderie took over.

There was concern that Sue Wagner's daughter and son be informed and brought to their mother's bedside from their campuses in Colorado and Arizona. They are children left fatherless by a plane crash 10 years ago.

Friends of Judy and Bob Seale said over and over that their marriage of going on 25 years was a marvelous partnership. They had no children. But they had each other.

In the ensuing hours, it is the story of the Seales, and the lessons their lives give us, that keep coming to mind.

93

Their final moments together were in the Cessna cockpit, he as pilot, she as his experienced copilot. We can picture Seale, candidate for state treasurer and heralded as a man of careful detail, battling to tame a plane that now refused his commands.

Surgical nursing leader Judith Seale's stricken last seconds were filled with concern for friends aboard the plane.

"We're going in," she cried. "Everyone tighten your belts!"

Bob Seale's parents have died, as have Judith's. An aunt of Seale's was with him as Tuesday dawned. Around 2:30 that morning, he finally asked about his wife and the aunt told him she was gone.

On the surface, they were different.

He is gregarious, plugging into new friendships rapidly. She was not one for the spotlight. He has this deep wish to serve the public, an urge so strong that, months ago, he gave up his Pangborn & Co. partnership, to avoid any potential conflict of interest amid his political run.

She loved horses and her life was spiced by a love of rural Nevada. He has been a force in improving our cultural environment, especially at the Nevada State Museum.

But as unlike as they seemed, each complemented the other.

She always reacted swiftly when something struck a wrong note and, frankly, she had not been pleased at his decision to run for the statewide office. Yet, as the campaign lengthened and Tuesday's primary drew near, she warmed to the mission.

She joined her husband on a recent Las Vegas swing and was savoring their quick weekend rural visits.

His days were chewed up by the campaign, especially by the long distances a statewide candidate must travel in Nevada. However, he could see that progress was coming, that he could overtake the incumbent, Ken Santor. The wife and husband shared the thrill of seeing the *Las Vegas Review-Journal* editorial, a ringing political endorsement of Robert Seale.

He was so right that progress was made. The voters, not many hours after the plane went down, gave Seale a resounding victory in the primary.

Sunday was their final full day together and, fittingly, they had the day to themselves.

They were accomplished equestrians, although the pounding tempo of the primary campaign had kept him from joining her on rides the last few months.

Instead, there had been the quiet barbecues at home out on the patio, just the two of them. She had kept riding on weekends, but invariably alone.

Sunday was different. It was a picture-postcard day, with our cloudless September sky, and a little early temperature nip that hinted the nearness of autumn.

On Monday, they would fly to Fallon for the cantaloupe festival and holiday parade.

But Sunday was theirs. They went to the place they loved to ride, on the beach along Big Washoe Lake. Judy was up on See, her favorite animal, and Bob Seale aboard his gelding, Twister.

They had a day to savor as outdoorsmen. As a team. Being together. Living for the moment. Until tomorrow came.

Sept. 6, 1990

Crash Survivor Fights through Pain, Tragedy

BOB SEALE flashed a bright smile from his hospital bed. His eyes twinkled. He spun me around with a little one-liner and we laughed together.

He alone remains hospitalized among those hurt so badly 28 days ago in the Labor Day crash of his campaign plane. But Bob Seale, reinforced by a cadre of medical experts and his own great strength, is well on the way to coming back.

A glow that is his personal trademark is rekindled.

He lost his greatest possession when his wife, Judy, died in the accident near Fallon.

"Over the years," he tells me, his voice husky as he speaks of her, "I would occasionally think that if I ever lost Judy, I, too, would be forever lost."

But he knows now that he must go on. For Judy, for himself, for those who've rallied to him.

He speaks of a Nevada army of supporters, of the medical help, and he speaks of now and tomorrow.

"I am overwhelmed by the love given me. Inspirational letters from Panaca, from Yerington, from Elko. All over the state."

A Saint Mary's nurse, Laurie, steps to his bedside. "Everything all right, Bob? Need anything now?" He waves her off, saying he's being smothered with attention and that he loves it.

With his left hand, steadied by an elbow-to-hand brace, he pokes his chest. "All these nurses and doctors have put this

Humpty Dumpty back together again."

Putting Seale's broken parts back in normal order has been one tall task.

His legs were broken. His left wrist was broken. His left heel was shattered. Ribs were cracked. There were deep burns, including ones on his throat and forehead. He laughs, gesturing: "I'm wearing my Olivia Newton-John headband."

In a delicate surgery three weeks ago, the small finger of his right hand was removed. But he is ever the optimist. "Fortunately, I am left-handed." Seale, finalist in the race to become the next Nevada state treasurer, is a veteran certified public accountant.

We talked briefly about the campaign and he took on an intensity.

"My team was back here yesterday," he related. "We went over who's doing what. Nothing's changed. Everybody has something vital to do."

He had to add a final thought on this, his maiden voyage into politics: "I've already lost too much to lose this race."

Bob Seale recognized from the moment he was told of the enormity of his loss that he would need special help. "A week after the accident," he said, "I asked that a grief therapist visit me. I have done much in my life. But I have no experience with how to handle the loss of Judy."

Such an expert is counseling him. Seale is learning there is joy in reflecting on his wife and what they had together and that showing one's grief not only is all right, but very necessary in the emotional healing. They would have been married 24 years on Nov. 18.

One of the toughest procedures he has been confronted with is the twice-daily changing of bandages, requiring one-and-a-half hours a crack. "They must think I'm Lon Chaney in those old *Mummy* movies," he says.

Seale's hardest work has come twice a day in sessions with a physical therapist, "To get me tuned up again."

His physical healing progresses ahead of the most optimistic predictions. Gone are the myriad drainage tubes. He has gained mobility. The little things we take for granted when healthy are so meaningful to him.

Last Sunday morning, he shaved himself for the first time. Two days earlier, he called a halt to being spoonfed.

"I'm eating on my own from here on," he said with a laugh, waving a fork at brother Wayne, a nuclear physicist and university educator in Sao Paulo, Brazil.

Except for the busted ribs, Seale, who turns 49 on Thursday, suffered no internal injuries. The shattered heel is the most serious hurt of all and will require much more healing time.

Additional skin grafts on his legs and forehead were done successfully last Wednesday.

His weight is down at least 15 pounds since the crash. The people at Saint Mary's have been badgering him to eat, loading him up with calories.

"I'll eat anything except okra," he says with a laugh. "People have been good about smuggling in goodies from the outside." A fortnight ago, candy-coated peanuts arrived. A filet mignon dropped in on him the other night.

Workmen have been reconfiguring his home, creating ramps so that he will have access while still in a wheelchair.

Early this week, probably Tuesday, Bob Seale will leave Saint Mary's. He will go home again.

Sept. 30, 1990

Experiment in Marriage Still Going Strong

I WON'T TRY to convince you my wife's a total saint.

She works her crossword puzzle first, then scans the comics, putters over the stories, pictures and weather page. An hour later, I'll ask if my column was OK, and she'll tell me she hasn't read it yet.

Three Sundays ago, I saw her read Dave Barry first, then Cory Farley, and me last. This hurt me bad. Especially Marilyn's putting Cory ahead of her own husband.

Marilyn tends to sing off-key, too.

While I insist on promptness, she takes her own sweet time.

Marilyn is so casual that she drives me nuts. Especially if we're preparing to go to a wedding. While she fusses about what to wear, or with her makeup, I pace and stare at my watch. Still, she won't rush.

She blows sky-high maybe once a year. It's the Irish on her mother's side. This is so scary that I then question why I ever hooked up with her.

But now for the beautiful part of my wife.

I met Marilyn Royle in spring 1952. We were students at the University of Nevada, and she was fun, artistic, totally unstuffy, pretty and genuinely interested in people and issues.

We dated for a year and decided to get married. Her parents urged us to wait until we graduated. But waiting didn't suit us.

I was close to broke, so Marilyn busted open her piggy bank and found $14. We went to a Reno hock shop and bought her a cheap, plain wedding band. We eloped to Minden on a Wednes-

99

day night, joined by our closest friends, Sue Casey Baker and Bill Griggs. Sue loaned us $25.

We were married at Justice of the Peace Bert Selkirk's home. The hour was 7 p.m. This was casual. JP Selkirk had on his bedroom slippers. I also savored an irony—he owned Gardnerville's *Record-Courier*. Me, married by a newspaperman!

I wasn't thinking of this as a milestone then. But it was!

A lot of differences can murder a marriage, so little wonder some worried that ours wouldn't last.

Marilyn is Catholic, I had no church. I was from small Fallon, she from big Reno. I boxed and played football, she disliked violent sports. Except for her black-sheep uncle, there hadn't been any divorce in Marilyn's family. In my family, every marriage had failed.

Our own marriage has been a charmed run, with a few bumps, but none we couldn't remedy. It's been our Happiness Express.

I am truthful in telling you that most of our marriage's success is because of Marilyn. Married to a career man absent from home too much, the biggest pressures were on her, as with countless wives. That our four great children survived intact is to their mother's credit.

I have worked with many outstanding leaders. But Marilyn has been my greatest leader. The longer we're together, the more I treasure her honesty, creativity, how she accepts all of us for what we are, and her justice. Her humor is gorgeous—you ought to hear her visit aloud with her imaginary dog, "Buster."

It may sound like I knew from the start she would be my perfect partner. But I didn't. I just lucked out and got the perfect wife.

We were married on March 25, 1953. Forty years ago today. Tonight, we will dine out, just the two of us, and savor our great blessings. Marilyn and I will toast family, friends and our love. I will toast my incredible wife.

March 25, 1993

Persistence Finally Pays off —in a Big Way

LONGTIME RENO couple Martha and Don Jessup were married back in their native Oklahoma in 1951. Their first house was a trailer, bought for $300. It was the first and last home they've owned outright.

Work-wise, they took vows of poverty and became teachers.

Two years ago, they took early retirement, she after 24 years at Brown Elementary School, he as professor of mathematics at the University of Nevada, Reno. (Jessup, 62, also was for a few years vice president of finance in Joe Crowley's administration. Jessup still teaches math once a week on campus.) She's now 61.

They live in a retirement home at tiny Tahoma, Calif., on the west side of Lake Tahoe. Despite the lowered income one gets when retiring early, they've not been on poverty row. Nor on Financial Easy Street.

Month by month, the Jessups whack down the home mortgage. They've been figuring to pay it off by 2001.

Retirement has been spent visiting their children, Kenneth, Rich and Cynthia; spoiling grandbabies; and driving to Reno weekly to see family and friends and to shop.

One of her few luxuries has been spending $1 a week on the California Lottery, at the PDQ Tahoma market—against the knowing advice of arithmetic whiz Don, who has reminded her, "You've got 1 chance in 21 million. Save the buck."

On Easter Sunday, about 11 p.m., the Jessups pulled up to a 7-Eleven at Tahoe City after driving back from Reno. She went inside for bread and milk and to check the numbers of the prior Wednesday's lottery. In the car, weary Don Jessup fell asleep.

He was jolted awake by a mob banging on the car. There

101

was Martha, never looking happier—or more stunned; and the jubilant store clerk, and about 10 others who appeared out of the night to cheer the Jessups.

To cheer what? Martha was screeching, "Don, Don, we're millionaires! Honey, we won!"

"Won what?" sputtered groggy husband.

"Don, we won the lottery!"

The Jessups hit all six numbers, sharing equally with a housepainter from Van Nuys, Calif., who said, "Now I can afford to send my five kids to college."

Martha and Don Jessup's gross share is $1.6 million, payable over 20 years. He's given up advising his wife.

This week, at Barbara Olson's PDQ Tahoma Market, Lotto officers from Sacramento will give the Jessups the first check—about $58,000—what is left after the 28 percent federal income-tax deduction.

On each succeeding April 7, for the next 19 years, they'll get a $58,000 check. The Jessups already pray for future on-time mail delivery.

They now deliberate on how to spend and/or invest the gorgeous new supplementary income. A Christmastime trip to Hawaii for the entire family is likely.

Friends' jolly kidding is proliferating. On Friday, retired University of Nevada, Reno president N. Edd Miller teased Don Jessup: "May I touch you?"

"Sure," Jessup said with a laugh.

"Fine," Miller said with a smile. "I'm putting the touch on you for $6,000."

April 18, 1993

Love, Tenderness Kept Couple Together

TODAY, in an era when one in every two American marriages ends in divorce, Ruby and Robert Swan of Reno celebrate their 60th wedding anniversary.

She is 79 and he is 81; he is tall and baldish; she is just an itsy bit over 5 feet; she has quit driving; he is her taxi guy; he vacuums their southwest Reno condominium without being asked; he slips over to Smith's at Virginia and Moana for pastry and coffee, and when he stays long, she teases: "Bob, you must have a girlfriend there!"

They have loved each other from the start. Two days before his 20th birthday, he got a job at a Columbus, Ohio, clothing store and immediately met 18-year-old coworker Ruby Everly. They eloped on March 24, 1929. "I didn't want to put my parents out for an expensive wedding," she says with a chuckle.

Listen:

Ruby: "How Bob worked! My mother used to say she never knew him when he wasn't holding down two jobs."

Robert: "Wall Street crashed six months after we were married. I couldn't find work. For a time, we had $36 a month coming in and Ruby was earning all of it."

Ruby: "At first we didn't have a bank account. We would just come home and throw what little money we had in a drawer."

Robert: "Ruby was so pretty and remains so beautiful!"

Ruby: "Everyone had things against them in the Depression and we worked to keep our sanity."

Robert: "In the first years we had to both dig hard to keep our belly buttons from touching our backbones."

Ruby: "What has counted most is that we love each other. It wasn't all peaches and cream. We learned to talk things

103

over and set goals together."

Robert: "When I first met her, I found out she had $200 in her bank account. That clinched it. I wanted to marry that girl (laughs)."

Ruby: "Bob kept doing different things—our dry-cleaning business and Internal Revenue Service work for a time, and then building custom homes in Columbus; I did interior decorating and kept books."

Their advice to young marrieds:

Ruby: "Be patient and considerate and learn to work things out."

Robert: "Don't go head over heels in debt. Remember the old saying, 'When poverty comes, love flies out the window.'"

Ruby: "Love each other."

Robert: "Be tender."

Ruby: "Neither husband nor wife is right all the time and you can't be under the same roof and not have disagreements. It helps to compromise."

Except for his hospitalization 18 months ago when he had successful lung-cancer surgery, the Swans have never been apart.

Robert Swan is a mathematical whiz (he majored in math at Ohio State). During our interview, he rattled off this statistic:

"You know how long 60 years of marriage is, my friend? It's 21,915 days, including those 15 additional leap-year days. What a beautiful 60 years!"

After enjoying their 55th anniversary dinner in the Prospectors' Room at Harrah's Reno, management told them, "Come back on your 60th!"

Back to Harrah's they are going—not tonight, because of the conflict with Good Friday, but for a Saturday dinner.

Among the 30 guests will be Ruby Swan's sister, Elaine Sawyer, and their brother-in-law, Gene Sawyer of Reno. And the Swans' only child, Sandra Westin, 40, of Palo Alto, Calif., regional sales manager for Convex, the computer corporation.

Their daughter gave me a lovely ending for this story:

"Mother and Father always give 100 percent to each other;

104

they share common values; they always realized they married not only each other, but each's family; they accept each other for what each is.

"They always strengthen each other."

March 24, 1989

A Masterpiece of Humanity Leaves Us

DOROTHY RAGGIO never made an epic speech, wrote a heralded book or felt a need to be famous. She could be shy; she never stood on pretense; she preferred being "Dottie."

For those who didn't meet her, let me explain why she was a work of art.

She was such a gifted listener. Her quiet disposition was as sweet as honey, and as the lyricist wrote, she was never fully dressed without a smile. Whether you saw her at a cultural gala, or steering a Raley's grocery cart, her manner of dress was immaculate. Fashion does speak a language of its own, and she was its Singular Sensation.

Dottie Raggio was a woman of her time, elegant in her tastes, her modesty, her sense of occasion. She had grace, serenity and a wry humor that often knocked the unwary off balance, especially during Wednesday night pasta grazings at the Truckee River Bar & Grill at Village Shopping Center.

Governors come and go. But her husband, William, has for 50 years been the epitome of high achievement. Some straddle their partners' celebrity, as if on a joyride. Dottie Raggio never did, for she was immune to feelings of self-importance, and balanced her generous disposition by putting those in her circle fully at ease.

She had lovely character, being the possessor of straight thinking. She knew that injustice of any kind was tacky, cruel and narrow-minded, and she was a woman who easily saw through people who needed to satisfy their vanities. Yet, she

106

was kind enough to tolerate egomaniacs. Most of them, anyway.

Through the couple's half-century together, whether he was the young district attorney, or the foremost legislative hitter, she was his omnipresent sounding board. She knew Bill Raggio better than did any other, and she was patient with his torrid agenda, and even with most of his critics, their invented myths notwithstanding. She had an intimate knowledge of what democracy is, and tolerated its menu of painful confrontation. Always, she stood tall and strong by her man.

Her husband relied on her intuitive power, valuing her judgments in family matters, in law, and in his influential governance positions. He long has been a champion of demanding that schools teach adequately, and in this area their philosophies were irrevocably intertwined.

No man ever had a more graceful, loyal cheerleader.

Her values, sense of rightness and steadfast bond with close friends remained to the end. As to her unwavering devotion to the institution of marriage, it remained absolute to the end of her life.

The passing of a work of art always is sorrowful, as it is this day. Dottie Raggio's death diminishes us all.

April 8, 1998

NEVADA PROFILES

Remembering a Man Whose Dignity Shined

IT SEEMED that Sol Dartch was every man's friend. Those who weren't his friend wanted to be. It wasn't that Sol was Mr. Personality, for he was a quiet man. It wasn't that he was a headline-maker.

What Sol had was dignity. He was a shoeshine man, and when you walked past his station outside Harrah's Steakhouse, he'd look first at your shoes. Whether you needed a buff job or not, Sol's gaze went up to your face, and he'd smile. That smile wasn't just saying, "Let me give you a shine, mister." It was saying, "Glad to know you, friend." The dignified man was never on the dole. He came to work.

Sol would shine my shoes, chatter on about all that he'd read and seen, and share what he'd picked up in idle talk, loose gossip, wild rumors. But he didn't deal in malice.

While he was shining, I'd sit there, seeing and feeling his financial straits. I could have shined my own shoes, and most of the time I do, but I'd come to him, as did so many of his other customers, to give him companionship, and to give him some income, but mostly to savor his dignity and serenity.

I'd sit there feeling guilty. As he leaned into my shoes, dispensing common sense, I was enveloped in the truth: Here was Rollan Melton, a white man, born into a situation where he could get educated.

The man hunched before me, Sol Dartch, was of a bleak circumstance. I never probed too much into his past, for fear of embarrassing him. You don't question people in a way that compels them to say, "Sure, I had it awful rough."

But I could speculate accurately on the peril he put up with. With the Sol Dartches, we see the familiar pattern. He was black. Therefore, the odds were heavily against him. It was plain that

111

Sol came from a poor background that denied him opportunity.

I came in for a shine months ago, but Sol was hurting bad. Cancer treatment a couple years earlier had blunted the disease, but it had resurfaced. The man who had had such lousy luck was to be harassed by bum fate right to the end.

I would ask for him each trip in, but Sol didn't come back. It was plain I had seen him for the last time.

The paper carried the obituary. Sol Dartch, 61, had died at his Reno residence. Native of Pennsylvania. Born in 1929. Former professional boxer. No survivors. No funeral planned.

Afterward, Reno lawmaker William Raggio took to the state Senate floor to memorialize Sol. What Raggio said is important to repeat, for all to ponder.

Raggio speaking:

"Sol, a black man, operating his one-chair shoeshine stand outside Harrah's gourmet Steakhouse, was the epitome of neatness and of courtesy. He knew everyone, took great pride in his appearance and in his ability to discuss with you the events of the day.

"He knew people, mingled with the high and the mighty, and he typified the little person who is probably taken for granted by many of us in our day-to-day routine.

"The reason I comment on Sol's ability to know what was going on," Raggio continued, "is because Sol could not read or write. I once made an effort to get him enrolled in a literacy program at Truckee Meadows Community College and he was about to embark on learning to read, when he discovered he had cancer.

"I share his story also because I know some of you (legislative colleagues) have great concern about literacy. I had asked Sol how he got along since he was living by himself. He answered that when he went into a restaurant, he usually ordered a hamburger, since they'd mostly all have it on their menu."

Raggio concluded: "I don't want this day to pass without Sol knowing that someone cares. This is probably the only time Sol ever had his name in a paper. But he made a difference."

March 10, 1991

All That Mayhem Was on the Silver Screen

FOR A FELLOW WHO has been so often beaten, pushed, dropped, bopped and killed off, Stanley D. Brown arrived at his 75th birthday last Friday in incredibly fine shape.

Fortunately, the mayhem was fiction. Boris Karloff didn't actually murder Stan Brown seven times. It was acting, Hollywood style.

Brown and his wife, Ruth, a former dancer on Broadway, have lived in Reno since the late 1970s. He had retired at 62 from a high-powered advertising executive job in Los Angeles, but was tired of doing nothing. Then came a call from Sam Auld, president of LearAvia in Reno. Brown joined the corporation led by Moya Lear, his friend since they were teen-agers.

LearAvia faded from view after a foreign interest bought it. But Stan Brown has continued to be active in community work.

He has been skilled arbitrator in union-management matters, and as volunteer trainer at the Reno Senior Center; he is the respected behind-the-scenes dialog coach of the annual *Sheep Deep*.

He went into the movies with Columbia Pictures after graduation from UCLA, signing a contract in 1938. He tested for the lead in *Golden Boy*, but the part went to an unknown named William Holden.

Brown was to have 150 speaking appearances in his film career, including the leads in five movies done for Republic Pictures at the tail end of World War II. Later, he toured Europe in the stage show *Hellzapoppin*, filling the part done originally by Moya

113

Lear's father, Ole Olsen, of the Olsen & Johnson comedy team.

Here are early entries in his movie appointment book:

• Newsboy in *You Can't Take It With You*, with Jimmy Stewart.

• Eight lines as college freshman in *Lady Lawyer*, starring Virginia Bruce.

• Mostly adlibbed lines as Margaret Tallachet's boyfriend in *Girl School*.

• Dopey kid in Andy Clyde comedy.

• First real part—young Legionnaire in *Revolt in the Sahara*. Got applause from crew after his death scene.

• Tested with most stunning woman Brown had ever seen. Her name was Rita Hayworth.

Once you get Brown to talking about his Hollywood days, the memories came in torrents:

"In *Blind Alley*, Charles Vidor cast me in a small but important part of a young student who is shot by Chester Morris. This started me on a career of being killed early in pictures in which I had good parts . . . (Boris Karloff, star of horror pictures) was actually a charming man who grew prize-winning roses . . . Henry Fonda was as nice a man as I knew in pictures."

Brown had to learn to deal with rejection. "I tested for a good part in the Howard Hawks picture, *Only Angels Have Wings*, starring Cary Grant. I didn't get the job. They told me I looked too much like Cary, which was better for my ego than saying, 'You were rotten in the test.' "

Brown had good roles in the *Blondie* series and with Joan Blondell and Melvyn Douglas in *Good Girls Go to Paris*. Then his career turned around because of his willingness to try anything.

"The casting office called and said, 'We see on your autobiographical form that you can ride a horse. Come in at 5 a.m. Monday to get your cowboy wardrobe.' The problem was I was no horseman, which became painfully apparent when I tried to mount my horse from the right side."

Nonetheless, Brown was typecast in Westerns.

Producer Irving Briskin told him, "You are the weirdest thing in a saddle I've ever seen. But you're a good actor who knows the lines. Next week, you start a picture with Wild Bill Elliott."

Brown finally mastered riding while filming *Arizona*, with Jean Arthur.

114

"The Western scripts offered me only two basic plots," Brown says with a laugh. "Either I was the hot-headed cowboy who got into trouble and the hero saved me, or I was the weak cowboy, and the hero saved me."

Brown was loaned to RKO and did a Tarzan picture with Johnny Weissmuller, then went to Republic, winding up his movie career with lead roles in five pictures. Trouble was, the scripts were lousy. So he left the movies for good in 1945.

He maintains his Hollywood friendships, especially with Lloyd Bridges. They broke into movies together.

The real Stan Brown is a fun man to be with, for he is gregarious and a marvelous storyteller. He is a Nevadan who also is a sterling civic spirit. And that's no act.

Aug. 21, 1989

Jud Allen's Life in Hollywood's Tarnished Tinsel

JUD ALLEN was Reno Chamber of Commerce president for nearly two decades, then a city councilman. But this column, for the first time, illuminates an earlier life.

As a Wisconsin boy, he dreamed of Hollywood. But after the dream came true, he found Hollywood to be a myth. Basically decent people were ruled by a ruthless system that discouraged ethics.

Following his wartime job as Army press agent, Allen got a job with Maggie Ettinger, cousin of Hollywood gossip columnist Louella Parsons. The thrilled young man was told to publicize Dorothy Lamour, Betty Hutton, Irene Dunne, Frank Sinatra, Parsons and many others.

He waited for stars to seek him out for interviews. None did. Finally, Paul Price, later a *Las Vegas Sun* nightlife columnist, threw movie files at Allen, growling, "Your clients are in here. Get busy and 'create' news." Allen obediently invented a story in which Betty Hutton's husband surprised her with a huge diamond. To Allen's amazement, the fiction appeared as truth in Louella Parsons' column. Allen's unease stirred.

He publicized bandleader Horace Heidt's talent show, but calls him the most miserable human he ever knew. "Once at a party, one man said, 'That's a nice horsehide jacket Horace is wearing,' and another replied, 'It ought to be; it's from the skins of three sax players.'"

After Rhonda Fleming was among 45 actresses auditioned to play opposite Bing Crosby in *A Connecticut Yankee in King Arthur's*

Court, an Allen gimmick got her the role.

Fleming had never been closer to the war than one visit to a military canteen. But at a gala dinner, with Allen's coaching, she came off as super patriot—all orchestrated by Allen to influence columnist Parsons.

The plot worked. The grand old lady of keyhole journalism wrote glowingly about Fleming, who was promptly awarded the part.

Non-names had to genuflect to stars' egos and put up with their abuse. Actress Joan Bennett reamed Allen for calling her, by previous day's agreement, at mid morning. "How dare you phone in the middle of the night?!" Sinatra was never accessible. Comic Bob "Bazooka" Burns was an obscene and unfunny bore. Howard Hughes somehow got the phone number of a showgirl Allen was dating. When Allen last saw her, she was being followed by a Hughes limousine.

The system and the fast life beat up stars. Betty Hutton destroyed her life with drugs. Heidt persuaded brilliant-but-innocent accordionist Dick Cantino to sign over 90 percent of his earnings for seven years. Actor Allan Jones didn't want it known he had a happy 20-year marriage "because it could kill my romantic image."

Before Jud Allen burned out after compromising his principles for three years, he publicized Atwater Kent, a retired radio manufacturer who moved to Hollywood to be a professional party-giver.

Colorless Kent didn't know one celebrity from another and was so tired and bored at his parties that he would nap before being photographed with stars.

Allen talked *Life* magazine editors into doing an elaborate picture spread, showing Kent with many stars. When the host saw the huge splash, Kent gushed to Allen, "There is no place for me to go after this. I've had the ultimate."

Two months later, Atwater Kent died, leaving token amounts to his servants while lavishing bequests on Hollywood's famous and rich. The will specified that bleachers for 5,000 people be erected at the cemetery. He wanted comfort for the hordes who would attend his last rites.

Five people came to the funeral of the man who purchased transient notoriety: three servants, Maggie Ettinger and Jud Allen.

Nov. 24, 1991

117

Coach Beasley's Lessons Run beyond Playing Baseball

BUD BEASLEY, the Methuselah of Nevada public education, is going strong as teacher, role model, inspiration and cheerleader for those he has taught and coached for 56 years.

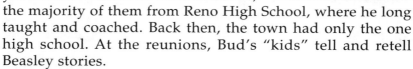

The 80-year-old Reno man is an institution who never appears to forget a name or face, although he sometimes jokingly tells a friend, "In your case, I'm willing to forget."

The fact is that it is his students who remember things he did, or said, from decades ago.

Beasley has just passed through yet another season of class reunions, the majority of them from Reno High School, where he long taught and coached. Back then, the town had only the one high school. At the reunions, Bud's "kids" tell and retell Beasley stories.

He has always dwelled on the need to stay physically fit. But he was also a crackerjack strategist, a winning coach who instilled the principles of mental toughness.

He had been a pitching star with the Sacramento Solons of the AAA Pacific Coast League, one step below the Major Leagues, and was as effective for his guile as for his throwing artistry. Beasley has been passing on such lessons to his young disciples all these years.

He has shown both athletes and academicians how to win by using psychology.

Here is an example: Today, George Young, 57, is the father

of three and grandfather of five. He is the owner of Reno Business and Professional Collection Service.

Yesterday—it was longer ago than that, but seems like only yesterday to Young—he was a ninth-grader at old Billnghurst Junior High School on Reno's Plumas Street. Reno High was a three-year school.

The year was 1948 and George Young was such a promising left-handed baseball pitcher that Coach Beasley called him up to the varsity. Relying on such a young player was rare in those days.

Here was Young, only 15, a "baby" among the older Husky players, who included his older brother, Jack, an outfielder.

As the season opened, Beasley took his team to Susanville to play Lassen High School. George Young was told he would be the starting pitcher.

It was a thrilling moment for the youngster, who wasn't shaving yet. He knew he would be relying heavily on his control, which was sharp, considering his youth and lack of experience.

Young was warming up just before the game started, when Beasley strolled over to him. Young vividly remembers the coach's orders:

"You've got to give those Lassen guys something to think hard about—BEFORE the game starts!"

Beasley told his rookie, "When the first batter steps up, I want you to uncork the wildest throw of your life! Aim it anywhere! Except don't hit the batter!"

The stunned George Young learned fast.

Reno went down in order in the top of the first inning. Then Young walked out to the mound to face the Grizzlies, who figured to feast on the green kid.

Southpaw Young cranked and threw as hard as he could. His streaking first pitch went into orbit, sailing over the backstop and out of the ballpark.

Lassen's leadoff hitter, suddenly rendered pale and trembling, wobbled in to face the gangly and "errant" flame-thrower from Nevada. The first batter never had a prayer.

Nobody wanted to dig in. Each went to the plate, fearing this wild man would stuff one in the batter's ear.

Thus did control-artist George Young sail to the first of his many varsity wins under the crafty Beasley.

Young became one of the school's all-time great pitchers and later was a standout for Coach Jake Lawlor at the University of Nevada.

Today, Young says of Beasley: "Bud was so exceptional. He has had a lot of impact on my life. I will always be grateful to him."

Oct. 6, 1991

Piazzo Family Proves You Can Succeed in USA

THERE ARE MANY new immigrants in Nevada who cannot yet speak English. Who may be confused by what now seem to be weird American customs. Who are confronted with not only a devilishly compli- cated new language, but are short of money be- cause their jobs are low- pay. If they've yet found jobs.

Chet (left) and Link Piazzo, back at The Sportsman after World War II.

But things can work out, as they have for ear- lier Nevada immigrants. Or for those born here to immigrants.

What was, and is, vital is being given a chance to work, doing well on jobs, trying the utmost to learn English, encountering luck and hospitable timing and finding established local people who will give them a chance. A cram course in learning is an indispensable ally.

This leads me today to a Nevada success story that has an im- migrant beginning.

Chet Piazzo, amiable Nevada entrepreneur and sportsman, was born in Reno on April 6, 1917, the day America declared war on Germany, propelling us into World War I. Last Monday, I talked to him on his latest landmark date—his 75th birthday—and he was pleased to talk about his roots.

The parents were Italian immigrants who, like many thousands of others, came through the immigration center on New York's

121

Ellis Island.

Once off the island, Santino Piazzo headed out of New York into the West, but stalled after he ran out of money at Portola, Calif., and couldn't continue the train trip to San Francisco. Instead, he walked the many miles to Reno and stayed. There, he met another recent Italian immigrant, Emma Pizorno, and they wed. A son and daughter were born before Chet arrived, followed by another son, Link, who came along on Dec. 11, 1918, a month to the day after the Armistice. The final addition was daughter Melba.

The immigrants put Chet in first grade at Mary S. Doten School (it was at Washington and Fifth streets). The family's home was up the hill at 10th and Bell streets. The little boy returned home the first day, crying: "They're speaking a foreign language, Papa." Santino soothed him: "They're talking American, and Chet, you now must learn to talk American, too."

In 1938, when Chet and Link were 21 and 19, respectively, having been raised by their widowed mother, they used their combined savings—$1,800—to open a little business they named the Sportsman Store. It was downtown, on the ground floor of their mother's St. Francis Hotel, which Santino had built on North Virginia Street across from what is now the Eldorado Hotel & Casino.

As kids, they had scrapped with each other, as boys will do. But now they were irrevocably bonded by their commercial vows, and a fierce desire to succeed. Their family was always ready to help, too—while Chet and Link fought in World War II, their sisters, Olga Dibitonto and Melba Cassinelli, managed the Sportsman until the war ended and the brothers came home.

The Piazzos worked slavishly hard, hired excellent people, treated them well, gave excellent service and had fun being with customers.

Bankers felt safe dealing with them because the Piazzos were true to their word. Thus did their enterprise soar. If you've been around awhile, you know that the Sportsman is a blue-ribbon business in Reno. Subsequent Piazzo ventures, including three shopping centers, also have done exceptionally well.

The Piazzo family story is a thrilling Nevada success.

Such successes will be repeated in Nevada as new immigrants are given a chance to prove that impossible dreams can still come true.

April 13, 1992

It Wouldn't Be the Christmas Tree without Gloria _____

ONE NIGHT at the Christmas Tree Restaurant up on Mount Rose Highway, a customer asked co-owner Mary Ellen Houston, "What would you do if Gloria wasn't working with you?"

"Simple. I wouldn't be here, either," she answered. Gloria, of course, is Gloria Michaels Stein, a Nevada and Lake Tahoe restaurant institution.

On a recent shivery night up on the mountain, happy diners collected at the Christmas Tree. Live music had the comfortable reception area jumping, a cluster of patrons camped around the cozy fireplace and, at the bar, a wide mix of patrons chattered while waiting to be called in to diner.

At the rear of the dining room and in efficient command of her open kitchen was Gloria Stein, chef extraordinaire. She was smiling—and making each cooking move count.

At times this month and in December, when business is at its peak, she will prepare up to 200 dinners a night, Wednesdays through Saturdays.

Stein's culinary magic and Mary Ellen Houston's growing reputation for quality draw customers from afar. But the majority is homegrown.

Diners wave to the gracious Gloria as she labors at the grill. They call out cordially to her and some stroll over to the handsome chef, bearing praise.

She is 62, the preparer of famous mahogany-broiled steaks, and she has been the Christmas Tree's affable star, on and off, since 1953. Mostly on, fortunately.

She and Guy Michaels were owners for many years and she kept at it after he died.

In the early 1980s, she was so impressed with her efficient cocktail server, Mary Ellen Houston, that she sold the Christmas Tree to the young woman and her husband, David, a Reno lawyer. But the Houstons wisely insisted that Stein remain to cook and give counsel. So, for nearly 10 years, she has stayed on to cook, spread her patented charm and offer her colleagues nightly on-the-spot "clinics" on how to do the right restaurant thing. "I could not operate without our precious Gloria," Mary Ellen Houston emphasizes.

Hear the Gospel According to Gloria:

"Be helpful and ultra-friendly to customers . . . Bend over backward for local people—they'll keep us going when no tourist is around. . . . Get to know customers personally. . . . Give them great food."

She coaches this generation of young restaurateurs to "treat everyone as a celebrity, because each is!"

The "Tree" is best known for its steaks, prepared on Stein's open grill. Her advice on cooking them:

"Buy top-quality beef. Hard mahogany wood makes the hottest fire. Turn the steak frequently, to seal in the juices. Don't overcook."

Gloria Michaels grew up around restaurants in Chico, Calif., moved to Reno in 1952 to be a Riverside Hotel cocktail waitress, and after a few months went to work at the Christmas Tree for owner Guy Michaels.

Years after he died, she married Richard Stein, a retired Los Angeles police officer.

She is Irish, is close to her twin son and daughter and is devoted to customers.

She prizes her quality-time Nevada life. And to her, high Sierra adventure is being snowed in, which doesn't impose hardship—Gloria and Richard Stein's home is next door to the restaurant.

Former Reno car dealer Herb Hallman gave an apt description of how much Gloria Michaels Stein is admired. He flew into Reno from his home in Canada, drove promptly to the restaurant, savored dinner, then told her: "There is something you must never forget, Gloria. You ARE the Christmas Tree!"

Nov. 17, 1991

124

Memorable Woman's Toughest Decision

FOR ALL OF HER 72 years, Genevieve Young was always at her finest when times were roughest. She was that way as the kid growing up in Reno; as the girl working in an adult world; as mastermind of her husband's runs for public office.

A leader in the purest sense, she had a gift for picking good people, of rallying them and of collecting facts. What made her an especially memorable leader is that she could make decisions, no matter how difficult they were.

Last week, confronted with the grimmest option of her life, she summoned her best advisers, got the facts, then made her decision.

She had just begun her 14th week of hospitalization at Saint Mary's Regional Medical Center, having been admitted on June 19 with a ruptured ulcer. But after surgery came grave complications. The wife of retired Washoe County sheriff Bud Young came down with pneumonia, which was then compounded by bronchial infection.

Doctors and staff had fought to save her life, and she had rallied. But she remained on the life-support system, in constant jeopardy.

As her 80th day of confinement approached, Genevieve Young asked doctors to her bedside. She wanted the facts laid out straight. She was told there was no hope of ever living normally again, without the life-support equipment.

There would have to be 24-hour nursing the rest of her life. Life spent in bed with the respirator, without the freedom she loved.

She also knew that the heroic measures that had kept her going, if maintained, could bankrupt both the spirits and purses of those she loved most dearly.

After the visit with doctors confirmed what she had suspected, she asked her husband and sister, Mildred Smith, and brother, Frank Menante, to come to her bed.

Genevieve was weak, but fully alert, and in full command. She didn't want to go on like this forever, she told them, because it wasn't fair to herself, or to anyone. "She was afraid we would fight her decision," Frank Menante later said, "and Gen was ready to defend her reasoning. But she didn't have to. We knew she was right."

Now she had what she knew was the luxury of deciding final matters.

She whispered and scribbled instructions. She asked the Youngs' lawyer, William Sanford Jr., to make a few minor changes in the will.

She gave her husband of 38 years, for whom she had campaigned so often and so hard, a long list of friends to call ahead of her death.

She wanted dear friend William Raggio to deliver her eulogy, and he will.

She chose the pallbearers and the honorary bearers and the place of her funeral (St. Therese the Little Flower Church). Little Flower pastor Robert Bowling had been at her bedside virtually each day and more often, near the end, and she directed that he officiate at the funeral.

Genevieve Young, thoughtful of friends to the last, even hoped her funeral might occur on a Saturday, so that "people won't have the inconvenience of leaving their work." (As it worked out, the service was held at 10 a.m. this Monday.)

She didn't miss a detail. She asked that visitation at Walton Funeral Home be a full day, and that the Rosary be on the evening before her funeral.

She must look her finest! She chose the dress she loved so much: silk, with the long sleeves and the high, ruffled neckline.

She asked also that her longtime hairdresser, Jo Davis, do her hair for the final time.

Everything then was in order, and to her satisfaction. She told them she had had the greatest life, and she told husband Bud that she was ready to go.

Genevieve Young, who had called everyone "Sweetie," was taken off the respirator last Tuesday about midday. The doctors had said she would be gone in a few hours, but she fooled them.

It was fully two days later before her brave heart stopped, and one of our finest leaders, and sweetest friends, left us.

Sept. 12, 1988

Visionary Lawyer Fought for Underdogs

RENO'S FIRST black lawyer, David Dean, was a visionary who four times asked for a chance at public office in Reno. That he was rejected by voters, and that he died too young and short of his glowing potential became Nevada's loss.

Dean (1934-86) grew up in Texas ghetto poverty, tethered to the existence that denies most youngsters a fighting chance at the good life. Yet he did break out over overwhelming odds. He did emerge with a solid education. He did get through prejudicial barriers without being consumed by hate.

He came to Reno in 1973, and was a law clerk for the respected Washoe District judge, Peter I. Breen, while preparing to take the Nevada bar examination. The following year he made his first run for public office, losing in the Reno Township justice of the peace race.

His leadership qualities were noticed by the *Reno Gazette-Journal*, which in 1974 "encouraged the newcomer from San Francisco to again seek a position of leadership."

He tried again, coming up short. The Reno of the 1970s to 1982, when he lost in a bid to become district attorney, wasn't ready for David Dean. Perhaps he sounded too many alarms.

Review what he was trying in 1978, in his first run for DA:

• Washoe will have to spend substantial time and manpower in the violent crime area.

• Dean would make no plea-bargain deals with habitual offenders.

• Dean foresaw a rise in child-abuse cases. Program he'd

128

create would provide special training to identify and prosecute child abusers.

If that wasn't accurate crystal-balling, take note of Dean's pledge when he ran for Reno City Council in 1975:

"Alternate north-south and east-west traffic routes must be developed."

"We must develop and firm action on Reno growth, and the impact of that growth on our environment."

Fourteen years later, we live with the crowdedness and dirty air that David Dean saw as a clear, future danger.

Dean's big-city background enabled him to see more clearly than most of us what was ahead. He declared in 1982 in his DA run:

"Reno is to have big-city problems. Ultimately, we will be faced with deciding whether to try every person who comes through here.

"I want to make crime prevention as high a priority as prosecution. ... We have got to promote neighborhood-watch groups."

Dean believed that attacks on anyone's rights debase all of us. If we could but stand and deliver for the underdog as did he, what a better place for all of us.

Reno lawyer Tim Henderson was one of Dean's closest friends. They studied together at Golden Gate Law School in San Francisco. "David could be tough as nails, but he always had that soft spot for those who were denied," Henderson said.

In the days following Dean's death from cancer more than two years ago, his wife, Jeanette, told me her husband's philosophy was to think not in black and white. "It's a lot of grays; I'm tired of people judging in extremes," he had declared.

So intent was he on taking swings for the have-nots that David Dean earned only enough money to get by on.

He was a country-doctor kind of lawyer. One time he took chickens as payment for legal service; he accepted a rattletrap car as a fee substitute, then gave it away to a poor boy; he took up the legal club for the American Indian family that had lost its home.

He used his own funds to bail out have-not clients, more often than not young, uneducated minorities, and when his own sleep wouldn't come for worrying about mapping strategy for a poor client, he screamed, "Damn it, they're sticking it to my guy, giving him a dirty deal!"

His special imprimatur was quiet and clean humor that kept him from caving in under defeats imposed by those who weren't ready for his farsightedness.

Dean had done many things that expertly prepared him for life itself. The youngest of five, he was raised by a strong, industrious single mother, went to work as an 8-year-old bowling alley pin-setter and, by the time he arrived in Nevada courtrooms, had been barber, college newspaper columnist, truck driver, musician, radio broadcaster and paratrooper.

What came through most clearly as he lay dying at Ioannis A. Louganis Veterans Administration hospital was the love he had for all. He had lived as a good and caring man and knew he was ready for pastures that were not black or white or even shaded.

Just gloriously green.

Feb. 26, 1989

Hundreds Pay Tribute to a Living Legend

The Harrah's organization tossed a honey of a party in Reno last month, the kind of gala Bill Harrah himself would have given. The event honored Bill Harrah's favorite executive, best friend and man he could trust his life to.

Bob Ring did more than any other person to help Bill Harrah build his modest little bingo operation—founded almost a half-century ago—into a corporate empire.

Harrah's genius lay in his vision and his keen knack of getting things done through others. He was fortunate to have had Robert Anthony Joseph Ring, who had an orderly mind, a beautiful personality and a humane streak that has endeared him to two generations of employees.

Had they been matched business bookends, one doubts they'd have been nearly so successful as a team. They presented sharp contrasts. Harrah was thin, while Ring, in his prime, was of blocky build; Harrah stood well over 6 feet, Ring of average height; Harrah was stiff when in unfamiliar company; Ring has never met man, woman or child he couldn't charm; Harrah's inventive mind was forever churning, but he was the Silent One. Ring became a whale of an operations man and his gregarious nature helped make him everybody's friend.

Their styles complemented each other from when they first met in Los Angeles. Harrah was running a bingo game on the Venice Pier when he hired Ring, then a student at Santa Monica

131

Junior College. Ring joined Harrah in a brief gaming venture at Palm Springs. They first came to Reno, along with Harrah's father, John, in 1937. After a false start in gaming, they retreated, then began anew the following year in a bingo parlor on Commercial Row.

The Bank Club was Reno's largest gaming operation during that period. But Harrah, Ring—they had had only four other employees at the outset—and colleagues were on the move. One by one, they overtook competitors.

Ring, the sidekick of the legendary Harrah for years, served as best man at several Harrah marriages; there wasn't anything Harrah couldn't confide in Ring and apparently there wasn't an assignment Ring couldn't handle.

The things Harrah liked most about Ring are the same qualities that endear Ring to his admirers. Harrah didn't respect "yes" men. Ring served up platters of truth to the big boss, whether or not it hurt; Harrah, a conceptual pioneer, concentrated on planning; Ring built goodwill both internally and externally. Nothing so captivates employees as knowing that the boss knows them. Ring knew the employees, and their families, as well. He cared about employees.

This was a two-man show at the outset, but as the company grew, both Harrah and Ring flew to the task of attracting superior executive talent.

Much of that talent was in the room when Ring was honored a fortnight ago. There were 350 guests and it was a coming together of the friends and colleagues Ring has admired all these years. To say there were yelps of recognition, lots of hugging and the retelling of stories of yesteryear would be putting it mildly.

The man who deserves so much credit in pulling together the night's program is Holmes Hendricksen, Harrah's executive vice president of entertainment. Initially, some thought the night ought to be a roasting. Hendricksen rejected that theme immediately, and with justification. Ring has been struggling physically lately, because of a hiatal hernia. Besides, he is a bona fide hero. At 74, and with an unbroken string of achievements, he is a legend in his own right.

About as close as anyone got to roasting were the repeated

references to his love of golf. To hear cronies tell it, his playing skills never approached the level of his love for the game.

Comedian Bob Newhart was the master of ceremonies. Speakers included longtime friends Charlie Gepford and Dr. Louie Lombardi, the latter who delivered both Ring's son and grandson; actor-singer Jim Nabors; present Harrah chairman Phil Satre and retired chairman Mead Dixon; Harrah's-Reno general manger Ron Jeffrey; Holmes Hendricksen, who delivered a stirring tribute; and Mark Curtis, who was witty and wise.

Ring, retired for several years, rose to respond to accolades. He is frail and, at first, struggled to speak, while every friend hurt for him. But then, steadied by Monsignor Leo McFadden, who was at the head table, Ring spoke, characteristically crediting all but himself for the organization's success.

When Curtis and wife, Ruth, married in 1959, Ring was the best man. Curtis seemed to best sum up what friends felt about Ring the other night, saying, "Bob, you're still my best man."

May 3, 1987

133

Reports of Mr. Brymer's Demise Premature

I WROTE HERE last Sunday about Joe Conforte and his late wife, Sally, and relying on another of my "always-right" sources, dutifully reported that Conforte's onetime bodyguard, Ross Brymer, also had died.

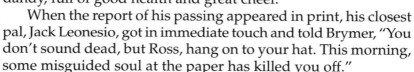

Not many hours passed before I began getting calls from Brymer's legion of friends, and some of his family members, saying that when last they checked, their pal Ross still was above ground. Very much vertical rather than horizontal.

As a matter of fact, the last time Brymer himself checked, he was dandy, full of good health and great cheer.

When the report of his passing appeared in print, his closest pal, Jack Leonesio, got in immediate touch and told Brymer, "You don't sound dead, but Ross, hang on to your hat. This morning, some misguided soul at the paper has killed you off."

Brymer, who lives in Sun Valley, was so intrigued and amused that he went out and bought a dozen papers, inspected the obituary page and was quite relieved to discover he was not among the decedents.

"But to tell you the truth," he would later declare, "at first I thought I was having one of those out-of-body experiences. You know, like in that movie, *Sixth Sense*."

This columnist already has survived one near-death experience this year. Now the prospect of dealing with Brymer, one of the toughest dudes in Nevada, wasn't something to which I looked forward.

I trembled as I recalled that long ago, Brymer could lick any

134

guy in the house, including a gaggle of University of Nevada football players who challenged him one by one and had the hell beat out of them.

Brymer did eight years in Nevada State Prison after being convicted of manslaughter in the 1976 shooting death at Mustang Ranch of heavyweight boxer Oscar Bonavena. Brymer encountered a lot of very tough fellow inmates. The youngest of them called him "sir." The guards kept themselves at a respectable distance and addressed him as "Mr. Brymer."

As it turned out, he was a well-behaved prisoner and received parole in 1991. He's not been in trouble since. He's the father of a daughter, 6, and a baby boy.

I hastened to apologize to the man I had laid to rest, and found him to be in robust health and high spirits. He put me at my grateful ease right off.

"To tell you the truth, Rollan, I am really pleased you were wrong in you reporting. Hell, I'm on the right side of the grass and that's what counts."

After reading that he had died, he immediately called his mother, Armenda Brymer, 80, a retired Reno nurse. His joy at living was such that he immediately tipped his favorite bartender $5 and spent much of the balance of the week autographing copies of the column.

Indeed, he reeks of good health. Brymer's dark-brown hair shows only a touch of gray at the temples.

He is a well-conditioned 6-foot-2, weighing in at 265 pounds and looking very much like a former National Football League lineman who has kept himself in good condition.

The native of Houston has a strong streak of musician in him. He started singing as a boy in a Texas church choir. He is an excellent guitarist, has a most pleasant baritone singing voice and presents his patented rock 'n' roll and Texas swing each Tuesday night at Abby's Highway 40 Bar, E. Fourth St.

He declares, "After learning last Sunday that I died, I'm thinking of renaming my act, 'Ross Brymer and His Pall Bearers.' "

May 14, 2000

135

Just Getting by Is Old Warrior's Latest Challenge _____

ONE MORNING last week, Jack Van Noy sat across the breakfast table, his ruggedly handsome old prizefighter's face beaming, and he told me, "Michael Spinks can beat Mike Tyson, but if he does, it'll be one helluva accident."

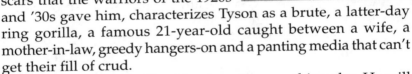

He was referring to Monday's heavyweight title fight in Atlantic City, N.J., the richest such event in history, with both fighters unbeaten. Hype is the mother's milk of boxing and, this time, we've got hype up to our eyeballs.

Van Noy, forever wearing the scars that the warriors of the 1920s and '30s gave him, characterizes Tyson as a brute, a latter-day ring gorilla, a famous 21-year-old caught between a wife, a mother-in-law, greedy hangers-on and a panting media that can't get their fill of crud.

Spinks, as seen by Van Noy, is quite something else. He will be the toughest foe Tyson has met, and the craftiest. He is guaranteed $13 million for showing up in Atlantic City, and that is enough incentive, speculates Van Noy, to light Spinks' fire to an all-time high.

Van Noy boxed in quite a different era. Not that it wasn't a brutal sport then, too—what sets the game apart is the INTENT to inflict harm. But in Van Noy's day, there were no hyped television gates, no closed circuit TV, no super paydays for even journeyman fighters.

Van Noy would make a few hundred bucks a night for cleaning some guy's clock. The most he ever earned was $23,000 for his non-title fight against champion Max Baer, a fight Van Noy lost on an eight-round technical knockout. "Oh, if I hadn't suffered that cut," Van Noy still grouses.

Van Noy was born more than 80 years ago on an Indian reservation in Oklahoma, the son of an Indian mother and a Dutch father. He ran away from home when he was 13. A roustabout youngster with natural athletic skills, he grew into a hunk of a prizefighter, standing an even 6 feet and weighing, in his prime, around 195 pounds.

I have seen Van Noy's boxing scrapbooks several times and always marvel at them. There is Van Noy, set in his posed fighter's stance, a Depression-era gladiator who might have driven latter-day palookas to the floor.

Van Noy had jet-black hair, never smiled for the camera and in the scrapbooks, today's reader sees him flitting from state to state, crisscrossing America to battle men now forgotten.

He was an intimate friend of Jack Dempsey and was nine years younger than that great heavyweight champion. Van Noy was Dempsey's sparring partner and, later backstage player, as Dempsey turned to promoting fights.

Van Noy has experiences that justify dwelling on past golden moments, but in fact, he doesn't get much hung up on what used to be.

Just getting by today is challenge enough.

He is a widower, having lost his wife of 50 years three years ago. He lived in Sparks for four decades. Around the casinos of our twin cities, everyone knew the burly, good-natured Van Noy. He was the veteran security man and, in the old days, before laws were enacted and enforced, he was a bouncer, pure and simple. There wasn't any troublemaker he couldn't handle.

When it became unlawful to throw the drunks into alleys on their faces, Van Noy easily made the transition to reasonable security man. Inside this warrior was intelligence and the ability to articulate.

But back to today's so-called Golden Years. For Van Noy, they are not as golden as they're cracked up to be. He moved to Denver a year ago to be near his sons, Carlisle and Jeff, and, frankly, "to find more reasonable living costs."

His health has been lousy. Last year, he spent more than 100 days in a hospital. That jet-black hair is almost totally silver now, and my old buddy of 35 years moved slowly, tugging at my arm for support.

He came to Reno a couple weeks ago to visit those he has known many years. The airplane trip was no picnic. He has to lug along the portable oxygen these days. But the magnetic tug of longtime friendship brought him back.

Visiting Jack Van Noy, I think again of how drastic change ultimately nails all of us. Children flee the nest, changing their lives and ours. Our own childhoods grow farther away and invariably we say in chorus, "It all went by so fast." When a spouse dies, the blow hits harder than any other.

I wonder, too, if there is any wisdom in leaving a place where you have lived so long, where most of your family and friends are. Van Noy didn't tell me whether he wonders, too, but I think he must.

As we said goodbye, he hated to let the handshake come apart. Before the old fighter faded away, I saw him reach for his handkerchief.

I was fishing out mine, too.

June 26, 1988

Tradition Carries on by Example _____

THE UNIVERSITY OF NEVADA, Reno's Homecoming Week featured the 50-year reunion of the school's 1947 football team.

The first Wolf Pack club to play in a postseason bowl game defeated North Texas State 13-6 in the Salad Bowl (now Fiesta Bowl) in Phoenix.

The reunion is a news peg on which to hang these thoughts about the event's orchestrator. For years, he has cheered Wolf Pack athletic traditions and helped sustain them.

Richard Trachok, UNR's former football coach (1959-68) and athletic director (1970-86), laid a solid foundation upon which his successor, Chris Ault, has carried sports programs to new heights.

Trachok's association with the campus began in 1946 when coach Jim Aikin recruited him and Trachok's running mate, Tommy Kalmanir. The two played in high school together in Jerome, Pa.

Trachok was a standout on Nevada's powerful teams of 1946-48. After his Nevada days, Kalmanir was a punt and kick-off return star for the world-champion Los Angeles Rams. Many others on the 1946-48 teams also turned professional.

What most contemporary and even old-line Wolf Pack fans don't know is that Trachok led Pack rushers in those seasons—noteworthy in light of the presence of other exceptional backs, including Kalmanir, Bill Bass, Johnny Subda, Lloyd Rude, Teddy Kondel, Ed Klosterman, Ted Ensslin and Sherman Howard, to name eight.

They were local sports celebrities, as were the quarterbacks:

Bill Mackrides, later a Philadelphia Eagle ace; passing star Stan Heath, United Press' 1948 first-team, major-school All-American.

Heath is the only Nevada player to earn that distinction; and Heath's backup, Alva Tabor, could have started on most major teams.

Trachok also was an outstanding defensive halfback. Today, print media tell the fan/reader how many tackles, interceptions, blocked punts, fumble recoveries and so on that players get. But defensive statistics weren't a staple in past years.

Nonetheless, a Trachok single-game feat 49 years ago is thought to be a record for Nevada.

His defensive gem occurred in Nevada's victory over the University of San Francisco in Kezar Stadium.

Trachok intercepted three passes and recovered two fumbles. Five turnovers in one game, by one player! Even top players don't approach five turnovers in a long career.

Trachok quietly achieved another hallmark. The No. 1 rusher, who also was a track sprinter, led football peers in grade-point average.

He turned down offers to try out with the Rams and other pro teams because he didn't want to waste time from pursuing coaching in Reno, and the city he always has loved.

Trachok became Reno High School football coach in 1949 after the unexpected death the prior year of legendary Herb Foster, at 50.

Trachok coached Reno to six state championships in 10 seasons. He became Wolf Pack head coach in 1959.

He remains the glue that binds past athletes to their traditions. He is the guiding force behind the university's athletic hall of fame. He knows where his teammates are, as well as how they are. He sorrows as they drop off. He comforts surviving families.

Richard Trachok is athletic director emeritus, in name and in continuing good deed.

Nevada is blessed to have him.

Oct. 19, 1997

Despite Fall, Verne Foster Still Dynamite in Small Package

THE INCOMPARABLE Reno grand dame, Verne Foster, remains indestructible.

Recently, the tiny lady took a fall and came up limping, and no wonder! Her hip was fractured. But surgery repaired the break. Just a few days afterward, she edged into Harrah's Steakhouse for lunch. She had one hand on her walker, the other on the arm of her host.

"No little accident like that is going to get me down," she told close friend Joyce Hall, on hand to greet her.

Verne Foster is the widow of legendary Reno High School football coach Herb Foster, who died in 1948 at age 50. The feisty lady was at his side through the glory years when he produced Nevada state championship teams in all sports, year after year.

I still see her in my mind's eye, prowling prep football sidelines or the perimeter of basketball courts, clipboard in hand, logging statistics, notations, on "suggestions for the coach." There are those who remember Verne Foster as "co-coach." That title wasn't far from the truth.

Her husband coached thousands of athletes at Reno in 24 years. The Huskies' Foster Field is named after him.

Athletes from the 1924-48 era remember wife Verne. A standout coach, Bud Beasley, colleague of Coach Foster, has said:

"Verne used to be more excited at games than Herb was. When there was any doubt in a referee's call, she was right out on the field, or the court, with her rulebook."

Modesto, Calif., stockbroker David "Bloto" Ryan, who played guard on Foster's 1946 and '47 football teams, remembers the First Lady of Reno football as a person "who was always there, rooting us on."

Verne Foster has been rooting for people all of her life, which began in San Francisco. Her father was Alex Wise, son of a prominent Winnemucca mine owner.

She lived in Virginia City with her family as a small child, until her family moved again to California. Then in 1919, they moved back to the Comstock.

Her life is recounted in a marvelous oral history, done by Thomas King, who heads the University of Nevada Oral History Program.

Her multidimensional career is covered in detail, with a strong focus on the Nevada Mining Association, which she served from 1953 until her retirement in 1988. As leaders came and went, the staying power of the wondrous Foster was the one thing you could rely on. She proved that dynamite, indeed, comes in small packages.

In her 35 years on the mining administrative scene, Verne Foster never took a day off as sick time. Even when she suffered a fractured pelvis, she got on crutches and hobbled to work.

She never took a vacation. "We had a one-gal office, so what was I to do?"

There were four mining association leaders in her 35-year career. Several times, she was interim leader. She was efficient and decisive.

She witnessed or participated in many events and decisions that were important to mining development in Nevada.

The history program's King says, "Mrs. Foster was a delight to interview, as were her former employees." The association made a substantial grant for the Foster history, and donated documents, photographs and manuscripts, which have been given to UNR's Special Collections department. Over the years, association leaders were Lou Gordon, Paul Gemmill, Robert Warren and the present CEO, Rod Higgins.

The history is great Nevada reading, the more so because Foster is totally candid and blunt about personalities.

142

Verne Foster long has been the epitome of voluntarism and remains so today. She helps out four workdays a week at the oral history program.

Her love of her late husband endures, though he has been gone more than 40 years:

"I never knew anyone I wanted to be married to after Herb died."

Aug. 28, 1990

A Century of Olsen's Memories Honored

ON MONDAY'S 8 a.m. television news segment, *NBC's Today Show* weatherman, Willard Scott, will declare words to this effect:

"Out in little Verdi, next-door to Reno, a beautiful little lady, Lillian Olsen, today is celebrating her 100th birthday!"

Thus will Americans hear of a landmark event in the fascinating life of a woman her fellow Nevadans know little about. Lillian Olsen, born a century ago in Piqua, Ohio, lived almost half her life with a famous musical comedy showman. Her daughter, Moya Lear, has become noteworthy in her own right.

Lillian Olsen, age 17, 1907.

Yet, the woman who will be honored throughout Monday never was comfortable in the celebrity spotlight. Tomorrow, however, she happily surrenders her privacy for a few hours. Her 100th is something she has excitedly pointed for.

She lives at the lovely Verdi home of daughter Moya, widow of the inventor of the Learjet, William Lear. A high tea Monday afternoon will honor Mrs. Olsen, and flying in from around the nation will be most of her nine grandchildren, great-grandchildren and their families and friends.

Her second daughter, Joy Surbey, an acclaimed professional photographer who lives in Camarillo, Calif., will help host the celebration.

Lillian Olsen stays in her bed or wheelchair most of the time and is attended around the clock by nurses. The tiny lady is

144

mentally alert, her humor ablaze, her love of books intact. She reads the Bible daily, without eyeglasses.

Mrs. Olsen drove her own car on Interstate 80 between Reno and Verdi until she was 94. When she was "only" 80, remembers close family friend Stan Brown, a California highway patrolman stopped her for speeding outside Sacramento. Glancing at her driver's license, the officer laughed and said, "Madam, you were driving your age—80!"

She has a treasure of memories. "I was one of the girls leading a 'protest' march back in '07, she reminded daughter Moya the other day. "Don't recall what we were protesting," she said with a chuckle, "But I remember what I wore that day."

"Nano," as her family calls her, is from a family of long-lived people. Her surviving sister, Thelma Wright, of Palm Springs, Calif., will be with Lillian Olsen on Monday. Little sister Thelma is 94.

For 48 years, the woman who was born Lillian Clem was married to the brilliant songwriter and comic John "Ole" Olsen (1891-1963), of the Olsen & Johnson comedy team. She met Olsen in Chicago on a blind date.

Olsen, extroverted, gregarious and creative, had studied violin at the Chicago Conservatory of Music. He was an unknown $5-a-week salesman when she married him in 1913.

Olsen began playing music with pianist Chic Johnson, and their similar clown instincts led them to team in vaudeville.

As celebrity built, young wife Lillian, now the mother of three, was a reluctant part of the scene.

As Olsen & Johnson took to the vaudeville road, so did Lillian, Moya, Joy and John Charles, the son who died in adulthood. The kids slept in hotel "beds" that mother fashioned out of dresser drawers or bathtubs.

Even as Lillian Olsen's backstage discomfort grew, the children loved being around famous theater people—the comedy team of Burns and Allen; the great Al Jolson; child stars Jackie Coogan and Jackie Cooper; Fanny Brice, the celebrated comedienne; and on and on.

Through all the hi-jinks, the transient life of theater people, the turmoil of constant moves, Lillian, a lifelong Christian Scientist, never permitted liquor in their Long Island, N.Y., home;

never smoked; and never took so much as an aspirin.

She ran a well-ordered house and has her own rich sense of humor—when the family settled in a Palm Springs home, she erected a sign at the door: "The house that laughs built."

Olsen and Johnson used laughs to build their fame. Their crowning clowning achievement, *Hellzapoppin*, a zany comedy, ran 1,404 performances on Broadway, from 1938 to 1945.

Ole Olsen's wife always preferred the hearth. She would squirrel away money in what she called her "for-fear account," but Ole would constantly invade it to "pay to get scenery out of storage," or "help a down-and-out singer."

Her diary says time and again that she had done her best to keep her children together as a family.

After the divorce, Ole Olsen, famous man, now contrite, wrote her that the divorce had made him know how sorry he was.

"I didn't understand," he told the woman he would always love, "how very precious you are."

May 27, 1990

SOLDIERS AND SACRIFICE _____

Heroism of World War II under New Attack

ON SUNDAY, AFTERNOON, Dec. 7, 1941, we sat by our radio, it being the only way to get the sketchy, scary news that so upset my relatives.

I was 10, old enough to believe that what my father and uncle were saying was gospel.

"This looks like war!" Father declared.

Uncle Jack was confident. "We'll lick those bastards in a few days. They won't stand a chance."

I believed my relatives must be correct. They were older. Actually, none in our house, or in our nation, realized the enormity of Japan's attack, and how it would change our lives, and the world's. Four days later, Germany and Italy also declared war on us.

Our neighborhood emptied as young men and women went into military uniform, or away to war work. Before Uncle Jack left for the Navy, he reassured my grandmother, "I'll be home in a few months." She lapsed into a nervous breakdown. Uncle Jack didn't come home for four years.

Fortunately, our country didn't break down, physically or emotionally. Today's revisionists, had they been around then, would have seen how everyone pulled together, and how committed and resourceful they were. Revisionists would not have seen apathy. There wasn't any.

I moved to Fallon during the war to join my mother and sister. There, the scene was the same as across America: fighting-fit people were off to the war. At home, sacrifice and patriotism ruled every life.

Today's second-guessers criticize Harry Truman's decision to drop the atom bombs. However, had the complainers been in Fallon, or in Anytown, USA, in 1941-45, they would have embraced his decision.

149

America and its allies were in a death fight. No wonder the American temper boiled, that we despised those who killed our soldiers, sailors and airmen, and tormented the free world.

Little Fallon, though thousands of miles from the fighting, was devastated by war, as was every American place. The ultimate pain came as our men were killed and wounded. Thirty-six times, Fallon's Western Union manager, Adele Bron, carried War Department telegrams to families. "We regret to inform you that your son was killed in action."

Then, on Aug. 14, 1945—exactly 50 years ago today—the town's fire siren, car horns, noisemakers and people's shouts rose together in a mighty chorus, after word flashed that Japan had surrendered.

It wasn't systematic firebombing of many Japanese cities that brought the capitulation. Japan's suicide planes and suicide submarines, and its fanatical military and civilian defenders were now neutralized.

The A-bombs at Hiroshima and Nagasaki had brought the enemy to its senses.

Today, President Harry Truman (1884-1972) is reviled by those who attempt to perform historical surgery, who diminish the B-29 Enola Gay exhibit, who argue that American leaders did not act in the best interests of humanity.

What revisionists do not admit is that Hitler and Tojo, had they been first to develop atomic power, would have used it on American and Allied cities in a heartbeat.

Truman's bottom line was decisiveness. He knew nuclear bombs would stop the killing by both sides. He used the bombs. He was right to do so.

A half-century later, gold stars no longer hang in windows of Fallon, or of Anytown, USA. Even as revisionist blather builds, the WW II veteran ranks grow thinner.

Nearly every day, obituary pages report the passing of the Americans who long ago were at war. The stories simply say, "He was a WW II veteran." But behind such obituaries are inspiring stories.

Regardless of where they served, or how long, they were heroes, every one. Men and women who bellyached neither then, nor now. Their task was to win WW II with the strategies and weapons given them. That they prevailed profits us still.

Thank God for our soldiers, sailors and airmen. Bless each one. Past and present.

Aug. 14, 1995

If You Remember Pearl Harbor, You Understand _____

FIFTY YEARS AGO, on Sunday, Dec. 7, 1941, the day when life irrevocably changed, I was a 10-year-old who had been sent to a movie matinee by my grandmother. The Gene Autry Western had barely begun when a terse advisory appeared on the screen.

It said, "All military personnel immediately report to Gowen Air Field!"

In this suddenly somber Boise, Idaho, movie house, half the audience hurriedly left. Then came a second message that said Japanese warplanes had attacked Americans in the Pacific.

At home a few minutes later, I found my father, uncle and grandmother huddled at the upright Philco radio. I was bewildered by their concern because, after all, war to me then was simply a game we neighbor boys played in vacant lots.

News trickled in agonizingly slow. But as that infamous Sunday lengthened, it became clear from hearing my family's reaction that America was in for some nasty moments. But I remember my father saying several times, "This will be over in a few days. We'll murder them fast." Millions were just as overconfident. All were sadly wrong.

The next day, in a scene common to most U.S. homes, we again were glued to the radio and heard President Franklin Roosevelt call the attack on Pearl Harbor the "day that shall live in infamy." We went to total war against Japan, Germany and Italy.

I remember in the days that followed that virtually every neighbor boy or man of 17 or older went downtown to enlist. My father was declared 4-F, but Uncle Jack made it into the Navy immediately, whereupon my grandmother suffered a nervous breakdown. The instant he came home safely four years later, she recovered.

152

The town and country I lived in were on the verge of mental breakdowns in the months following Pearl Harbor. No matter how newspapers and radio imposed censorship on themselves, it was patently clear we were taking an awful beating in the South Pacific.

Regardless of people's ages on the home front, World War II was the constant that affected all of us. We went through night blackout drills. Food and gas rationing became an accepted way of life and I can't remember hearing a single complaint.

Everybody from school kids to the aged talked incessantly of buying war bonds, of saving scrap iron, of treating uniformed people with dignity.

We were urged to write to the men and women in the service, and people sent off daily tons of V-Mail. Cautions were commonplace about enemy agents in our midst. "Loose lips sink ships."

The horrors of Corregidor, the Bataan Death March and Hitler's atrocities built genuine hatred of the Axis. To say "Japs" today is impolite. But in 1941-45, it was "Japs" and "yellow bastards."

To me, it seems just yesterday when we heard of the incredible achievement of the Jimmy Doolittle Raiders. Col. Doolittle, who had been a barnstorming stunt pilot in the 1930s, led a band of 16 B-25 warplanes off a carrier 700 miles from Japan. They bombed Tokyo and a few other enemy cities.

Much later, the world would know that the Doolitte fliers inflicted little damage; but in April 1942, the improbable strike was electrifying news that sent military and home-front morale skyrocketing.

Despite my youth then, living through the war deepened my love of America as no other event could have. It made me completely understand how miraculous freedom is, how fleeting evil men can make it, and how the brave people saved freedom for all of us.

Dec. 8, 1991

Her Memories of Pearl Harbor and Lost Love Still Sharp _____

THE MARCH OF TIME ultimately dims even the most epic American chapters. This is so with the anniversary we observe today.

After Japan's sneak attack on our military in Hawaii, President Franklin D. Roosevelt noted that "Dec. 7, 1941, was a day that shall live in infamy."

Infamy or not, time is eroding the nation's memory of both the Pearl Harbor tragedy and the catastrophic war that followed.

To some children, Dec. 7, 1941, may as well be in the Ice Age. Recently, a Reno autograph party saluted the marvelous book by the University of Nevada Oral History Program, *War Stories*, and the 21 World War II fighters whose experiences it chronicles. However, the veterans were jolted as a teen-age passerby asked, "What was World War II?"

Yet, there remain those who, beginning years ago today, were swept by a patriotic tide. The vow of our country was fiery: "Remember Pearl Harbor!"

In Reno, those who vividly remember are the 60 living members of the local Pearl Harbor Survivors Association.

About 100 other people will attend tonight's Reno Navy League Pearl Harbor Day dinner-dance.

At her home in Coronado, Calif., a former Fallon schoolgirl today vividly relives the Pacific event that shattered the nation, and her romantic dream.

Wanda Temple Abarta, her sister, Merle, and their parents lived in Fallon from 1939 to early October 1941. Wanda spent her freshman and sophomore years in the farm town. Merle, 19 months younger, attended Oats Park Grammar School.

In mid October 1941, the family went to Honolulu. Civilian Samuel B. Temple had been hired there as a heavy-construction worker.

Through Dec. 6, the sisters had a joyous time. Wanda, age 16, was reunited with a Fallon boy she had been writing to for a year. Richard Walter Weaver, 18, was a seaman on the battleship USS Arizona. It was based at Pearl Harbor.

They were dating regularly. The mother, Nan Temple, was famous for her southern cooking and had Weaver and shipmates Richard Brown and Dick Goshen to dinner each Sunday in November. "Given more time," Wanda acknowledges, "Richard and I would have been talking marriage."

But they were young. Time was what they believed they had plenty of.

The Temple girls and the sailor boys enjoyed Sunday band concerts in the park, saw movies and had dinner at home.

Richard's notes from the ship grew affectionate. Small and dimpled, "He was a handsome boy-doll, in sailor suit," Wanda says. "I've never adored anyone as much."

But what neither of them, nor most of the world, knew was that Japan's spies had infested the Honolulu American consulate, systematically noting U.S. shipping and aerial movement at Oahu's five military installations, including Pearl Harbor.

Japan was finalizing its scheme to attack the United States.

Wanda and Richard last saw each other on Sunday, Nov. 30. The Arizona left Dec. 1 on a brief maneuver. It returned Saturday, Dec. 6, the same evening Wanda, Merle and their parents strolled Waikiki Beach.

Weaver was told during the maneuver that his Christmas leave was granted. On Friday, Dec. 5, he wrote to Fallon advising his folks, Marge and Ray Weaver, that on Monday, Dec. 8, he would board a transport ship bound for San Francisco.

Early on the morning of the day that would live in infamy, Weaver and Richard Brown, former star high school athlete in Chowchilla, Calif., had breakfast in the ship's mess. They probably checked signals: Shore leave at 10 a.m., then to the Temples' home.

At 7:55 a.m., the first of two waves of Japanese bombers and Zero fighters from carriers pounced on Pearl Harbor. Our forces were caught totally by surprise.

As the USS Arizona's general alarm sounded, Gene Goshen saw Brown and Weaver race for their battle station.

155

They were killed at Gun No. 6 when the Arizona was shattered by a single armor-piercing bomb that sliced through several decks, exploding in the forward magazine. The stricken ship sank in nine minutes.

Among the 47 Arizona officers who died was Ensign Eric Young of Reno, a Naval Academy graduate. Weaver's dear friend, Gene Goshen, suffered horrible burns. Altogether, 1,177 shipmates were killed. Richard Weaver and Eric Young were the first Nevadans to die in World War II.

The second enemy airwave arrived at about 9 o'clock, further pulverizing Pearl and the air bases. By 10 o'clock, the U.S. Pacific fleet was in ruins.

The enemy had scored a mighty victory. However, its act doomed Japan—it united America, as never before, or since.

Wanda cried a river of tears after Richard's death, as she vowed to someday try to memorialize him.

The USS Arizona's dead remain entombed in the ship at Pearl Harbor. Its decks are partially exposed in a solemn shrine.

Wanda, now 70, has visited the memorial many times. She gazes up at his name, her memory linking today and yesterday. She also remembers the other lost Fallon boys. She had known 11 of the 36 killed during WW II.

After the war, Wanda often wrote Richard's parents. She visited them twice. On the last trip, Marge Weaver told her, "I wish Richard had lived, so we could have had you as our daughter-in-law."

Wanda Temple Abarta married an Air Force officer in 1947. They had one child, a boy.

Wanda did then memorialize Richard Weaver.

She named her baby Richard.

Dec. 7, 1995

A Shadow 50 Years Long Falls on Bataan Survivor

FIFTY YEARS AGO today, in 1942, tattered, weary and half-starved airman Ralph Levenberg was among the thousands of Americans who surrendered to Japanese troops on the Bataan Peninsula in the Philippines. But if he believed it would be the most awful day of his life, he misjudged. The worst was yet to come.

President Franklin D. Roosevelt said Dec. 7, 1941, was the day that would live in infamy. But a momentous calamity, the fall of the embattled defenders of Bataan, and the butchery that followed was the other infamous American tragedy. Unlike Pearl Harbor, this catastrophe did not conclude in a few hours.

Reno's Levenberg, now 71, was in the eye of the epic military storm. For six days, Japanese captors brutalized Levenberg and several thousand others on the infamous 57-mile Bataan Death March. Levenberg was kicked, cursed and beaten with rifle butts. But through the whippings, the days without food, water, medicine or sleep, he was lucky. He lived. Thousands died.

The horror is indelible: Seeing buddies beheaded. Friends falling from exhaustion, pleading for water in the jungle heat, begging for food. They were shot, bayoneted, stomped or decapitated.

Bataan defenders, outnumbered 100 to 1, had resisted for four months after Japan hit the Philippines on Dec. 8, 1941, the day after our Pacific fleet was crushed at Pearl Harbor. Finally

157

came Bataan's surrender and the death march.

The murder toll grew as the march lengthened. Levenberg could barely walk as he reached the destination prison, Camp O'Donnell in North Central Luzon. There, an additional 1,500 American and 22,000 Filipino prisoners of war would die of starvation, disease and torture.

Though he survived the death march, he would be held at O'Donnell and in Japan for 44 months—"my 1,244 days of hell on Earth," he declares.

World War II prisoners of the Germans believed their POW life was a waltz compared to being at the mercy of the Japanese.

Levenberg and others were beaten if they faltered as slave laborers. Starvation rations were rice and water. Disease was as grotesque as the guards. Malnutrition, beri-beri, malaria and especially dysentery killed prisoners every day.

News leaks into Camp O'Donnell were scant. "But as months rolled by, I could tell we were starting to win in the Pacific," Levenberg says, "because the guards became more brutal."

With the war tide turning, Levenberg and buddies were transported to camps in Japan, aboard infamous hell ships. A 17-ship convoy sailed from Manila in mid July 1944 and the journey was 33 days of agony, "As agonizing as the death march," Levenberg says.

His ship, the only craft with POWs, was packed with more than 900 prisoners jammed below deck, a space so tight that men slept standing up. A lone toilet—a pickle barrel—was lowered to them once a day. Heat was a killer. There was little food or water. American submarines hounded the unmarked convoy and 10 of 17 ships were sunk.

Over nearly four years, Ralph Levenberg was beaten, starved and given only one mailing from home. Weighing 145 pounds when taken prisoner, he was a pathetic, shrunken 72 pounds on Sept. 3, 1945, his liberation day.

He continues as a national leader in the long effort to win compensation from the Japanese government for the dwindling Bataan survivors, who long ago were hailed by their countrymen as heroes.

So far, the campaign is fruitless. No member of Congress or any American president has been the passionate advocate-leader these forgotten heroes of Bataan so desperately need. Nor have the sleeping media championed them.

Long ago, Ralph Levenberg's mother said, "Son, it will do no good to hate the Japanese." So he does not. But he wonders still.

Why, after all these decades, has Japan not given one word of apology for what was done to the victims of Bataan?

April 9, 1992

Remote Spot Held Pain, Hope for Americans _____

UNTIL A HALF-CENTURY AGO, the only Americans who had heard of Guadalcanal were mapmakers and military doodlers. But then the Big Shootout began.

For awhile, we took an awful beating out in the Pacific. Back home, those of us old enough to understand war, and what we stood to lose, were aching for good news. There was little to cheer us.

But at last we got a big dose of hope, because in April 1942, Jimmy Doolittle's Raiders bombed Tokyo, doing little damage, but making American spirits spurt high.

Then on Aug. 7, 1942—50 years ago—the U.S. Marines invaded Guadalcanal, one of the lower Solomon Islands, in the South Pacific.

It was our first offensive of World War II, the beginning of the end for Japan.

All at once, Guadalcanal was a household name. To some, it even had a lyrical, almost romantic sound. But to three Reno men, retired United Way leader Chuck Clipper, engineer Jack Means and retired Reno city manager Henry Etchemendy, and thousands of other Americans—Guadalcanal meant jungle, rot, slop, scum, dysentery, leeches, combat, death.

The Japanese were fanatical, resourceful fighters, maybe the best in this century. However, just as treacherous was Guadalcanal heat, rain, humidity and the alternating fever and chill of malaria.

Author Jack London had said of this part of the world, "If I were king, the worst punishment I could inflict on my enemies would be to banish them to the Solomons."

Chuck Clipper fought in five World War II campaigns—36 months of combat—and was awarded five Bronze Stars and a Silver Star. He was wounded in 1944. Guadalcanal was his first fighting.

Listen: "We went in there with old bolt-action Springfield rifles. My regiment hit the beach Aug. 7 with no opposition. Our hell began days later.

"You can't imagine jungle warfare until you've done it. Our shoes rotted. You tried to bathe. You had bugs in your beard. For awhile, we had no bread, sugar, no nothing. Finally, we ate captured rice and oats.

"My attitude was that we were living on borrowed time, fighting off patrols and snipers. There was this silly saying, 'Try to avoid the bullet with your name on it.'

"The scariest time was the night. The trick of staying alive was obeying orders, watching out for your sick, lame and lazy, and keeping yourself and the equipment in working order."

For Clipper, Guadalcanal hell lasted five months, until early December when the First Marine Division was relieved by the Army's American and 25th divisions. The battle-scarred island was finally declared secure in February 1943.

The Guadalcanal campaign's human toll was enormous— 7,100 Americans killed and four times as many Japanese dead. The enemy had the right name for this hellish place.

The Island of Death.

Aug. 9, 1992

Memories Were Always Close to Home

GARDNERVILLE—A woman always remembers her first love, all the more so if they marry.

This is true with Nola Lummus. For more than 50 years, the men in her life have had military connections.

Beloved second husband, Aubrey Lummus, with whom she founded Draperies by Lummus, was a U.S. airman. Son Kenneth served in the Army National Guard. Son Ray, retired 25-year U.S. Marine officer, survived a year of Vietnam combat.

Husband Aubrey died five years ago, after their five-year marriage. She and Ray and his wife, LeAnne, still operate the family's store here.

But after more than a half-century, she still smiles and cries when she recalls her first love, Winfred (Winnie) Kobler.

She was 19, he was 22 when they met as students at Fort Hays State College in Kansas. World War II had begun. Soon, Winnie Kobler took Nola as his bride.

After baby Kenneth was born, they agreed that Winnie would join the Air Corps. Winnie left college before graduating to begin flight training in Texas. She and the baby moved to Haviland, Kan., and she taught school.

Early in 1945, Winnie won his wings, and shortly after, they met at Lincoln, Neb., where Winnie had flown to pick up the 10 crewmen in his B-29 bomber.

Nola and Winnie then spoke of love, joys, of the baby, and they held, kissed, and she cried. But he soothed her, "Soon I'll be home."

Days later, he and his crew were fighting.

Their first plane was hit and fell into the South Pacific. Miraculously, every man survived.

On their second mission, May 25, 1945, while raiding Tokyo, anti-aircraft fire shattered their ship, which was precisely like the Enola Gay, which 16 days later incinerated Hiroshima

162

with an atomic bomb.

Winnie and his crew were out of miracles, and their plane spiraled to earth.

The War Department told Nola he was missing, and later confirmed him dead. He was 29.

The Air Corps said just one crew member had survived. But it could not locate Harry Slater, the waist-gunner.

For 51 years, in each town and state she saw or lived in, Nola vainly sought Slater's name in newspapers, magazines, military publications and phone directories. No military entity, including Veterans Affairs, knew of his location.

At last, she concluded he had died. Yet, she remained watchful.

The Melton column is now in its 19th year, and the most stunning coincidence in its life span has occurred. I recently wrote that a National POW/MIA Day would be observed in Carson City. Speakers would include a WW II prisoner of war, Harry Slater, the only survivor of a B-29 crew shot down over Tokyo in May 1945.

Nola Kobler Lummus spotted his name and phoned me. Our ink was barely dry. She told of her long search. I gave her Slater's unlisted phone number.

That night, Nola and son Ray drove to Harry Slater's Carson home. Her nationwide quest was ended. They live 15 miles from each other.

Slater, 73, described the disastrous hit and the fire, and the story of "Capt. Kobler desperately yelling into the intercom, 'Everybody out!' " Only Slater was able to jump.

Fire from exploded fuel tanks burned him and his clothing. As he floated down, he saw his buddies in the plummeting plane perish below.

He landed in a field, and Japanese civilians, long tormented by American firebombing, beat and stoned him. In a prisoner-of-war camp, he was tortured and starved. He was liberated after the enemy signed unconditional surrender documents on Sept. 2, 1945.

Slater remains bedeviled by the pain of friends lost, of torture, and by the unanswerable question: "Why was I alone spared?"

Nov. 11, 1996

163

History Behind the Column about World War II Hero's Survival

HERE IS THE GENESIS of Sunday's column about the World War II survival, and the death 56 years later, of an authentic American hero.

Gazette-Journal reporter Phil Barber's mid November stories told of the traffic death, near the Peppermill Hotel Casino, of a pedestrian, Lester Zook, 80, of Springfield, Ore. He was said to be among the 10 survivors—of a crew of 698—in the 1942 sinking of the cruiser, USS Juneau.

From left: Joseph, Francis, Albert, Madison and George Sullivan stand around a hatch door aboard the USS Juneau, Feb. 14, 1942.

The name "Juneau" stirred my memory. Yet, I couldn't recall why. But as often happens, a news source with keen historical interest phoned. William Randall, veteran postal inspector in Reno, asked if I knew of the fatal van/pedestrian accident. I did.

Randall, an American history buff, especially of the 1930s and '40s, then wondered, "Did you notice reference to the USS Juneau?" I had.

He continued, "What made this tragedy more infamous was that the five Sullivan brothers were on the ship. Each was killed."

By 1943, everyone knew of the Sullivan tragedy, including me. I was then 11. "Remember the Sullivans!" became an American battle cry to war's end, in 1945.

164

Thanks to Randall, a few facts surged back. The U.S. Navy foundered fatally after the torpedoing, off the coast of Guadalcanal, where Americans and Japanese were fighting epic battles. (The movie, *The Thin Red Line,* is about that pivotal campaign.)

Months went by before a famed radio broadcaster, Gabriel Heater, told the story: American naval officers, sailing close by, saw the Juneau explode and disintegrate. But they sailed off, ignorant that an estimated 140 sailors had initially survived. Wounds, horrible weather and sharks were to claim all but 10 sailors.

Heater's focus on the deaths of the five brothers alerted the media. The recurring theme was the loss of the Sullivans—history's most catastrophic event in an American military family. There was then a ban on siblings being in the same unit. However, the Sullivans, of Waterloo, Iowa, had insisted on being together. The Navy had relented.

After admitting the facts, the military strictly enforced the "no sibling" rule. It still does.

The Sullivans were memorialized in a movie, *The Fighting Sullivans,* and on an American postage stamp two years ago. There have been several Juneau books. A Navy destroyer bears the Sullivans' name.

Randall came to my office to loan me the best of such books. *Left to Die: The Tragedy of the USS Juneau,* by Daniel Kurzman, was published in 1994 by Bantam Books, a division of Simon & Schuster.

Lester Zook is mentioned many times in *Left to Die,* from the killer torpedo, his fight to live, the lethal sharks, and searchers finally rescuing him and the nine others.

Mr. Zook may be the last Juneau crewman to die. The only other known survivor, Frank Holmgren, who would be 75, was last known to live at Eaton Town, N.J. I called for him, but his phone was disconnected. There isn't a new listing.

Except for William Randall's alert, I could not have passed on to readers the story about Mr. Zook, and his special place in WW II history. This postal inspector's sense of history and of contemporary life is a great example of how readers can shape a newspaper, making it more accurate and enlightening. Thanks to him.

Long live the memory of Lester Zook, the Sullivan brothers and their USS Juneau shipmates.

Dec. 28, 1998

Fallon Men Gave Lives for Freedom ____

(NOTE: *I was the keynote speaker at the Fourth of July dedication of a monument honoring Fallon's 20th century war dead. My remarks were reprinted in the following column.*)

Before war stole them away, they were brimming with happiness and liberty. Such talented, diverse, young peacetime achievers!

There was the rodeo rider; a hunter; pianist; construction workers; Fallon town league basketball player; lawyer; several farm boys; two service station attendants; a trombonist; engineer; horseman; all-state football star; yearbook staff member journalist; Churchill County High School's 1937 student body president; a track competitor; Little Leaguers; school singers; a Golden Gloves boxing champion.

Before war devoured their future, the work of the ill-fated 51 Fallon men widely varied: Dairyman, ditch tender, Reno Riverside Hotel clerk.

One was an orphan; one was an alien, begging to serve; one was accepted, after his three failed attempts to pass Army physical exams; three who died were from families of 10 children; a widowed mother's only two sons went to World War II. Each was killed.

There were among them infantrymen; artillery men; a medical corpsman; combat fliers; bombardiers; a radio technician; machine gunners; riflemen; a Navy torpedo man; navigators; B-17 Flying Fortress and Liberator bomber gunners.

Among them were a West Point Military Academy graduate and several from Stillwater Indian Reservation; a Sheckler District farm kid; a Naval Academy graduate; numerous Fallon boys just out of high school.

The two world wars, and Korea and Vietnam were crueler than any of them had imagined.

Military ground and aerial accidents claimed several; myriad illnesses fatally stalked them—including influenza, pleurisy, yellow fever, malaria, a heart attack, meningitis and, in one instance, a ruptured appendix.

The men we honor here were lost in all combat sectors where Americans rallied for freedom, from 1917 in World War I to 1970 in Vietnam.

They died in Italy, France, Korea, Vietnam, Cambodia, Tunisia, the Philippines; on Luzon; near Saipan; in Belgium and Austria; a U.S. Marine from Fallon died at Guadalcanal; airmen perished in Scotland and Yugoslavia. Two were victims of 1942 Bataan Death March butchery.

The youngest victim was 18 when he was killed at Pearl Harbor in the first moments of Word War II; eldest of the 51 was 38 when his plane exploded.

Such tragedy:

The youngster in Vietnam, killed in a napalm-bomb explosion; the infantryman, slain by a German sniper in an obscure French village, 54 years ago today, on the Fourth of July; the Stillwater lad, killed in the D-Day invasion at Normandy, France, on June 6, 1944.

On Feb. 2, 1968, a conscientious objector was the first Fallon man killed in Vietnam. A medical corpsman, he was fatally shot by the Viet Cong as he tried to rescue wounded countrymen.

Of the Fallon dead, six were married. Three of the widows were left with babies.

One of those lost was posthumously awarded the Congressional Medal of Honor, the only Nevadan ever so honored.

But it is imperative that we know and remember that each was heroic.

Each gave his life, that we could have the most magnificent gift: Freedom.

July 5, 1998

167

On V-E Day Anniversary, Remember Sonny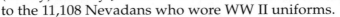

FOR SONNY ROWLEY, there would be no girl to marry; no children; no home of his own; no future job to prove his worth; no savoring of combat tales with Army buddies.

He did not live to enjoy Victory in Europe, for which he fought; or to prove how valued his adult life might have been.

As with 549 other Nevadans killed in World War II, Sonny was much younger than the leaders whose wretched mischief caused this war.

Today, on the 50th anniversary of V-E Day, let the story of Fitch H. (Sonny) Rowley Jr. also be a tribute to the 11,108 Nevadans who wore WW II uniforms.

He was the blond Reno tyke, dancing merrily on Lake Tahoe's warm beaches; a squirt learning to ski in the Sierra; the boy smacking younger brother Richard one minute, and defending his sibling the next; the Sonny who scrawled an Easter note: "This is a little bunny, to my dear little mummy."

He was the cocky guy battling an older Billinghurst Junior High bully to a standoff; the maturing teen, wrestling hay bales in steamy Nevada summers; the emerging kid rodeo star; the teen who loved dancing and loathed school.

Bored in class, dreaming up shortcuts to action, he enlisted in the Army National Guard in Reno in May. At 16, three years too young, he merely listed his birth year as 1922, rather than the correct 1925.

In Europe and over England, the Nazis were having the best

of it, and American unease grew. Then Sonny's Nevada Guard unit was activated. His brother and their mother, the celebrity *Nevada State Journal* columnist Gladys Rowley, were among the large Reno crowd rallying at the Reno train depot, to bid a loving goodbye.

While training, feisty Rowley broke his hand and confided to his brother, "I punched my fist through a shower wall. Better that, than hitting our lieutenant."

Now, his country was in the war all the way and Sonny yearned for an ultimate challenge. His requested transfer to the paratroopers was granted. Tough and nervy, he sailed through training jumps at Fort Benning, Ga., as one-third of his class washed out.

In November 1943, he came home for what would be his final furlough to Reno.

He was yet to meet the foe, but the charismatic lad won a hero's welcome, which military men did in those anxious times. Proud, neatly uniformed, his parachute emblem glistening on his chest, combat boots spit-shined, Sonny lit up the town.

Girls flocked to the fun-loving sky jumper. He danced nights at Club Fortune. Lew Hymers, a noted Reno artist, drew Sonny's portrait for the *Reno Evening Gazette*. But time sprinted by and then he had to race back to reality.

He jumped behind German lines at Normandy, France, on June 6, 1944. Death was everywhere in his 82nd Airborne Division, and among the enemy. Shrapnel nicked him July 1. He joked in a letter home, "Fortunately, I was hit in the head and am all right."

The last ordeal began Sept. 17 when he and thousands of liberators jumped into Holland. Four days later, he was driving a Jeep with three buddies aboard, racing to crush German guns. Behind in a second vehicle was his roommate from Ely, Al Ponsock, who survived to tell the story to Sonny's family.

Everyone heard the shell coming, and dived for cover. All got up, except Sonny Rowley. His promising life was over, at 19.

Days later, Gladys Rowley wrote a beautiful tribute to her lost son, ending it with this:

"Soar on my darling, brave and joyous spirit that you are. I, still earthbound, would not hold you back. Go with God."

May 8, 1995

169

War Hero Warren Remembered _____

WALLIE WARREN (1908-1987) was revered in Nevada as a legendary public-relations star and political consultant. But he was always understated about himself, and few of us knew very much about his exemplary World War II combat record.

Early in my friendship with Warren, I asked if I might interview him about his war years. He answered, "Someday."

I was confident "someday" would soon arrive. But it would be long in coming. Years passed without another word on the subject.

But in early 1987, as his health grew unsteady, his thoughts increasingly went back to the war. He called me one morning to say he was ready for the interview. I sensed some urgency in his voice.

During our visit the next day, Wallie Warren was fascinating and articulate. He was proud to have witnessed Pacific battles and the formal conclusion of history's most tragic war.

I intended to soon write a column based on the interview. But shortly thereafter, Wallie Warren died. So I wrote a column that reviewed his life, but with no in-depth treatment of his WW II experiences.

My interview notes were put aside until now, and for an obvious anniversary reason.

Through the last two years of the war, U.S. Army Sgt. Wallie Warren was a combat correspondent-photographer in the Pacific. He was among the first ashore in nine assault landings, as the noose tightened around Japan. He survived some of the most wicked fighting in six campaigns.

He would turn his film over to the Signal Corps, and bat out the captions on a portable typewriter, while holed up on scarred islands. Because he was constantly on the run, Warren never would see the historic pictures he made.

But on the home front, including in Iowa, his native state, his voice was regularly heard—through six campaigns, he was a featured reporter on the radio show, *Army Hour.*

On Aug. 14, 1945, the Japanese at last quit the war they had started in 1932 by invading Manchuria.

The following day, Warren was driving a Jeep on Okinawa when a sniper fired a bullet through the windshield—on the vacant passenger's side. "It was a guy who didn't get the word," Warren said with a laugh during our 1987 visit.

I am aware of at least three Nevadans present in Tokyo Bay on Sept. 2, 1945, a half-century ago this weekend, when Japan and the Allies signed the surrender documents—sailors Carl L. Whitaker, of Sparks, and V. James Eardley, of Reno; plus Wallie Warren.

It was Warren who had the catbird seat at the historic ceremony that ended a war that cost at least 50 million lives.

He came aboard the battleship USS Missouri at 7:30 that morning, photographic equipment at the ready. At precisely 9 o'clock, the brief ceremony began.

Warren remembered vividly. "The Missouri hadn't been spit-shined. She was still battle-ready, with every gun aboard loaded, in case anything went wrong. I straddled a 16-inch gun, just above and to the left of Gen. Douglas MacArthur. I was so near, I could see the surrender text.

"Gen. MacArthur had arrived moments earlier. The leader, whose strength and determination was so vital to our recovery in the Pacific, still had on the same old military hat he had worn since he evacuated Corregidor in 1942. I looked down at its crown and saw that an oily spot had accumulated.

"It was so quiet you could have heard a pin drop," Warren said. "I took my pictures rapidly, using a telephoto lens."

Wallie Warren noted that, "As Gen. MacArthur read from the script, I could see his hands trembling.

"Then, at the conclusion of the signings, Allied planes flew right above the flight deck," he said.

And Wallie Warren wept.

Sept. 4, 1995

SOLID CITIZENS

Bickfords Traumatized by Burglary

MARY BICKFORD is the gracious, efficient morning hostess at the Reno Airport Plaza Hotel restaurant. The 35-year-old charmer greets visitors with her positive demeanor and cheery smile, as if her life is strewn with roses.

How deceiving appearances can be. This articulate single mother long has battled alone to give her four children the best life. She has never gotten child support in 10 years. She limps along on her modest income so that the kids can play Pop Warner football, hop the bus to the Boys & Girls Club, see a movie.

The family lives in a tidy but cramped $620-a-month, two-bedroom apartment.

Bickford grew up mostly in Klamath Falls, Ore., where people didn't have to lock their doors. In Reno, crime had never touched her. Until now.

Thousands of burglaries occur each year in Nevada, hundreds of them in Reno. Now, Bickford and her family are victims. What happened on a recent night, as she and her children slept, hits her like an emotional and economic sledgehammer.

The stealthy intruder got in through a window and he apparently knew the precise location of rooms, closets, clothes and Bickford's purse. The family awoke the following morning, discovered their stunning losses and were terrified.

Taken was the small purse of daughter Shantell, 14, containing the $38 given to her on her recent birthday. Stolen were the new school clothes of sons Chris, 16, Ronnie, 15, and Michael, 12.

The most horrendous loss was Bickford's purse. It contained $645 in cash that two days later she was to use to pay November's apartment rent; her prescription eyeglasses; driver's license; house key; police card; and—worse—her car keys.

She rushed outside. Her 1995 Suzuki Swift hatchback was gone. The chief suspect, a teen-age boy, has vanished, too. The stolen car is teal green, bearing Nevada license WEW 152.

Bickford has no savings. Friends have helped her pay the month's rent and for new locks on the apartment doors. Reno State Farm Insurance provides her a car until the end of November. She has no stolen car insurance, so she must somehow pay the $5,700 she owes on the stolen Suzuki.

What a bummer! Now Bickford owns no wheels. Debts accumulate. She will try for a second job on her days off. Her two older boys speak of giving up basketball, the sports love of their lives at Galena High School, to work after-school jobs. Bickford wept fresh tears the other day when her four precious children told her, "Mother, you have always given up everything for us. Don't think of giving us gifts for Christmas."

She says, "Hearing this from my precious children is the greatest gift I've ever been given."

There is great compassion in this remarkable woman. Here she is, painfully tormented by crime. Yet, she says, "If only I could talk to the troubled boy who did this and help steer him onto the right path. I hate for him to ruin his life, as he has ruined ours."

Nov. 18, 1999

Wagner's Indomitable Spirit Marches on Road to Recovery _____

SACRAMENTO—It is eight days since Sue Wagner was hurt so cruelly in the Labor Day plane crash near Fallon.

She since has been in three hospitals.

She has undergone surgery on her neck.

She is tethered to medical equipment.

She is looked after around the clock by staff in the 14-bed neurological intensive care unit at the University of California, Davis, medical center.

Yet everything, declares this indomitable spirit, is coming up roses. To hear her, you'd think she's rich as Rockefeller.

"All is looking well, Rollie," she greets me.

"The nurse just washed my hair."

"My two kids are back safe on their campuses, and studying."

"They tell me my Reno neighbors are practically arm-wrestling for the right to water my lawn, flowers and shrubs."

Wagner's new Sacramento neighbors aren't nearly so lucky as she, to hear her explain it.

They are the other patients.

Sue Wagner will walk again and no doubt run again—the 50-year-old Nevada state senator and lieutenant governor candidate is a physical-fitness devotee.

Some of her fellow patients will not be so fortunate.

This is the trauma unit, for those severely hurt in accidents, especially car and cycle accidents. Some have damage that will rob them of hand and foot use.

Wagner escaped without paralysis.

Her surgeon, Dr. Pasqual Montesano, is enthused by her recovery path. He performed a four-and-a-half-hour surgery on Wagner five days ago.

"Her age is an advantage," he told her family. "Her bones seem just pliable enough to have averted a radical break."

This week, they'll have Wagner sitting up. In due time, she'll be on her feet.

The intense pain experienced in days following the crash is lessening.

Sue Wagner's thoughts focus more and more on the campaign ahead. In last Tuesday's primary, she walloped Republican Pro-Life Andy Anderson. Her challenger in the Nov. 6 general election for lieutenant governor is Jeanne Ireland of Las Vegas, a political newcomer.

The first order is Wagner's return to fitness. "My aides and friends will fill in until I am out of here," she declares.

Nevada's response to her situation has given her strength.

Letter-carriers have been lugging in mail by the bushel.

A tidal crush of flowers arrives at Wagner's Independence Square campaign office in Reno. "One of the first floral pieces came from Andy Anderson," she said, most pleased.

Phone calls have flooded her office, home and the hospitals.

Fraternity and sorority friends of her son and daughter, Kirk, 21, and Kristi, 20, paid for plane fares so the children could be with their mother. They are collegians in Boulder, Colo., and Tucson, Ariz.

The children's father, Peter Wagner, a Desert Research Institute scientist, died in a crash 10 years ago in a DRI weather plane.

Sue Wagner has carried on the past decade as widow, mother, legislator and development officer at DRI.

She was embarked on her first run for the state Senate when her husband was killed. Her campaign manager then was Barbara Weinberg, of Reno.

Weinberg has been at her friend's side much of these past

eight days. "It is hard to believe how much improvement Sue has shown since I first saw her at Washoe Medical Center after the accident," Weinberg said. "Her comeback power is unbelievable."

Present indications are that Wagner will return home next week. Her sister, Joan, of Flagstaff, Ariz., will stay with her in Reno over the near term.

Her brother, Richard Pooler, and his wife, Jackie, live in Danville, Calif., and have been making the long daily commute to Sacramento to support Wagner.

Wagner asked me to thank Nevadans on her behalf. "People will never know how important they've been," she said. "They are the best medicine."

As for the flowers people have sent—she hopes they approve—she has ordered them taken to Reno-Sparks senior centers and convalescent hospitals.

Sept. 11, 1990

Churchill Gym Honors Very Special Educator

FALLON—Standing on Churchill County's impressive new high school campus is a state-of-the-art gymnasium, and it now bears

the name of one of the finest Nevadans and top public educators.

In Fallon, where Elmo Derrico has been superintendent for a record 20 years, people respect him as a practical, frugal, caring leader who makes good things happen.

But if you're thinking of him in the old stereotyped fuddy-duddy school leader role, forget it. Dericco works tremendously hard. But he plays hard, too. A Nevada native who for two years was Pershing County High School's student-body president, he has been U.S. Marine, superior athlete, teacher, honored coach and song-and-dance man at Churchill faculty parties.

This is an emotional Italian who cries easily but who, at 60, is the first guy to plunk his spit-shined shoes onto the dance floor; witty cheerleader at party time, he also is pasta cook extraordinaire; he laughs a lot.

Elmo Dericco's work ethic is his hallmark. As a boy, he toiled in hayfields at odd jobs to help his widowed mother. At the University of Nevada, he was industrious student, waiter at the storied old Blue and Silver Restaurant and varsity basketball player. His coach was Glenn "Jake" Lawlor, and Dericco is still known among his university cronies as "Little Jake."

The thought of a vacation revolts him—he has never missed

a day of work on account of illness since signing his first Fallon teaching contract on March 28, 1955. Dericco has accumulated 240 days of sick leave and has accrued 100 weeks of vacation, but wouldn't draw on it, even if policy permitted.

Behind Derrico's rollicking good nature is political savvy. In his two decades as Fallon's top school gun, he has worked effectively with a total of 37 trustees. Among the present Nevada public school superintendents, only Mineral County's Arlo Funk, with 22 years, has served longer.

Derrico spent nine years as assistant superintendent, so come 1989, we are talking 30 years in central school administration, most in the state.

Staying power not withstanding, it is Derrico's continuing achievements that win respect. As Churchill's population churns ahead—20,000 will be reached by 1990—Dericco keeps his district apace of the rising pupil tide.

When the public was asked to approve a school-bond issue for the new high school, Dericco was in the front lines, emphasizing the urgency of the issue. It passed. Now, analyzing escalating population statistics and the growing number of young families, he knows the district soon must go again to the school-bond well.

Churchill's student dropout rate is among the lowest in the state; teacher and staff morale is healthy; Fallon graduates continue to perform well when they move to university-level studies.

Retired Churchill school district business manager Don Johnson says, "Elmo Dericco is a terrifically caring man—accessible to students, parents, staff, trustees and citizens." Fellow superintendent James Kiley, of Pershing, declares, "You can count on Elmo." Fallon high school principal Don Travis, Derrico's longtime colleague: "Boy, can he chew on people! But let someone pick on his staff, and Elmo is a ferocious defender! He is respected!"

Dericco is the stuff of which legends are made. He is a rare Italian because he won't drink wine—it gives him heartburn; he fears heights—his devoted wife, Donna McGowan Dericco, who is his tower of strength, claims her husband makes her do all the ladder-climbing around home; he is fiercely patriotic—it is said he won't approve a high school band leader's contract "unless the guy knows every John Philip Sousa march."

There is no more quotable Nevadan, without trying to be: When workers erred in installing boys' locker-room urinals at pygmy levels, Dericco raged, "What are these things? Foot baths?"

He is trainer of St. Patrick's Church altar boys and is "culinary chief" at Knights of Columbus dinners. Longtime colleague Ed Arciniega looks his dear friend right in his cherub face and says, "Elmo, when you flash that holy look, you remind me so much of Friar Tuck!"

No more honored name could go on a Nevada building than Elmo Dericco's. Thousands feel in his debt for his countless good deeds, for sneaking sunshine into their lives and for being an education champion.

Aug. 23, 1988

Beloved Teacher Receives Another Deserved Honor

FALLON—In May, a few weeks before she received an honorary doctorate at the University of Nevada, Reno Commencement, the most influential classroom teacher in my life, Anne Gibbs Berlin, nervously told me, "You will hear from me soon again, as I develop new qualms."

Now it is time for another case of the qualms. Many honors have piled up for her over the decades, and next Sunday afternoon there will occur the latest.

A wing of the high school is to be dedicated at 2 p.m. in the name of the woman who taught English here for 31 years.

But not to worry about her qualms, for she will be the ceremony's calmest, most eloquent person.

Should matters grow too serious, she'll simply order us to lighten up.

Anne Gibbs Berlin, 77, also may remind the 100 people present about a few of the spelling lessons she gave us years ago: "It behooves you to make a PAL of the principal."

The widow of John Berlin remains the grand and grammatical lady of Fallon, living in contented retirement in the Union Lane home where she has spent most of her life. A typical summer's day is spent tending her beloved indoor plants, reading good books and neatly typing out her lovely, witty letters to former students.

She will visit a neighbor, or chat on the phone a bit, or look west, hoping for a hint of rain.

There were no teachers in her family. Yet, from the time she was little, she knew she would become a teacher.

After her 1937 graduation from the University of Nevada she went out to McGill, where she began to shape a style that would make her a model by which other teachers measured themselves.

Her students loved her humanity and wit.

When she decided to leave for Fallon to teach, McGill seventh-graders took up a collection to buy her a present.

"What she'd really like," said young Billy Ireland (later UNLV's athletic director), "is a case of beer."

What was she like at Churchill County High School? She pumped our esteem, but never praised beyond what we had coming.

Without saying as much, her actions told you, "I know why you are here and I want to help you all I can." None of us remember her ever ignoring a student's needs.

Her language and examples were so simple that all of us couldn't help but understand.

I can still hear my first journalism class teacher, Anne Gibbs Berlin, define the newswriter's mission: "A good story is like a well-focused snapshot of a place in time."

She also was a lovable piece of work because she did not favor one student over another—read this teacher's pet. Whether you were the daughter of Fallon's wealthiest, or the kid from the farm, or the son of the waitress, she gave you equal time. Which is to say you received Mrs. Berlin's undiluted commitment.

Anne Berlin, role-model teacher, felt she needed to get students to think interesting thoughts.

Then there was no telling what might happen, when they were given opportunities.

Aug. 23, 1992

Alice Smith Asked No Thanks, but Her Name Will Live on

FIFTY YEARS AGO, a black couple, Alice and Alfred Smith, trying to put poverty and prejudice behind them, left Mississippi and came to Reno. But life seemed just as shabby for them in Nevada.

Nobody wanted to rent to black folks; Reno casinos were off limits to the Smiths; the restaurants didn't admit them. Alfred, an expert tailor, found work at last, for grubby wages; Alice finally got jobs as a domestic, for a few cents an hour.

Her husband went into the military when World War II came. His wife stayed in Reno, cleaning homes, raising their two children and going to town to meet troop trains—black soldiers and sailors weren't admitted by Reno clubs and cafés, so Alice Smith would board the trains and give the young men doughnuts and coffee.

Alfred Smith came home when the war ended and he and his wife founded the Reno-Sparks branch of the National Association for the Advancement of Colored People. At last there was a Reno place where blacks could talk over ways to minimize their problems.

Alice Lucretia Smith in 1945 was a Nevada delegate in San Francisco at the founding conference of the United Nations; she became a Red Cross worker in Reno; she signed up with the Washoe Democratic Women's group in town.

Her poise and confidence were stirring.

In 1947, her husband fell ill—because he was black, he was

185

wait-listed by the Reno veterans hospital and died while still trying to be admitted.

At his death, his widow pledged "to devote the rest of my life to help my fellow man, without pay or thanks."

She continued to live in the home they had acquired earlier—the only way they bought in the all-white neighborhood was to have friends, a white couple, pose as Alice and Alfred Smith.

She carried on after her husband died. She loved doing church work and helping people. The color of those she supported made no difference. "We are all God's children," she declared.

She became a charter member of the League of Women Voters in Reno. She impressed people with her gentleness, with her strength, with her burgeoning leadership qualities.

Not that she was a female Uncle Tom who would sit and smile amid troubled times. She could and did speak with passion, crying out for justice.

Charles Springer, now a justice of the Nevada Supreme Court, who in those early years represented minorities on many occasions, says of Alice Smith: "She was cordial, courtly and strong."

Nevada leaders admired her emergence as a role model for all of us. While he was governor, Mike O'Callaghan had her represent Nevada at a White House conference on aging. His successor, Robert List, named her to the state advisory committee of the Department of Human Resources.

She joined the State Welfare Board and reached into the community to help blind people, kept up her steady work for several churches and, foremost, championed education as the passport to an improved life.

At civic board meetings, Alice Smith shared her wisdom openly, letting her years of pain and joy inspire people. She always understated her own pain and she rallied people, declaring, "When we work together, life improves for everyone."

Poor health overtook her five years ago and circulatory illness led to amputation of a leg. She has been a patient since 1983 at Physicians Hospital. She is 86.

To this day, she sees education as the great ally in curing

individual and societal ills.

As this year began, Washoe school trustees were asked to name new schools. In 1988, elder Luther DuPree Jr. of the Northern District Churches of God in Christ had submitted Alice Smith's name for consideration.

Two weeks ago, Washoe school curriculum coordinator Jerry Holloway spoke eloquently to trustees about the woman who "devoted her life to people, without pay or thanks." The school board reaction was unanimous.

The new elementary school in Golden Valley, north of Reno, will be called the Alice L. Smith Elementary School.

It is the first time in Truckee Meadows history that a black person has been so honored.

Jan. 22, 1989

You Never Know Whom You'll Meet ____

THIS BEDRAGGLED GUY walks into the Home Depot store off McCarran Boulevard in Sparks, appearing for all the world like a fugitive from Devil's Island. His soiled work clothes hang at half-staff.

He is overdue for a shave and a haircut, but they're no doubt out of his reach because he looks broke.

He could easily be mistaken as a newly arrived transient who just creaked off a Union Pacific boxcar.

As the unkempt shopper ambles along the aisles, poking among the work tools, customers gawk and possibly speculate how long it has taken him to walk from the railroad tracks to the Home Depot.

As he later admits, at this juncture he is so tattered, even close friends would hate to be seen with him.

Poor down-and-out fella. Onlookers stifle the urge to advise him, "Next time you shower, also get lots closer to the razor."

The man places a few items in the shopping cart and gets in line at the checkout counter. The young female cashier forces a smile. "How may I help you, sir?"

The old duffer pats his empty pockets and admits, "I don't have cash on me." Not news that surprises the wary cashier.

He extracts something from his rumpled pocket. "Been working in my shop at home," he apologizes. "I don't have my credit cards on me, either." So what else is new, wonders Miss Cashier.

"But I do have my checkbook."

"All right, sir. Here's the total amount due. You can make it payable to Home Depot, and sir, please write your address and phone listing, if they aren't on the check already."

As he begins making out the check, she must be thinking, "I'll surely have to buzz our manager about how to handle this one."

The scraggly fellow hands the check to the young lady. "This'll do the trick," he says.

She quickly looks it over and sees the imprinted name of Robert McQueen. There is a listed address on Wedekind Road in Sparks.

"Fine, Mr. McQueen. Just wondering, sir, this McQueen name. Is that any connection with the high school in Reno?"

He gives her his impish grin. "Yes, there is a connection."

"And what is that, Mr. McQueen?"

"Well, I'm the school's namesake. You know, they named it after me when it opened in 1982."

The young lady rolls her eyes, bursts out in disbelief, laughs at the smudged curmudgeon and declares, "Yeah, and I'm Princess Diana!"

If this disheveled shopper is the sort, which he isn't, he can modestly remind us of major headlines in his life.

World War II soldier in New Guinea in the South Pacific (his two brothers and father also were in uniform); married 52 years to Shirley; father of three; longtime respected professor of psychology at the University of Nevada, Reno; scholarship chairman for 29 of his campus years; served 20 years as a Washoe County School District trustee. Yes, "Princess Diana." He truly is namesake of the school.

Which reminds me: When McQueen High first opened, its charter principal, John "Slug" Flynn, was giving the namesake an inaugural tour when a student asked, "Dr. McQueen, was our school named after your father?"

Nov. 21, 1999

THESE WERE GIANTS

Marion Motley: the Player from 'Eli' ___

MARION MOTLEY grew up in rural Georgia, and was barely out of his teens when Coach Jim Aikin asked him to play football at the University of Nevada. Shy, the only black on campus in 1940, Motley took odd jobs to get by. Washing dishes. Cutting grass. Babysitting the daughters of assistant coach Jim Bailey.

Aikin, anxious to avoid non-resident tuition, told Motley to say he lived in Ely. Answering the registrar, Motley drawled a legendary Wolf Packism:

"I'm from Eli."

Years later, the greatest National Football League fullback admitted, "When I return to Nevada, my teammates kid, 'Marion, are you still from Eli?' "

As a first-year student, Motley lived in Lincoln Hall, the men's dormitory. He was lonely. His social life was dull. Yet, his teammates, all of them white, welcomed him into the Wolf Pack family. At first, Motley had difficulty relating numbered plays to what he was to do. To his rescue came offensive captain Wes Goodner, who told Motley in huddles, "Marion, carry the ball right." Or, "Knock down that left linebacker."

Marion Motley, who fumbled the Eli pronunciation, never fumbled the ball. Yet, he was a marked player on two counts:

He was a star. He was black.

In his second season, two other blacks joined the squad. "Rival players intimidated and battered us, and referees often didn't call obvious fouls on them," Motley said. He was a football Jackie Robinson, quietly enduring racial torment.

"We were determined not to fight. The way I dealt with the intimidator was if I caught one in my way, I just ran over him," he explained. Marion Motley, a Nevada teddy bear off the field, was an irrepressible terror playing with the Pack and then the Cleveland Browns of the National Football League, and was elected to the NFL's Hall of Fame. Critics hailed him as the league's consensus runner/blocker/tackler of the century. When he died early this week of prostate cancer and diabetes complications, his legend blossomed anew:

Run blaster inside. Olympic-quick sprinter outside. Revered 60-minute-a-game marvel. As great a linebacker as ever played. Only the fourth black player in the NFL (Kenny Washington, Woody Strode and Bill Willis came earlier). At 26, Motley was signed by the Browns so that lineman Willis would have a black roommate.

Today, Motley's legend outshines all.

He was a brilliant rusher on what was essentially a passing team, led by Hall of Fame quarterback Otto Graham, who called him, "Best I ever saw, better all-around than (immortal) Jimmy Brown."

Motley was honored as the premier fullback on the 75-year all-NFL team. In 1968 he was the second black, after Emlen Tunnell of the Giants, to enter the NFL Hall of Fame in Canton, Ohio, where Motley grew up. In 1973, the University of Nevada, Reno inducted him among its first Wolf Pack Hall of Fame honorees, and he was a consensus selection on the Wolf Pack all-century squad last winter.

Motley's rookie professional salary was $4,500. In his last year, he earned $15,000. Today, he would command millions. What was worth gold to him was that Nevadans treasured him. In 1973, he returned to Reno for the Pack Hall of Fame induction. His Nevada contemporary, renowned Reno dentist David Melarkey (1920-78), saw that Motley had several front teeth missing, and that "Mot" was sensitive about it.

Before the superstar left Reno for Cleveland, Dr. Melarkey presented Motley with a perfectly crafted dental bridge.

A gift from Nevadans who cherished him.

July 4, 1999

Robert Laxalt: Friend, Literary Great Remembered

(The following column reprints the text of my eulogy delivered at Robert Laxalt's memorial service.)

CHEERFUL, LIKABLE, profound, witty. Epitome of great citizenship. Brother-lode of wisdom. Plainspoken.

Incapable of writing anything that wasn't lively and brimful of his profound intelligence.

Supremely modest. Graciously personable. Free of bombast. Free of ego. Free of bluster. Free of insecurities that shackle others.

He spoke and wrote at times with the softness of a shy child. However, on other occasions he communicated with the brash toughness of the Marine drill sergeant.

Robert Laxalt.

An idealist in an increasingly cynical world.

The teacher who made literature come alive, who enriched his students with his episodic fiction and fact, who urged young writers to read the classics.

The teacher who cherished his students' literary potential, who brilliantly developed their characters and talents.

As much as this supremely modest man tried to camouflage his incredible skill, he failed.

Failed, because amid his pageant of teaching and nurturing, his own books poured out—17 in all.

195

In his works, he reduced what would be complexities to plain language. From his books, there inevitably emerged the unfailing kindnesses that made him so especially attractive.

Robert Laxalt.

The writing office at his and Joyce's home seemed to be an intensive care unit for his Royal manual typewriter's malfunctioning margin releases. For the cantankerous carriage returns.

However, the chattering machine at which he toiled was the bridge to the world that so intrigued him: Literature.

His literature was a lyrical symphony. His literature enabled him to view the faults and frailties of the world with compassion and his belief that the best in mankind would ultimately win out over the worst.

His literature flowed, for he was addicted to daily writing the way others are addicted to water, food and oxygen.

To Robert Laxalt, literature was the spiritual food that was so essential to the human diet. What also was essential to him was friendship. When those Nevada writers to whom he was closest slipped away, he was enveloped in both sorrow and gratitude.

Among them were Walter Van Tilburg Clark, Anthony Amaral and Guy Shipler Jr. Each had accurately regarded friend Robert Laxalt as the high priest of Nevada authors.

Now, Robert Laxalt, the last of our state's 20th century literary giants, also is gone.

Today, you and I are bathed in our sorrow and gratitude. Sorrow for the myriad reasons said here today.

Gratitude? Yes indeed! His 17 books will outlive each of us, and those generations yet to arrive.

We shall remember that he was incapable of saying, "No, I cannot help you."

To the end, we shall recall that our shy friend never forgot his own impoverished, but treasured, boyhood.

As far as I know, he only misspoke about one thing: He said that notoriety was only transitory.

Well, transitory to the majority, who usually can expect no more than 10 minutes of fame.

However, Robert Laxalt shall remain, to our own final days, the famous man whose presence and legacy blessed us.

April 1, 2001

Mark Curtis: Energetic, Savvy, He Set High Ad Standard

MARK CURTIS SR.

Earnest, confident and superb Reno advertising/public relations star who, long before today's local marketeers were potty-trained, or born, set a high standard against which young counterparts are measured.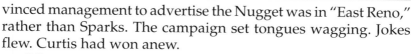

Creative and persuasive, he thrust the Harrah's name on the American and international stages.

It was his lively mind that hatched the notion that the "Bill & Effie's" truck-stop name be scuttled in favor of a winning zinger: "Boomtown."

It was his novel scheme that convinced management to advertise the Nugget was in "East Reno," rather than Sparks. The campaign set tongues wagging. Jokes flew. Curtis had won anew.

I first encountered him in 1950 when we were in Journalism 101 at the University of Nevada. He was older and seldom gave an opinion in class; but when he did, we listened well, for the slightly built man had a giant's knack of lobbing stimulating questions and beliefs. I knew then that he was one of the returning military veterans flocking to campus. But I would have no inkling until much later of how profoundly World War II hardships had shaped him.

The time of his heaviest public influence coincided with Reno's golden era as a destination city, circa 1950-75. It was a period when a rich menagerie of marketeers and writers were

197

holed up in the still small town.

They included such publicists as Roy Powers, a onetime Curtis PR agency partner; Max Dodge and Bob Dill, who flogged the promotion drums for the Holiday Hotel; Gene Evans, a Harrah's PR operative; Harry Spencer, the advertising/PR voice of the Mapes property; Faith Greaves, who teamed with Roy Powers at Harolds Club; and many hard-charging newswriters, including Bob Bennyhoff and Clark Bigler, of United Press International; Ed Olsen, Paul Finch and Dwight Dyer of the Associated Press; and William Berry, the godfather of Reno-based freelancers.

If this flock could be labeled a parade, then Mark Curtis was out front as a drum major, a man able to remain at an occasional colleague party without a bit of a wobble.

He was the wellspring of creative energy that oozed ideas. Though he came off to some as reserved, he did have a delightfully wry humor, and also an undisguised exuberance for the city in which he made a handsome living.

While he was with Harrah's, he was close to entertainment big names, a few of whom were superstars (Frank Sinatra and Sammy Davis Jr.). I never heard any, even the most temperamental, say anything but nice things about Mark Curtis.

Bill Harrah once fired Curtis, but later realized he had booted the major PR heavyweight, re-signed him, and it was a good thing for Harrah!

As the Harrah's Corp. did its dog-and-pony show, leading up to becoming publicly owned, Mark Curtis was superb in convincing Wall Street that this first gaming property to go public was No. 1, inside and out.

He also was a wonderful writer with a gift for saying much in few words. He had credibility with media professionals. I couldn't begin to say how many times Curtis' newsy tips wound up in Herb Caen's enormously influential columns.

Curtis had far-reaching knowledge and perspective, and being with him in person, especially as he grew older, was like having a significant conversation with Reno's past.

There were so many things to admire in him. His brush with death, and imprisonment in the Nazis' infamous Stalag 17 prisoner-of-war camp surely sobered his reflective being.

While the wartime episodes seemed not to have embittered him, they did deepen his sensitivity to suffering.

A few years ago, he at last went fully public about being the B-17 Flying Fortress gunner who, thanks to a crewman, escaped as their stricken plane went into its death spiral. The man who saved him was killed.

The harrowing WW II experiences are told by Curtis in the University of Nevada Oral History Program's all-time bestseller, *War Stories*.

At the urging of friends, Curtis completed the writing of a memoir, *It Was Great While It Lasted: A PR Man Reflects on Nevada's Heyday, 1950-75*. The book focuses on Curtis' public relations career, especially with Harrah's. UNR's Black Rock Press agreed to publish it.

With no attempt at sentimentality here, I need to affirm that Curtis had a deep patriotic streak and lived to the beat, "My Country, Right or Wrong."

The man who totally lacked mediocrity also lived by a personal rule: "Have fun." Indeed, he made things so much more fun for the army of coworkers and friends whose lives he brightened.

June 26, 1998

Ty Cobb: Journalism Houdini, Light in Our Lives _____

(The following column reprints the text of my eulogy delivered at Ty Cobb's memorial service.)

HE WAS THE JOURNALISM Houdini whose daily magic act was getting out the *Nevada State Journal*, in superior condition, on time.

He was the master who always came fresh to the task of writing history, in a hurry.

He was king of the Nevada journalism vineyard, and each of us bowed to his virtuoso literary concerts.

He did not rewrite, revamp or retreat—because he wrote it right at first impulse.

He was the Ernie Pyle of his beloved Nevada.

He was the silver-and-blue humanitarian.

He was the occupant of Reno's most littered news office, toiling amid paper stacks; hastily filing stuff—on the floor, trying feebly to do office housekeeping before the visits of Dempsey, DiMaggio, Patrick McCarran, Gwen Leonard.

He was the bespectacled, cigar-chomping sportswriter, being regularly visited by bleary, needy guys who seemingly stepped out of a Damon Runyon page.

He was the one who would work until 1 a.m., fall into his bed exhausted, and then be jolted awake at 3:30 in the morning by the telephoning drunk who asked, "Hey, Ty, who hit the winning double, in the ninth inning, of the seventh World Series game in 1947?"

200

He was the one who was unfailingly patient and kind to the have-nots.

He was the person who regarded the blue-collars as the noblest of them all.

He never publicly knocked; he held no grudges; his kinder and gentler example was shaped while he was a boy.

He was a son of the Comstock, where isolation, the lack of water and inhospitable weather made people bond as family.

He grew up, and went away, and became a household name to the unknowns and the unwashed and the very famous. But always he remembered.

Remembered and practiced the boyhood learning.

He was in love with sports, and athletic participants, and sports fans, and he adored being their messenger man.

He was able to convey not only the scores of games, but the lessons that accrue to winners, and especially to the also-rans.

His was an encyclopedic memory. He was a living library and museum. He was a Western Traditions devotee, spewing history.

He would grow agitated at even the faintest disrespect for ethnic minorities. He would scold such acts publicly. Long before others in the media awoke to prejudice, he was attacking such bias with his typewriter and printing press, and with his torrent of beautiful speeches.

He, more than any other Nevada news person of his generation, put American Indian and African-American athletes up on a news pedestal, where they could feel and touch respect. He made it appear that somebody else did the deeds he had set up.

He was a fantastic teacher—readers, educators and peers learned from him. So did track sprinters, churchgoers and benchwarmers.

He was the man who never kept a running joke file—he used his own humor masterfully. He invented nicknames. Three-finger Brown. Limping Louie. Bull-nose.

He admitted at fuel oilman George Basta's 80th birthday party, "I'm not an oilman, like others here. But I've been oiled a few times."

He was the Kid on the Comstock, an 81-year-old kid, on May 15, 1997, at his final public appearance. Ty Cobb, facing a standing-room-only gang, deadpanned, "This is Comstock Preservation Week. I think I'll preserve myself by sitting down." Ty spoke two hours. He was Mark Twain, and Will Rogers, and he was the Man to Match Any Mountain.

He was frequently believed to be only a sports journalist. But that was mistaken. He was a total journalist, respectful of all people's rights, yet slavishly devoted to the task of telling all the news that's fit to print.

He faced attempted news censorship many times. He would not put up with it.

His *Journal* teammates glowed as he declared to the snake-oil sales visitors, "Our news columns are not for sale."

His editor, the late Paul Leonard, called Ty Cobb the best that ever was, or will be.

People fawned over him, not for his favor, but for the affection they felt for him. A typical for-instance:

Flashback to 1971. It is still another Ty Cobb night. A grand dinner. Paul Laxalt, then Nevada's governor, asks to be master of ceremonies. In San Diego, a retired boxer hears about the tribute, asks to say a few words, flies to Reno, and gives a brilliant keynote speech. He is the world's former light-heavyweight boxing champion, Archie Moore.

No man would laugh harder when the joke was on him. Example: A Sparks Little Leaguer runs up to him, asks Ty Cobb for his autograph, and chirps, "I've always wanted to meet a baseball Hall of Fame immortal."

Fifteen years ago, as Cobb continued to write his wonderful *Gazette-Journal* column, his faltering eyesight was misdiagnosed. Glaucoma had gotten an irreversible head start. His vision grew dimmer.

In darkness, Cobb continued his bright, glowing, inspirational life. As friends learned of his challenge, they increased the frequency of contacts. That is what friends are for!

Miraculously, the Ty Cobb weekly column continued, and it blossomed even more. He sent out a torrent of stories about good deeds, human pratfalls, ironies, laughter, and about treasured Comstock, and Nevada, and Reno history. He told his thousands of readers, in essence, "It's better when we work together."

What he called "Killer Corner" nagged him and worried him.

202

"Get a traffic light up at Skyline and McCarran boulevards," he wrote, "before someone gets killed." Silence from the city of Reno. Ty Cobb kept phoning them. "Get that corner lighted."

After wife Olga's passing, Ty Cobb carried on, warmed by memories, enchanted by the successes of children Patty, Ty and Bill, and charmed by his delightful grandchild herd.

For the last five years, he had a daytime housekeeper, Beverly Rivera.

For four-and-a-half years, she cooked him oatmeal twice a week. Six months ago, he finally confessed, "I hate oatmeal." Beverly answered, "Heavens, why didn't you tell me?" And Ty Cobb replied, "I didn't want to hurt your feelings."

Mrs. Rivera is from Beatty, the daughter of a construction worker and a school janitor. She has had a few classes at Truckee Meadows Community College. Now, thanks to Ty Cobb, she is like those he taught for 60 years.

He told her, "Don't cheer for the Rebels; you're a Wolf Pack girl now." She didn't know much about Nevada in 1992. Now she's an expert.

Every morning, she read him the *Gazette-Journal* and sometimes he would yell out, "They missed that angle! Why do *we* do that?"

She read him his column, on Sunday mornings. He'd either say, "Good," or mutter, "They left off my last 'graph."

She read him the *Comstock Chronicle*, *Nevada* magazine, *Silver & Blue* alumni magazine and the New Year's flood book.

He had the perennial martini with dinner, Beefeater's, with Martini & Rossi vermouth; and an onion. After the first one she made him in 1992, he told her it was awful. He drank the whole thing anyway.

Ham Robb, his lifetime pal, would come by to drive Ty to Wolf Pack games. Housekeeper Beverly would say, dead serious, "Now, you boys behave at the game!"

To the end, Ty reveled in Paul Harvey's broadcast humor. Ty rallied heroically to write his final four columns, and he did a superb job on each of them. They appeared in last Sunday's Sierra Style section.

Ty Cobb's deeds endure brightly.

Two weeks ago, housekeeper Beverly arrived at Ty's house

in the morning, all excited, and told him, "They're installing a traffic light at the Killer Corner!"

Ty Cobb, never cynical, yet skeptical, answered, "I don't believe this! Thank God they're finally doing something."

At 11 o'clock this morning, Harker & Harker Engineering reported it was going to turn on that traffic light the next Friday.

So, just as he did for us, for all those beautiful decades, Ty Cobb keeps lighting our way, bringing us home happy, and safe.

June 8,1997

Walter Cox: a Nevada Original _____

WALTER COX was a golden man who, for much of the century, sprayed Nevada with humor, wisdom and unbridled skepticism and hope.

For 50 of his 95 years, he spouted views in his *Mason Valley News* column; uttered crackerbarrelisms from his tidy garden or his porch, or on daily walks in Yerington.

Everywhere he went, he sent up cigar smoke, flicking ash on friends and strangers, or grinding it into wife Vivian's carpet to "kill the moths."

He punctured egos, jolted political pretenders and described lovely flowers seen on his city walks. He once described then new Lyon County physician Robin Titus as "a fine doc, running around like a cute little chick in jeans."

Born in Virginia City in 1900, a decade before Mark Twain died, Cox seemed a reincarnation of the legendary humorist. He also was every bit the curmudgeon H.L. Mencken was, but without venom.

He called himself not the smartest University of Nevada graduate, but boasted he went to college longer than any student. His hoaxes would have warmed Twain's juices. In 1924, Cox pulled a revolver on a blowhard college senior, and shot him dead. Then the "victim" and Cox left for a beer.

Shortly before he died on Nov. 19, the "Sage of Pizen Switch" entranced his lawyer, William Carpenter, with a yarn about selling rattler juice as a lubricant. The lawyer swallowed the snake-oil hype.

The sign at his back door said, "An old bastard lives here." When Tom Magee was a 5-year-old, Uncle Walter advised him, "You should sue Yerington for building this sidewalk so close to your ass."

Jack Carpenter of Dayton calls his former *Mason Valley News* and Chevrolet dealership partner "the craziest guy I ever knew." Wife Jewel Carpenter adds, "Walter made Nevada laugh."

He did big deals on a handshake, admired candor and wrote that Reno's traffic was crap. He said, "There are more award-seeking journalists than officers in the Mexican army."

He had a genius for talking up to readers.

So dominant was his humor that his political brilliance didn't sink in with everyone. But he was a star councilman, assemblyman and then state senator. Cox in 1945 authored the first Nevada gaming-tax bill.

Media slobbered over him. I publicly pouted when Cox stopped writing his great column in 1990. Ty Cobb called him curmudgeon cum laude. Elko publisher Chris Sheerin knew Cox since journalism school, and loved each day of their friendship. Journalism professor Jake Highton wrote a lovely portrait of him in a history of state newspapers. Bob Sanford cherished his newspaper partner and sweet friend in Thursday's *Mason Valley* eulogy. Cox's four-star journalism buddy, Jack McCloskey of Hawthorne, composed a tender farewell.

Cox sent scores of kids to college and medical school. Devoutly religious, he adored his wife of 56 years. He once said, "I bought Vivian a rake for her birthday. Since she stopped cooking, I have her in charge of outdoors maintenance." After her death in 1990, he sat by her picture and talked to her.

He created America's most famous journalism slogan, "The only newspaper in the world that gives a damn about Yerington."

It turned out that all who ever knew this incredible man gave a damn about Walter Cox.

Dec. 3, 1995

Herb Caen: He Was Funniest when He Laughed at Himself

FROM THE FIRST TIME I read Herb Caen 50 years ago, it was impossible to forget him.

What hit me almost as hard as news of his death on Feb. 1 was his earlier column, telling us he had inoperable lung cancer. But how typical he was then in declaring his predicament. Factual, yet riotously humorous in describing his own peril, he was bracing us for his inevitable death.

I began reading Caen in 1947 when I was a 15-year-old printer's apprentice at the weekly *Fallon Standard*. I'd haunt Vina Woods' little newsstand each morning until the *San Francisco Chronicle* arrived, bearing my writing role model's words.

On many a high school morning, I read Caen on the sly, learning much about the real world by making Baghdad by the Bay my daily habit.

He had by then been writing his column for nine years. He was just 30, but already a master journalist. I was in awe of his energy and his results, and I was to read him over the next five decades—even when I went away to the military.

He influenced me more than any other contemporary newspaper writer. His cultivation of a vast Caen army of news sources and his magical gift with the language stirred me to ultimately become a columnist.

Later, he and I visited occasionally, the last time when he phoned to check a quote I had used about Leslie Sferrazza.

He always was cordial, but not big on small talk. In our visits, he was an efficient manager of his, and others', time.

The general public was aware only of Caen's column-writing. In truth, he was prodigious in answering mail, in thanking people for items they sent him, and for occasionally praising other writers. Among the notes from him I prized most was the one after I extolled San Francisco, following the 1989 earthquake.

Each Caen column was a clinic, laced with Herbspeak; but in each he also revealed his unique strength as both reporter and writer. During his 60 years at his manual typewriter, each column blossomed with creativity, each done under relentless deadline stress. Never was he short on fresh ways of saying things.

He was nominated for a Pulitzer Prize dozens of times, and at last, in 1996, he got a special one. God, it was about time!

Herb Caen was never funnier than when he laughed at himself, which was often. In its obituary, the *New York Times* reminded us that Caen once described his own daily output, pounded out with two fingers, as "journalistic stoop labor."

He was a friendly, humorous man in person. At the typewriter, the real Herb Caen emerged: Kind, irreverent, funny, deep, skeptical, happy, sad, thankful, investigative, playful and, foremost, responsible.

Over the years, Bay area newspaper competitors trotted out their versions of Caen. It was like dispatching the fledgling artist to unfrock Michelangelo. No other columnist ever got within 20,000 leagues of the master.

For decades, I savored the delight of watching him puncture egos, prod community and state leaders, extol the poor, champion minorities, and celebrate magnificent San Francisco, while noting with sorrow its diminished glories.

Alternately witty and caustic, Herb Caen was at his best in glorifying people, at explaining their pain and potential and setting the city's evolving agenda. More than any person, he made San Francisco world-famous.

In his final months, he uttered no self-pity about his lung cancer, and the approaching conclusion of his vaunted life.

Only once that I know of did he admit a fear. That was many years ago when an interviewer asked what Caen feared most.

"Only that when I am gone, they might forget me."

That was a misplaced concern. Forget Herb Caen?

Impossible.

Feb. 7, 1997

Santini Leaves Legacy of Courage, Kindness, Laughter

WHEN LEE HERZ DIXON learned that her precious friend, Clark Santini, had died, she wept, as much of the City of Trembling Leaves today weeps. And instantly, she remembered the poem memorized from her girlhood.

Certainly, she knew that Edna St. Vincent Millay's classic must have been written about remarkable lifetime Nevadan Clark Santini, who would tar and feather his Reno in an anguished shout, then lovingly tell at gargantuan length why Reno was the gem of America.

My candle burns at both ends;
It will not last the night;
But ah, my foes, and oh, my friends—
It gives a lovely light!

A month ago, news of Santini's desperate illness flew to neighborhoods he championed, to sorrowing friends, to strangers who felt empathy for him, to foes, now willingly conceding that his tenacity, his "mouth that roared" and his enduring courage were remarkably unique.

The truly great person always is surprised to learn he is widely appreciated, and this was so with Reno's gadfly, godfather of protest, creative wunderkind, community cheerleader and thousands-of-words-a-minute friend.

He always touched lives profoundly. Now people touched him back.

The published words about his throat cancer, and friends

and strangers spreading the sad word, both stunned and pleased him. He quivered at the outpouring. But there was nothing for him to do but surrender to the lovely avalanche of moral and financial support, flooding into the Saint Mary's Regional Medical Center mailroom.

Many more than 600 cards and letters. "Thanks for turning Rancho San Rafael into our great park." "We love you, friend." "I never thought I'd miss your talking, but God, I do!"

The mail tumbled in from as far as Germany, across the nation, Las Vegas, and every city, village and wide spot in northern Nevada.

Gifts ranged from children's coins to $5 bills to a Reno resident's $1,000 personal check.

Ex-girlfriends wrote; one woman mailed her picture, saying in charming longhand, "Marrying you would do me just fine, Clark."

The cancer wrung off his wonderful voice, so he merely scribbled his reaction. "I've never met her, but I'd like to." The notes and checks were still stacking up Thursday morning from Nevada who's who, kids, students, pals and strangers.

In those pained 27 hospital days, as chemotherapy and radiation sought to beat the unbeatable foe, people missed him.

None more than Donna Horgan and son, Mark, who one year ago today opened their popular café, The River Walk, perched at the Virginia Street bridge, across from the muted Mapes Hotel. Clark Santini, who seldom missed new things, didn't find the place for several months.

When he did, he was charmed, for curling around its exterior, facing our life-giving Truckee River, and winding around to face Virginia Street, is a stunning mural of trees, leaves and a young boy reading a book.

Santini instantly saw that muralist Marsha Crawford had captured the essence of Reno, circa 1920s and '30s, as lovingly depicted in Walter Van Tilburg Clark's beautiful *City of Trembling Leaves*.

The thrilled Santini, nephew of the brilliant author, waltzed into the café, became its permanent patron and verbal shill. Seated always at the lone window table, he praised the Horgans. "You've got the perfect café, and here is how to improve it." He brought in kinsmen and a corps of friends, paying the checks with his shrinking monies.

Then he vanished. The owners missed him and did not learn until Thursday afternoon that he had been so sick, and that never would they again hear Clark Santini tout their café, or recite true stories that made people's sides ache with laughter.

As when Lee and Richard Dixon invited him to their home for dinner, urging, "Bring a lady friend if you wish." Santini headed to the Dixons', stopped for gas, and overheard motor-cyclists at a pump, hotly arguing.

The man sped away in a huff, deserting his pretty person, clad in the beat-up cycle uniform.

"Join me for dinner," Santini said. "Fine," she said.

At the Dixons he was uncharacteristically stalled for words. There was no introduction. He had forgotten to ask the pretty person for her name.

In the last days, cancer having stolen a great voice, he scribbled gratitudes, sprinkling his final mailings to near, and to far.

They let him go home to his little apartment Wednesday. He neatly arranged things. Bereft of voice, his greatest tool, ever an activist, captain of his own destiny, he would not wait in agony.

On Thursday morning, on Riverside Drive, along the Truckee he cherished, he ended his life, as the November leaves trembled down.

Later found, neatly arranged on his apartment table, was his final statement, one he wanted people to hear. At the top were recent columns by Cory Farley and me, telling of Clark Santini's nobility. And three sheets of music:

I'll Be Seeing You.
The Impossible Dream.
What I Did for Love.

Nov. 17, 1996

Vernon Durkee Sr.: a Jet-age Pioneer ___

WHEN VERNON DURKEE SR. opened a one-man travel agency in 1946, with little more than the best of intentions, his friends despaired for him. They had reasons to. It was the only such business in Reno.

William Brussard had first tried such a fling in Reno at the end of the 1930s. But war came and the firm vanished.

Durkee didn't have much savings to tide him over. Reno's population in 1946 was only 34,000 and people figured a travel office needed a city with at least 40,000. Then there was the uncertainty of the postwar economy.

But Durkee already was expert at getting people from place to place. For 12 years, he had worked for Western Greylines, much of that time as superintendent of the Reno-Salt Lake City run.

Trains, buses and cars were the way most people got around in 1946. But Durkee felt certain that airplanes would revolutionize travel. He wanted to be at people's service when that big change occurred.

His first workplace was really kind of laughable. He set up shop in the lobby of the Overland Hotel, where now stands Harrah's Reno's parking garage. He had a secondhand desk, two telephones, a typewriter, a few airline-reservation forms and some travel posters taped to the wall.

Even old-timers have to strain to remember who Durkee's commercial neighbors were on Center Street and Commercial Row. Across the street were the Golden Hotel, the Bank Club and the Palace Casino. The Francovich family's Wine House

Restaurant was a few steps away. The Greyhound depot fronted Center and was just south of the Overland.

Harrah's casino was 9 years old. But men such as William Harrah and Raymond I. "Pappy" Smith of Harolds Club sensed the huge potential of tourism. People loved Reno, once they managed to get here. But getting them here was the trick.

Vernon Durkee Sr. became the professional travel pioneer who helped Reno truly arrive as a prime destination point.

He knew the old Nevada intimately because he and his family were an integral part of it. His father, Samuel C. Durkee, graduated from the University of Nevada in 1895 and worked in South African mines until the Boer War forced him home. He married Teresa Hinch, a teacher at the Fourth Ward School in Virginia City. Their son, Vernon, was born in 1911 in the historic Nye County mining town of Manhattan.

Samuel Durkee took the family to homes around the state— Elko, Silver City and, finally, Reno. Later, he lost to Ted Carville in a gubernatorial race.

Vernon Durkee mainly grew up in Reno, working odd jobs, including usher at the old Wigwam Theater, where he wore a tuxedo. He attended the University of Nevada, then joined Greyline in 1934.

Today there are nearly 75 travel businesses in greater Reno, and Durkee Travel Agency continues to hold a significant market share in the industry, under the leadership of the founder's son, Vernon Jr., who took full charge when his father retired as chairman in 1980.

Vernon Sr. steered his company through peril, momentous changes in travel and an era laden with opportunity.

Upon his death in Reno last Saturday, the community he impacted so much felt a sense of real loss. It was Durkee, along with then-Reno Chamber of Commerce manager Jud Allen, who in the 1960s created the Reno Fun Flight promotion. It became United Airlines' No. 1 tour package to any destination. Allen, now a Reno councilman, will eulogize Durkee at a memorial service at 11 a.m. Monday at the Walton Funeral Home, Reno.

The commercial jet came on line in 1958, and Durkee Sr., with his travel savvy and instinctive need to serve people, sailed along with the new trends. He was soft-spoken, had the warmest of smiles, never knocked people and was the epitome of the highest integrity.

He and his late wife, Marge, to whom he was married 50 years, became globetrotters after their son and daughter, Sharon, were raised. Vernon Sr. circled the world several times and visited all the continents.

It mattered not whether conversation was of the Inca ruins, life in Beijing or the Pope's summer residence at Castel Gandolfo—it seemed that he had visited all places.

He was a gentleman's gentleman, a man who adored his wife and cherished his friends. Ann Mandelstan calls him the sweetest man she has ever known. Retired chiropractor Robert Jenkins, who had lunch with Durkee nearly ever Tuesday since 1952, along with businessman John Humphrey, calls his friend irreplaceable.

Vernon Durkee Sr. summed up his personal and professional philosophy in a conversation not long ago. He said, "If you treat people with respect, and honor their traditions, you will be treated kindly, no matter where you travel."

July 10, 1988

Native Son Russell Was an Innovative Leader _____

WHEN NEVADA'S 20th governor, Charles H. Russell, died last month, news coverage was minimal. Some weeklies didn't even mention his passing.

That happens when a man reaches 85, has been out of sight and mind of the public for a long spell, and hasn't lived at the Governor's Mansion in more than 30 years.

Hardly anyone is left among print journalists who knew Charlie Russell, and who covered his career as legislator, congressman, diplomat, governor and University of Nevada officer. To the younger media generation, he was merely a clip from the newspaper library.

Hawthorne publisher Jack McCloskey and Yerington columnist Walter Cox, now 89, eulogized the two-term governor. The *Las Vegas Sun's* Ruthe Deskin, his friend, remains active, as does Cy Ryan, the veteran UPI man in Carson City, and columnist Melton.

Someday, historians will tote up scores of which Nevada governors were true innovators and had foremost leadership skills. The quiet, efficient and courageous Russell is going to be right there, topside.

Russell was a native son; of the six men who occupied the statehouse since he left office in 1958, only one, Paul Laxalt, also was a native.

As a homegrown person, Russell was intent to know everyone—for he had a vested interest in what in his day was the

215

least populated state, a place so devoid of people that Gov. Fred Balzar had as his slogan, "One square man for every square mile."

Elected to the Nevada Assembly from White Pine County in 1929, when he was only 31, Russell already had packed a lot of achievement into his life.

He had been Elko High School student-body president, ranch cook, grease monkey on a ship in the Pacific, collegian, time-keeper at the Ruth copper mine and Ely editor. He had cam-paigned enough to know that liquor ought to be consumed in limited quantities, that you'd better make friends in the opposi-tion party, and that when you visited little Nevada hamlets you saw everyone, so nobody would feel left out.

He knew, even as a young fellow, something he would tell his five children later in life:

"When you're in political office, you are catered to. As soon as you're out, you are dropped. Completely."

Russell was the last widely known Nevada state official who won office without benefit of lots of media. In his era, there were only a couple of low-power radio stations in Nevada; there was no television; the state's dailies were small; Las Vegas, a wide spot in the road, had no clout, and apparently no future.

It was man-to-man campaigning that let Russell win all but two of his campaigns. He went door to door. He went into the mines. He carpooled with other candidates. He'd rent a motel room in a rural place, pull in a couple of extra beds and split costs with other Republicans.

He and his Marjorie, to whom he was married 50 years, for-ever scrimped so he could run. Once, she let him cash in her insurance policy for $1,200, to finance a successful congressional run. He drove beat-up cars, walked to his Capitol office when he was governor, and earned only $7,600 the first year he was state chief executive.

What he sacrificed to serve proved how much he wanted to serve.

He had to sell his beloved *Ely Record* to his foremost politi-cal and newspaper rival, Vail Pittman, to make ends meet. Russell printed his own placards, political cards and other lit-erature.

216

On his first run for governor, in 1950, he had to borrow a car from friend Archie Pozzi, in Carson City, to campaign around Nevada.

Russell told Mary Ellen Glass in his oral history, published in 1966, when he was 63: "I'd get so tired campaigning, I'd sometimes find a little motel late at night, go to bed and sleep all next day. Sort of hide out."

But there were the light moments. After he lost a 1946 bid for the U.S. House, he and Margie drove to the Carson home of her father, Judge Clark Guild Sr., to break the sad news to the Russell children.

But the kids dashed out of their grandparents' house to the Russell car, yelling, "Goody, goody, Daddy's defeated. Now we can stay in Nevada!"

He was ahead of his time as public servant. In his two terms as governor, Nevada got a true gaming-control organization for the first time. Russell revamped the state's education system. He pushed through a personnel act to protect state workers.

Charles H. Russell left public life in 1958, a man who had never built a political machine.

He later said he had tried to make his family proud by doing the right thing.

No one bettered him at living up to a vital pledge.

Oct. 1, 1989

OUR BACK PAGES _____

A Reno Columnist's '50s Reminiscences

(The following story ran in Fun & Gaming *magazine in August 1995, to coincide with the summer special event Hot August Nights.)*

MEMORIES OF THE 1950s Reno that was small, yet pound-for-pound the most exciting city this side of New York:

Today's classic cars were shiny new then—if you could afford to shell out up to $3,000. The young ladies in poodle skirts fretted about calories, and none had ever heard of fat grams. As 1950 arrived, the long,

Raymond I. "Pappy" Smith (right), Pop Southworth (center) and Harold Smith Sr. with the Silver Dollar Buick, 1949, outside Harolds Club.

lean Bill Harrah, who had settled in a small-joint bingo place, had four years of running a full casino. Later, he constructed a gaming empire, started wearing his hair in weird bangs and, all of a sudden, he was called William F. Harrah.

By day, newsboys cried out to passersby any and all big headlines that would return them 10 cents. The best newsie corners were Becker's Bar and Grill on Commercial Row, and Les Lerude's Wigwam Coffee Shop on West Second, a place everyone loved, though "not recommended by Duncan Hines."

Young Don Carano, just before leaving Reno for law school, swept sidewalks at his family's bakery, where one day his Eldorado enterprise would rise. The district attorney, Bill Raggio, wore a trench coat with turned-up collar, and every hood in town cringed at the mention of his prosecutor name. But all was not always well

221

in the Biggest Little City in the 1950s. Bud Baker was the worst mayor in memory. We periodically manned sandbags when the Truckee River rebelled for lack of upstream storage.

Later, historians alleged the young of the day were the Quiet Generation. Not true. A collegian mob, angry at autocratic University of Nevada President Minard Stout, hung him in effigy from the Reno Arch—with all-conference football lineman Clay Darrow affixing the noose.

Northside Junior High shook in its boots when trains roared past, and today at the same site, National Bowling Stadium patrons get the same Southern Pacific jolts. There wasn't a freeway in sight, or planned. Our airport was of Podunk stature, until 1960, when the Winter Olympic Games at Squaw Valley compelled us to think modern. The Mapes, opened in late 1947, was the closest thing to a high-rise, and the wondrous joint featured world-class entertainers. Across the river at the aptly named Riverside Hotel, Sinatra, Durante, Paul Whiteman's Orchestra and a slew of big-league counterparts were simply dazzling.

The late '40s and '50s was the period of unforgettable characters and emerging entrepreneurship. LaVere Redfield, a super-rich Reno eccentric, would dress in a shabby plaid jacket, wander into the Riverside or Harolds Club looking for all the world like a bum. From a tattered paper sack he withdrew quarters, silver dollars and currency, while a crowd collected to eyeball him. He usually cleaned the house's clock.

Pappy Smith, tall and lean, with a giant Good Samaritan's heart, proclaimed, "Harolds Club or Bust." His place set the standard for casino marketing. Pappy Man publicly cautioned, "Don't gamble more than you can afford to lose." Unfortunately, his late son, Harold, the club's namesake, didn't heed father's sound counsel. Eventually, Harold was put on a spendthrift account.

Entertainment joy erupted in unexpected places. Lee Liberace pounded out piano tunes in a small room on the second floor of a new casino, Club Cal-Neva. Three blocks west, on Arlington Avenue (earlier called Chestnut), Tony Pecetti's El Patio Ballroom drew local dancers. On special promotion days, every Italian tyke in town waltzed in, accordion in hand, to compete for honors. Reno had just one television station, *KZTV* (later

222

KOLO). TV sets were made in America. Today, none is.

High school kids dragged the main after each game, and in between. In bustling Douglas Alley stood the Reno Turf Club, which produced for salivating patrons the best pastrami sand-wiches and New York cheesecake west of the Rockies. Reno's first supermarket, Sewell's, rose in 1948. The Silver Legacy now towers on the site.

Restaurants, and familiar passersby:

Johnny Petrinovich, of the Grand Café; Newt Crumley, of the Holiday Hotel; Pop Southworth, of cigar-store fame; the fam-ily that ran Armanko's Store; Leon Nightingale, who ultimately was a principal owner of the Club Cal-Neva; Frank Menante, the classy clothier; the Tomerlin brothers who ran the Golden Hotel (later wiped out by fire)—all these and many more were important business figures of the '50s, who erected the base on which the next generation would build. One of the early ones, John Ascuaga, was for a time grilling Awful-Awful hamburgers at the Nugget on North Virginia Street.

Johnny's since done A-OK at another Nugget. The one in Sparks that bears his name.

No final word can fall here without talking of the social head-quarters of my 1950 college years. It was the Little Waldorf, on Virginia Street, between Third and Fourth streets. Lance Morton, now 89, was the owner. The bartenders who later became fa-mous in their own careers, including Johnny Hart, Bruno Benna, Dean C. Smith, David Ryan and a flock of others. At "The Wal," political deals were struck by our elders; young women met young guys, and vice versa. The enterprising photographer Don Dondero took some of his best pictures at the "Wal." Fortunately, most of them were never published.

Physically gone now are many of these haunts, and others, too. The newsboys grew up. Sierra Beer passed from our scene. LaVere Redfield died and didn't take his wealth to wherever millionaires go. The fantastic gaming pioneers are gone.

Everyone and everything from that era left a mark, however.

Delicious memories are made of these precious things.

August 1995

Images of a Reno with Majestic, DJ Cactus Tom

WHILE SOME busily recall what happened in 1991, Don Hartman is thinking back a lot further—to the early 1950s and the Reno in which he grew up. Hartman, 48, teaches fifth grade in Davis, Calif. He remembers:

Buying bread from Welsh's Bakery, doughnuts from Rawhut's and goodies at the Spudnut Shop; listening to Bob Stoddard on the radio; the place to go was the gorgeous Sky Room of the Mapes Hotel; it was so much fun hearing Reno's very own country-western disc jockey, "Cactus" Tom Cafferty, on the radio.

People hung out around the Grotto Bar and the adjacent Little Waldorf Saloon (featuring such bartenders as Johnny Hart and University of Nevada students Bruno Benna and Dean C. Smith) at Fourth and North Virginia streets, the site now occupied by Don Carano & Co.; the world's best ice cream was made by our own Chism Company; you drank Coke out of 16-ounce glass bottles, at a cost of 15 cents per; admission was 25 cents at the Tower, Crest, Granada and Majestic movie theaters, and you could get a reasonable slug of popcorn for 10 cents, plus butter for a few more pennies; at Saturday movies at the Crest, kids got in free with a red cap from a Model Dairy milk bottle.

Radio brought listeners such entertaining programs as *Jack Benny, Fred Allen, Don McNeil's Breakfast Club, Big John and Sparky, Mark Trail* and the soap show, *My Friend Bill*; youngsters flocked to the Sears windows in the 100 block of North Sierra Street to gawk at Lionel toy trains; Farmers and Builders Hardware had a wonderful model railroad layout.

With supermarkets still in the future, grocery shopping was done at such small and cordial stores as Santa Claus Market on

224

Vine Street, University Market and Ralston Market, both on Ralston Avenue, and at Sewell's on North Virginia and the Akert Market on East Fourth; the best apple pie (and sauce) in town was offered by Les Lerude at his Wigwam Coffee Shop (northeast corner of Sierra and Second streets).

Swimmers did their thing at Idlewild Pool, or at Lawton's Hot Springs west of Reno on U.S. Highway 40; the Mapes was the tallest building in Reno and in Nevada, too; the largest casino was Harolds Club, and other casinos included the Riverside Hotel, the Golden, the Bank and Palace clubs and Harrah's. Oden Cycle Works was where you went for bicycle repairs.

At (old) Mackay Stadium, now campus site of the Effie Mona Mack Building, the University of Nevada Wolf Pack football team played before crowds of up to 1,800. Shrine Circus performances, also held there, thrilled the children and outdrew football; Reno's first fast-food place was possibly Bud's Burgers (19 cents apiece); a candy bar cost 5 cents.

The only area high schools were Reno, Sparks and new Manogue, which opened in 1948; the Reno junior high schools were Central, Northside and Billinghurst. Happiness was tooling around Hudson Lee's Drive-In.

Trains rolling through town were the City of San Francisco, the Overland, Gold Coast and fast mail; kids yearned to catch the prizewinning trout at the annual Idlewild Park fish derby; Arlington Avenue, north of Second, was called Chestnut Street. Center Street, north of Fourth, was known as University Avenue.

Hale's Drug Store sold ice cream cones for 5, 10 and 15 cents; you got records at Stampfli's, clothes at Gray-Reid's; in wintertime, a Reno-to-San Francisco drive on Highway 40 could take seven or more hours.

Some homes in southwest Reno cost upwards of $30,000; there were two daily newspapers, one television station (*KZTV*, now *KOLO*), which didn't go on the air until 3 p.m., and United Airlines flew DC-3s in and out of a small airfield.

Jan. 2, 1992

Some of the Best Things in Life Are the Smaller Things ───────────────

TODAY IN PICTURESQUE Rancho San Rafael Regional Park, close to 2,000 older folks are here to celebrate the high school days they spent in a tranquil, picturesque and small Reno.

The reunion picnic is a first-time, all-old Reno High School rally, and people from many states will be present. A majority of them were once students in the building that was a high school from 1913 through June 1951. The Sundowner Hotel-Casino and the Seasons Inn and Bonanza Inn motels on Fourth and West streets stand where old Reno High used to be.

When the idea for this reunion first came up, planners hoped it might attract a few hundred people, mostly from northern Nevada. But overnight, registration doubled, then tripled!

Why the nostalgic surge?

First, there is the lovely pastime called reaching back to one's youth—such exercise is safe, and it is a joy.

But there is something additional with this particular reunion: These people, who are now in their late 50s or considerably older, are excitedly eager to both commemorate the small and hospitable Reno they grew up in, and to mourn its passing, as well.

The Reno these celebrants lived in as youngsters was small, intimate, safe—a known territory that was both hospitable and Family, with a capital F.

The Reno back then had not experienced the Jet Age. There were no television, nuclear power, computer, supermarket or freeway, nor was there a Rancho San Rafael Regional Park— that area was then farm land.

The word "casino" wasn't used. Gambling places were called "the clubs." Little and friendly grocery stores dotted the small neighborhoods and you knew the cordial proprietors and they called their customers by name, asked about all the family, and told their patrons about their own families, too. Grocers at times routinely billed some customers by the month.

Reno was a place where guests were called visitors, rather than tourists. It was a town where you knew nearly all the people you saw on the street. It was a place where high school kids always seemed busy, though there was no television to watch. Few kids had a car, certainly none owned a "new" car, and most students either walked to school or pedaled a bike, or hitched a ride in a buddy's jalopy.

Small Reno didn't have a housing subdivision until Westfield Village materialized in the late 1940s, nor was there a shopping center until Village Shopping Center was erected on California Avenue.

The Reno that has now vanished had a downtown area that was intimately small, but jammed with little interesting stores. They were owned and operated by fascinating shopkeepers who seemed to invariably have gregarious personalities. Reno had characters, LaVere Redfield and Pappy Smith, to name two decidedly different examples.

Downtown Reno contained neither dirt, nor homeless people, nor vacant commercial buildings.

Kids and older folks came downtown because it was fun. There were things to do, and nobody did you harm. Once in a full moon, there was traffic congestion.

That little city began to surge in size precisely as old Reno High School was replaced by a new building on Foster Drive. Growth overtook the town. A new high school rose about every 10 years.

The cozy stores vanished. Television revolutionized our era. A way of life was gone.

Today at the reunion picnic, that wonderful little old Reno of their youth will be spoken of with something akin to reverence. Such memories are to treasure, for it was a school and a city that truly was Family.

There also is reason to mourn its passing, for it was a living example of how smallness often means the best things in life.

Aug. 25, 1991

In Its Heyday, Mapes Was City's Very Best

IN HER GLORY YEARS, the Mapes Hotel was our Baghdad by the Truckee River.

She was invariably exciting. Predictably romantic. Ever grand.

Opened by owner Charles W. Mapes Jr. in 1948, the hotel was a national hit from Day One. Reviewers extolled the architecture. Copycat critics found nothing to criticize. The Mapes became an instant "fun destination," before the phrase became a cliché.

It wasn't just that the Mapes was the tallest building in Nevada—a distinction the publicists seldom ignored.

It wasn't simply the celebrities, who were forever on the premises.

It wasn't the food alone—the restaurants were excellent.

The Mapes Hotel had a blend of attributes.

It had atmosphere.

It seemed it was barely out of diapers and it was behaving like a mature institution.

Employees were confident, but not cocksure. The best service was theirs to provide.

It was a place where Somebodies and Nobodies collided in harmony, where East met real cowboys, without turning up its Eastern nose.

The lobby, with its heavy traffic, was nonetheless cozy. You sank into the carpeting and into the lounge chairs. The eleva-

228

tors weren't the automatic mechanisms of today but were operated by live, "Hope you're enjoying your stay" humans.

The Mapes was a local joy, attracting, from the beginning, an avid Nevada following.

You never knew from one night to the next whether you'd encounter a dining party of Reno's old rich or a collection of yelping fraternity-sorority youngsters, down from the university on the hill.

The crowning glory was at the top—the Mapes Sky Room was made for lovers, for stargazers, for dancers and show-goers, who could watch the world's best entertainers in the intimate showroom.

There were gathered at the Mapes the famous and the no-names, the gadflies, the gawkers, the tourists and the real Nevadans.

A torrent of change finally overtook the Mapes, drying up its profits and dragging it off its pedestal.

But before the financial showdown, Charles Mapes did things that truly showcased Reno. Back then, Las Vegas was a Scout in walking shorts and Reno was Numero Uno.

Today, casino management retreats to tapes while live musicians scramble to make a living in other ways. Showrooms—Harrah's Headliner Room is the latest—convert to cheaper fare.

In the "old days," the Mapes brought in some of the best entertainment in the world. People still on top of their singing and dancing game, not fading stars on a downhill slide! Singer Nelson Eddy; the stripper Lili St. Cyr; the wonderful Ames Brothers, before sibling Ed split to do his own magic; Judy Garland and Mae "Come Up and See Me Sometime" West; incomparable Sammy Davis Jr.; and so many others.

Competition with the Riverside Hotel's lineup of stars really lit up life along the Truckee. The Riverside, then owned by the Wertheimer brothers, paraded in Jimmy Durante, the Paul Whiteman Orchestra, Ted ("Me and My Shadow") Lewis, Maurice Chevalier.

People with dim memories and no compassion demean Charles Mapes today. They would have you think he was the total reason for the decline and fall of the Mapes Hotel. True, the Mapes Enterprise ship did sink after expansion spread cash flow lethally thin.

But change had then arrived, altering the way casino management had to do business, if they were to survive. Competition surged. Interstate 80 supplanted primitive Highway 40, the visitors poured in around the calendar, and they increasingly searched for more than one hotel-casino destination.

All people, businesses and things have a beginning, a high point and a decline. The Mapes story went that way, too. Birth. Stardom. Death.

But in its star period, the Mapes was the glorious best. A place with the good sense to cater to local yokels, a trait that got the Mapes through lean economic winters. A place where you encountered gawking tourists, lunching business people and real stars, who behaved real friendly.

The Mapes seems in retrospect to have been a sort of social downtown home away from home. If a modern owner—Texas developer Hollis Walker, let us hope—could recapture the old Mapes moments, going home again could be our new beautiful journey.

July 22, 1990

Coach Room Gets Brief Time to Shine

FOR A FEW GLORIOUS HOURS on Saturday night and Sunday morning, a cherished part of the Mapes Hotel legend—the wonderful old Coach Room—came alive again, bursting with music, dancing and camaraderie.

For seven years the Mapes has stood padlocked; not a single event broke the silence imposed by the business downfall of Charles Mapes.

But on Saturday, the Coach Room became "Edna's Speakeasy." The party Edna and Bruno Benna threw there will be talked about for years.

Edna

Today is CB Concrete owner Bruno Benna's 60th birthday. Wife Edna, Reno's creative party planner, started wondering months ago where to honor her husband on his "big even-numbered day."

She settled on the Mapes Coach Room, hoping it wasn't Mission Impossible. She tried the idea on George Caradanis, one of three principal owners of the Mapes Hotel property. He let out a gasp. "All right, but you've got to get it by several local agencies!" he commanded.

Bruno

Edna Benna, believe this, talked approval out of the fire department, the health people and security folks.

She thought she'd better go see the Coach Room. She remembered what it was from 1948 to 1982—one of the happiest luncheon and dinner and entertainment places in town.

They let her inside the Coach Room, at the southwest corner of the Mapes, at street level, next to the Virginia Street bridge.

The party-giver wasn't prepared for what she saw and felt.

The elongated room, which stretches east-west, was dank, cold and black. Cobwebs and 18 tons of dust. Unwashed dishware, aprons draped over chairs.

Edna Benna sailed into the huge cleanup task, working for weeks to get the place shining again. She got the invitations in the mail—"dress for the 1920s, '30s or black-tie."

There was an unbelievable bit of lousy luck five hours before the birthday gala commenced at 7:30 Saturday night, when ceiling pipes burst in the Coach Room, dumping water into the bar area. The cleanup crew worked feverishly.

The party was a smashing success, laden with nostalgia. Only a few of the 200 guests had never before been in the Coach Room. One, Robin Sanford, said, "Oh, this must have been such a grand place!" So correct!

Sharon and David Quinn, the First Interstate Bank executive, told friends they had had their first dinner date in this room 30 years ago, on Feb. 6, 1959, her 18th birthday.

CB Concrete's sales manager, Bill Adcock, Benna's senior employee, used to join fellow Kerak Shriners for a Coach Room nightcap, "While Joe Karnes had us singing along at his piano."

The Speakeasy dress theme let the ladies bring out their Flapper Era finery; the guys either went the tuxedo route or imitated the mobster manner of dress and out-of-the-side-of-the-mouth jabber.

Violin cases, supposedly containing gangster hardware, were in vogue, including those lugged in by Clark Santini and Don Thompson—the latter in agony with a bad back.

Insurance man Dick Lowden, seated with "flapper" wife Toni, showed off a shoulder holster, with .32 Smith & Wesson pistol.

The place was made toasty warm by six propane heaters, courtesy of Jay Read; while two fire inspectors paraded vigilantly, Palmer House employees served catered goodies; two overworked bartenders ran themselves ragged.

232

A great three-man combo concentrated almost nonstop on the grand songs of yesteryear, as wonderful Cami Thompson belted out lyrics about laughter and love.

Gitta Tome, remembered as Reno's roving nightspot photographer from 1952 to 1980, returned to capture this party with her Graflex.

Everybody wondered aloud about the ultimate fate of the Mapes Hotel. Perhaps nobody knows for certain. Bruno Benna expressed people's trepidation: "I'm afraid this is the Mapes' last party hurrah."

Maybe so. But they wound it up with one of the best parties ever!

Feb. 13, 1989

Reno Photographer Snapped 'Misfit' Marilyn

LIKE MANY entertainment legends, Marilyn Monroe lived fast and died young. What is certain is that people who saw her during her fame, no matter how brief the meeting, remember her as fresh and young, and they'll never forget her.

Clark Gable, Gloria Mapes, Marilyn Monroe and Charles Mapes in 1960 in Mapes Hotel.

With the 30th anniversary of her death on Aug. 5, memories are especially strong for Reno commercial photographer Don Dondero.

He captured close to 150 pictures of Monroe in Reno and at Lake Tahoe in 1960, when she was in Nevada to film the movie classic, *The Misfits*.

What is gratifying about Dondero's pictures is their candor. The one you see here is typical of the Marilyn of that time—she seemed relaxed, even playful, flashing the patented smile, the undisciplined blond hair meandering across the forehead, her hospitable glance sweeping left.

Dondero has photographed thousands of people, in every manner of setting, for 60 years. Of the countless celebrities, he recalls her as one of the most relaxed and unaffected.

Somehow, she kept the young-girl innocence and vulnerability, but at the same time was regal.

234

Whether at the Cal-Neva at Lake Tahoe alongside Frank Sinatra, or being greeted at the Reno airport by then-Nevada First Lady Bette Sawyer, or shown in the receiving line at the Mapes Hotel Sky Room party, Marilyn Monroe was alternately joyous, languorous or meditative. She didn't perform for Dondero's camera, yet seemed always aware of the lens and of the man who made her his focus.

She was 34 then, and Dondero says she was beginning to show some aging. But his photographs do not reflect her total years, or reveal that, in fact, she then was living in the hard lane.

While *Misfits* shooting was being done at Dayton and Reno, Monroe was under great personal stress. Her marriage to playwright Arthur Miller was coming apart. The man who wrote the *Misfits* screenplay was always close by. But Miller seemed inattentive to her.

She sparred with director John Huston, who was exasperated by her failure to memorize her movie lines and by her habitual lateness to the set. Nor did her unreadiness sit easily with costar Clark Gable, who suffered a fatal heart attack six weeks after filming ended.

Amid Nevada filming, Huston had to fly Monroe to Los Angeles and hospitalize her because of her increasing dependency on drugs.

Yet, she appears for all the world on Dondero's film as the carefree queen.

Nothing has occurred in the ensuing 32 years to diminish Dondero's 1960 declaration that Marilyn Monroe was the most photogenic person he ever dealt with.

Even had he tried, he would have found it impossible to take a bad picture of the actress. "No matter what the angle was, or the lighting aspects were, or regardless of the emotional events swirling around her, she always looked terrific on film," he says. Little wonder that in Dondero's book, *Dateline: Reno*, she appears 23 times.

Though she has been dead 30 years, his Monroe pictures remain in demand. With the rising new tide of Monroe articles and books, there are fresh requests for prints of her.

Thus, does the magic of her life and the mystery of her death intertwine to make Marilyn Monroe live on.

Aug. 10, 1992

235

Boxer Always Remembered Fans, Friends

THE TOUGH GUYS I've interviewed leave indelible memories.

Rocky Marciano, rollicking at a Holiday Hotel party, was the happy-go-lucky retired warrior.

Henry Armstrong, lightweight king, was the funniest.

The 1932 Olympic Games swim champion, Johnny Weissmuller, the most famous movie Tarzan, was by the time I met him in 1959 a bumbling drunk.

Jack Dempsey, as I interviewed him in 1964 in Reno and later in New York, had the elegant gift of making you forget his celebrity.

But my richest memories are of Archie Moore, the incredible world 175-pound boxing

Rollan Melton Sr. with Archie Moore.

champion for nine years. I first met him 40 years ago, when I was the 27-year-old sports editor of the *Reno Evening Gazette*. Moore was here, offering me his famous Aborigine diet and lying about his age.

It was summer 1958, and he was training at Carson Hot Springs for a non-title fight against Reno's Howard King.

Moore, grinning, told me he was 40. After the champion's

236

death last Wednesday, his family fixed his birth date: Dec. 1, 1913. Thus, when he fought at old Moana Ball Park on Aug. 4, 1958, he was 44, a relic in a sport reserved for men in their 20s or early 30s.

The fight was ruled a draw, a decision so hometownish that locals in the $5 ringside seats gagged.

Archie Moore was unique for many reasons. He was history's most prolific knockout hitter. He had stunning recuperative power. In 1958, before Howard King, Moore survived four knockdowns, then blasted out Canada's Yvon Durelle. Moore was almost 50 by retirement.

The noble giant never forgot kids or his adult friends. For years, he wrote me at Christmastime, as he did thousands of others.

My father, Rollan Sr., idolized Moore, so I invited my dad down from Boise, Idaho, to see the 1958 match in Reno. Later, I said, "Dad, Archie wants to see you in the dressing room." Father reacted as if he was to visit the executioner. I dragged him up to Moore, who sat exhausted on a beat-up bench. He was draped only in a sweaty towel.

By pre-arrangement, Reno's top photographer, Don Dondero, was there as the champion yelled, "Mel, come sit and visit." Afterward, Dad glowed about being with his "old friend." Dad was one year older.

Months later, I visited my father, and he hauled me to homes of Boise friends. Displayed in every home was the framed photo of Rollan Sr. and his old friend, Archie.

Dec. 13, 1998

Big Nose Tony, Meet Jelly-Jack _____

IN 1979, I WROTE a column about White Pine County residents' penchants for hanging nicknames on local residents. It was George Charchalis, an Ely native, who had suggested I publish such a list. After seeing the names, I couldn't resist. Some of them:

A virtual stable full of men named Joe, as in Antler Joe, Candy Joe, Mustachio Joe, Coaldock Joe, Tire Joe and Little Joe.

There were characters called Seldom Seen Slim, Heavy Archer, Fat Pete, Banjo Baker, Saxophone Blanche, Bugsy Moran, the Professor, Dirty Steve, Donkey Murphy and Big Tommie.

Also adorned with nicknames were Big Nose Tony, Tony Baloney, The Soldier, Sawmill MacDonald, Digger Bill, Bicycle Mary, Charlie, The Blum; Thimbleful Millie, Dragline Miller and Cockeyed Mamie.

The list went on: Bubbles, Peanuts, Whispering Elmer, Whiskey Bill, Silly Willy and Plain Pete.

Not to be outdone by uniqueness, there also were The Black Basquo, Preacher Bob, Mahogany John, Johnnie the Sheik, Bulldog, Crazy Mike and Tiger Flowers.

I hadn't run across such stellar "different" names, rivaling White Pine's, until recently.

Retired gaming executive-turned-author Dwayne Kling of Reno has written a powerful, enlightening, fascinating book, *The Rise of the Biggest Little City*, which will be published this year by the University of Nevada Press. It covers the years 1931-81.

The Kling/press undertaking is monumental—an atlas, if you will—of licensed Reno casinos, and casino-connected people who have come, and, now, mostly gone. Kling spent 14 years on the research, and the results are stunning, placing gaming in a perspective never before achieved, let alone attempted.

Returning to names: Kling is including nicknames of many

involved in gaming in that 50-year period. The names by which they were known help spice the text. When the book arrives, readers will get insight into such individuals as:

Smiling Jesse, Ma Bull, Russian Louie, Rocky, Jelly-Jack.

You'll come face to face with a man they called Sugar Plum; there was a Jelly, and several fellows named Frenchy. Also, Bodie Mike; Buddy, as in Baer; a gaggle of guys known simply as Swede; "Pick," as in Hobson. "Pick" first owned the Overland Hotel, and later the Riverside. Few were aware that his actual given name was Richard.

There are in the manuscript some guys known as Shorty; there's a Baldy, and a Doc, and, of course, a Tex here and there; and a man known as Mohair, and another who was called The Galloper.

It was William Fisk Harrah, himself, who hung a nickname that stuck to a respected colleague, who avoided letting his facial expressions give away his inner thoughts. Harrah called him Joe Deadpan.

When Kling's history is issued, you will see many powerful quotations from gaming notables. Two are shared here for now:

Richard Graves, owner of the Sparks Nugget, after selling it to John Ascuaga in 1960: "I didn't want to be the richest man in the cemetery."

Mert Wertheimer, a co-owner of the Riverside Hotel, after he moved from Detroit in 1946: "The thing I like is that here in Reno, you don't have to pay anyone off!"

Jan. 25, 1999

NOTABLE NEVADANS

Puttin' on a Shine

A YOUNG RENO entrepreneur is aiming to make her mark in a business that operates down on the ground level.

Aileen Martin, the newest bootblack in Reno, breaks into a field that once was the exclusive turf of males.

Defying a trend that's seen shoeshine operations do less than polished business, Martin has customers lined up four deep at times at Reno Cannon International Airport, waiting for her patented brand of happy talk, humor and a shine you can almost see your reflection in.

Standing there in her customary uniform—jeans, cowboy boots, shirt and bootblack smock—Martin laughs as she recites her basic price list:

"Yes, sir. Well, it's $3 for shoes, $4 for boots, $10 for BS, and $15 for serious jazz.

Until he died last September, Charles Hill operated the airport stand. He had been there 15 years.

After his passing, nobody seemed interested in picking up the business.

Then Bernice Martin, who heads Silver State Skycap Inc. at the airport, said to daughter Aileen, "Hey, let's go for it!"

The mother, daughter and former Nevada Wolf Pack and Canadian Football League star James Curry are the firm's principals.

A handsome and personable woman, Aileen Martin is single, 29, grew up in Reno, is a graduate of Wooster High School and active in social and business circles. She's a member of the board of directors of the Nevada Women's Fund.

She started seven days before Christmas, determined to be the best bootblack she can be. She hadn't done this sort of thing previously.

She sought professional advice, going to Nevada Shoe Factory on Sierra Street in Reno for counsel. "The guys there were just super, showing me the best way to treat shoes, to make them glow. I got advice on polish, creams and waxes." She also flew to Las Vegas to acquire advice of shine pros at McCarran International Airport.

Once upon a time, the shoeshine stand was an institution that dotted the American landscape. It mattered not whether the community was huge or just a wide place in the road. You didn't need to hunt for a shine.

Shiners set up shop in neighborhoods. Hustled bucks in bus depots, train places and at hotels. A barbershop looked only half-dressed if it didn't feature a guy shining shoes.

Kids hawked business on any street, setting up impromptu portable shops. You didn't need a license to smack polish on the leather, bang it with brush and cloth and charge two bits.

In the old days around Nevada, you could get a shine in Battle Mountain, or Lovelock, or in Eureka, Yerington or Minden. In Fallon, where the population was 1,500 as I was growing up, a fellow named Art held forth at old Nick Jesch's barbershop on Maine Street.

While Jesch dozed waiting for a head to shear, Art did land-office business, tucked away in a corner.

When you wanted gossip, news tips and laughs, you saw Art.

But shining shoes these days is not that great a business. Occasionally I'll pop into the Scissors & Comb Barber Shop on Lake Street for a trim, and edge over to Stanley Boweak's shoeshine setup. He's a wonderful professional bootblack, a friendly, quiet man. But I've yet to hear that his business is swell. Stan simply isn't into expanding the facts.

Same for Sol Dartch, who has a stand in the lower level of Harrah's Reno. Sol's been at Harrah's 15 years. Business hums upstairs at the gaming tables and slots. However, Sol's business is slow. Each time I ask, it's slower.

Things have changed so much!

Guys shine their own footgear, or don't shine 'em at all. Or shoes nowadays don't take a shine. Try smearing paste on suede and you're aiming the shoes to ruin. Folks wander in, and automatically Stanley and Sol cast their eyes downward. If you want to see grown men cry, just take a peek when folks are wearing

244

sandals, tennis shoes or walking barefoot.

But Reno's newest bootblack isn't shedding a tear. Aileen Martin aims to batter down the notion that bootblacks can't make it in a big way.

At her two-seat stand on the ground level at Cannon, Martin is stopping traffic with her engaging chatter, the snap-crackle-pop of her flashing brushes and rags, and a string of one-liners that doesn't let up from the time she opens for business at 7 a.m. until she shuts down some 12 hours later.

Jan. 23, 1990

Reno Man Hunts Down Spot for Costner Film

IT'S TRUE THAT Hollywood doesn't award an Oscar to the foremost location manager.

But it also is a fact that no matter how superb the screenplay, the acting and direction, you don't necessarily get a winner without an outstanding person to manage the moviemaking locale.

If such an Oscar were given, a surefire contender this year would be a man reared and educated in Reno. Tim Wilson, 34, still makes his home here with his wife, Denise, and son, Alexander. But for much of the past two years, he was deeply involved in the creation of *Dances With Wolves*.

The current hottest guy in moviemaking, Kevin Costner, picked Wilson to be the epic film's location manager. Costner directed the movie and stars in it. *Dances*, with a final budget of $18 million, has done close to $50 million in gross revenues to date. It continues to pull in sizable crowds at the Granada in Reno and at the UA Sparks Cinema.

If you had told Tim Wilson 10 years ago that he would be part and parcel of the Hollywood scene, he'd have laughed in your face. In 1980, Wilson was still a year away from getting his psychology degree at the University of Nevada, Reno. The Wooster High School graduate was then uncertain of precisely what he would be doing after his UNR days.

But 1980 was the year Costner came to Reno to film a portion of *Double Down* (since retitled, *Stacy's Knights*), a gaming movie in which Reno Little Theater founder Edwin Semenza had a role. I remember Semenza telling me back then, "Watch this Costner. He's a young man who's going places."

Tim Wilson had that sense about Costner, too, and also about

Double Down location manager Jim Wilson. The two Wilsons became fast friends after a first meeting over dinner. This is the Jim Wilson who is such a dynamic partner in Costner's TIG company, which produced *Wolves*.

Tim Wilson has been associated with Costner and Jim Wilson since he got his UNR degree. "Essentially, we've been starving moviemakers," the Nevadan explains. But Costner's rise has been meteoric. He's taking people he can trust onward and upward with him, Tim Wilson among them.

Wilson's next likely linkup with TIG Productions and Costner probably will be with a movie titled *Mic*, still in the writing stage. The story is centered around Michael Collins, a founder of the Irish Republican Army. Filming will be in Ireland.

Wilson was present at the creation of *Dances with Wolves* in Los Angeles, as TIG colleague Michael Blake wrote it. The book now tops the *New York Times* bestseller list. Costner, who believes innovation through risk will be rewarded, was persuaded that a movie had to be made from Blake's book. Blake also wrote the screenplay.

Filming location was of paramount importance, as TIG moved forward to sympathetically portray the plight of Native Americans, as they were oppressed by 19th century white people and events.

Wilson, given the location manager assignment, painstakingly drove Plains states routes between the Mexican and Canadian borders.

His scouting recommendation: "South Dakota ought to be the place." Wilson brought along pictures to support his recommendation. Thus, South Dakota is the locale of all footage, including the movie's dramatic Civil War battle opening.

The film was made over six-and-a-half months in central and western South Dakota, not many miles from Pierre and Rapid City.

Wilson, working 80-hour weeks and using two assistants, managed a multitude of tasks, including feeding, housing and the erection of huge tents to house hairdressing, makeup and costuming. He prepared South Dakotans early for the Hollywood invasion. "Yet I'm not sure they were fully prepared when our 40 semi-trucks rolled in," Wilson says.

247

It was a long, tough haul, the greatest challenge of Wilson's life. He saw his wife just twice over a half-year. Prairie winds tormented the entire crew. So did Dakota snow. But in the end, after all the shooting (eight hours of film was distilled to the final three hours), Tim Wilson knew that *Dances with Wolves* would touch millions of lives, enriching us with its powerful truth.

He was a vital part of that truth as location manager, and in another way. In a flashback to the girlhood of the character played by leading lady Mary McDonnell, Wilson portrays her father, who is slain by Indians. Costner put Wilson in the film as another way of thanking him for a job well done.

Dec. 30, 1990

Journalism Hero Graces Us with Some of His Pearls _____

I'D WALK 100 MILES to hear Frank McCulloch speak about newspaper journalism, for of all the print media talent in our nation, this is the fellow who tops all. Furthermore, he's true-blue Nevada, a Fernley kid who reached the journalism big time, but who has not been spoiled by the heights.

McCulloch will appear as keynoter Friday at a Peppermill luncheon put on by the Reno Ad Club and four other organizations that relate to marketing, advertising and communications. The public is welcome.

McCulloch, 71, retired at midyear as managing editor of *the San Francisco Examiner*. Such is his celebrity that a retirement party to end all parties saluted him. Co-masters of ceremony were premier columnists Jack Smith of the *Los Angeles Times* and Herb Caen of the *San Francisco Chronicle*.

But it was McCulloch who was the star of the show. His gospel-according-to-McCulloch went straight to the heart of what newspaper people ought to be doing for readers. Among admonitions to his audience of contemporaries:

• Some newsrooms are so far removed from real life that we couldn't find our way to it with guide dogs.

• Editors have been talking to each other in great, pear-shaped phrases, which we then publish as great pear-shaped abstractions, when what our readers really want to know is why the chuckholes in the street haven't been filled.

249

• We tell readers about the socioeconomic implications of a debate in Botswana; what they really want to know is what the guy next door sold his house for. We feed them quiche and Evian water. They want hamburgers and Coke.

McCulloch graduated in journalism from the University of Nevada in 1941 and has spent the ensuing half-century learning his craft and teaching others how to publish meaningful newspapers.

The former *Reno Evening Gazette* sports editor, then *Gazette* reporter, went on to a distinguished career with *Time-Life*, producing many *Time* magazine cover stories.

He was the last journalist to interview Howard Hughes, an exclusive the reclusive billionaire would grant only to McCulloch.

He was night managing editor of the *Los Angeles Times* when then-young publisher Otis Chandler was seeking the innovative young leaders who would transform the metropolitan giant into a first-rate newspaper.

He was Far East bureau chief for *Time-Life* during the Vietnam War.

I shall not forget what my dear friend, Ron Einstoss, the late *Gazette-Journal* publisher, said of McCulloch. Einstoss, before joining us in Reno, covered the Los Angeles County Hall of Justice for 10 years. For much of that period in the 1960s, McCulloch was the rising star. Said Einstoss: "Everybody wanted to work with Frank because he was the best newspaperman anywhere."

McCulloch's message on Friday ought to be right down the alley of the people who are publishing today's *Gazette-Journal*. We are embarked on a self-started crusade to give readers more of what they want and need, and numerous community meetings are in progress to help us define that mission.

What Frank McCulloch is likely to include Friday is something he shared at his retirement party in Los Angeles:

"We admit the free press is not what it should be. But the inescapable truth is, it's all we've got. For better or worse, so long as this remains an open society, you and we—a free people and a free press—are stuck with each other. Shouldn't it behoove both of us to try to understand each other better?"

Aug. 18, 1991

250

Many Years, Many Words, from Just One Pen

FALLON—In 1925, Allene Baumann was 19, single and had lived in Fallon for all of seven years. The rural Georgia girl moved here with her parents in 1918, the year the "war to end all wars" ended.

Calvin Coolidge was president in '25 and he didn't say much, then or later. They called him "Silent Cal" for good reason.

Allene Baumann was pretty quiet until 1925, too. But suddenly, her pen commenced to chatter a lot. She started saying many things, for many people. All in print. And for what became an apparent record span for a continuously published Nevada column.

In 1925, the weekly *Fallon Eagle* asked her to temporarily write the Harmon District news. This would be "just until the regular correspondent had her baby."

The lady had the baby. But she never wrote again.

Allene Baumann didn't quit talking to people in print until a few weeks ago.

A month after she wrote her first column, she married Louis Baumann (1896-1957), a Churchill County rancher. She kept house and raised four children.

Until now at 86, she never halted her prodigious output.

She wrote millions of words about generations of Churchill people, filling the column with the stuff of life.

People's life journeys. What befell them along the way.

I don't think a longevity tally is kept on column-writing Nevadans.

We do know that Mark Twain lasted one year with the *Terri-*

torial Enterprise on the Comstock. He left to become famous.

The Rollan Melton column passed its 14th anniversary last October. Is this a longevity big deal? Compared to what Mrs. Baumann has done, I'm a speck in a column bucket.

Allene Baumann has retired her column in the *Lahontan Valley News* after an incredible 67 uninterrupted years of writing.

Her agile mind still crackles with wisdom and humor and the fondest remembrances of past Fallon newspaper colleagues.

Today, many wars and decades later, America has itself a new president, a verbal young chap named Bill Clinton. The year he was born, Mrs. Baumann turned 40 and had been writing a newspaper column for 21 years. She can't help but draw a contrast to the American leader back in '25.

If her eyesight had only cooperated, she would have kept writing through a few more Silent Cals and Verbal Bills.

She kept writing in her neat longhand—she never took up typing—until her final column, published on Jan. 2.

It wasn't hard for her to think. But she was using a magnifying glass to read and to proofread her writing. So she decided to call it a career.

In her farewell, to hear her tell it, it was the readers who did all the work for three score and seven.

In fact, it was Mrs. Baumann, soliciting news, handling phone calls, talking to folks, for all those tens of thousands of days.

On a recent weekday afternoon, she told me her long news watch has been a real adventure. "Most of all," she said, "It was great fun."

Her advice for young journalists? "Stay with it. That applies to all career paths."

What is news? Answering instantly, she said, "News is everything of consequence.

"I hate to give up writing news. I love news."

Jan. 24, 1993

252

Half-Way Club Brings out Poet in Some People

SOME OF NEVADA'S most eloquent poets can't differentiate between meter and a declarative sentence. They didn't win their degree from Poetry College, or matriculate to doctoral work at Literature University.

Such poets won't have words etched in marble, or printed for all time in books. They will neither be in the Nevada Writers Hall of Fame, nor be cited as Distinguished Nevadans, nor be declared Laureates.

All they do is let out what's in their hearts, to be heard, recited—most often by poet himself, herself, themselves. They write elegantly, simply, and the tumbling words flow most richly when they can feel, touch and embrace the subjects they love.

Charlie Flores is day bartender at Casale's Half-Way Club, 2501 E. Fourth St., west of Sparks, east of Reno. The little restaurant-bar is where some of the best pasta this side of Rome is savored. The club has existed since September 1937.

Inez Casale Stempeck is a lovely, sensitive, workaholic, long-widowed Sparks native who has traits that should be chiseled on Permanent Mount, where we might study, memorize and attempt to imitate them.

Traits such as staying power, integrity, work ethic, Stand By Your Kids and Your Friends; mottoes such as "treat the customers right and they'll be back."

She remembers people's names, and the times they became parents, and how happy they were the day they wed. She strokes the poor woman who married a guy who has betrayed her. Inez regularly spreads genuine charm by building her friends' self-esteem.

Bartender Flores works with janitor-dishwasher Erik Madden, and the guys and girls who cook, pour drinks, serve food—and forcefully take car keys away from an occasional diner-driver who can't find his hunkers with both hands. Customers line up for great food, at prices everyone can afford, unless they've been living cold and hungry along the Truckee; or their last Social Security check came back in January.

Inez Stempeck, 64, isn't a poet. She continues to cook 100 percent of the Half-Way Club's food. Her face wasn't typecast in Hollywood, she does not get her hair done at a salon each week. Inez dashes so hard from kitchen to dining room to bar, from patron to patron, that she resembles a marathon woman dispensing pizza, spaghetti and love, along her daily 26-mile work run.

Poet of the Club is bartender Charlie Flores, 45, Inez's son. Tony, 34, is head bartender. She had six of her own, plus an adopted son. Her husband and their father, Steamboat Stempeck, former all-Navy defensive football star, was hit by his first heart attack, and his last, in 1969. Gone forever at 45.

Inez Casale Stempeck, without a husband these 21 years, has carried on with her legion of family and friends and beloved customers.

A month ago, day bartender Charlie sat down and, in minutes, wrote a poem. Printed neatly, in his hand, it is posted on the club's west wall, at the kitchen entrance.

My friend, Debbie Brander, told me that Nevada poet Charlie Flores has written this:

"The Club: I'm sitting in the middle table in this little pub called the Half-Way Club. I look at the folks that are gathered here—they know, as I do, that love is near.

"The people, they speak of Old Times, and new, and they laugh and jest and rekindle anew, that sacred gift that blesses this place, the kindred spirit that engulfs our face.

"We smile, we laugh, we cry at times, with a special feeling that is in our minds. People live, people die, people come, people go. They all take, from this joint, I know it's so, a special gift. I think it's neat, from this simple place, on East Fourth Street."

April 4, 1991

Businesswoman a Worldwide Hit _____

Reno's Krestine Corbin looks like she was typecast in Hollywood.

Handsome, trim, fair-skinned, with blue eyes, she is a regal dresser who designs many of her own clothes—her 1978 book on fashions sold 200,000 copies worldwide. She is a gifted writer, a sought-after public speaker, an electronics whiz and an intuitive judge of who can do the job best.

Most of all, Corbin, a Reno native, is a brilliant entrepreneur. Under her hands-on leadership, her global company, Sierra Machinery, Inc., won 1989 honors as Nevada's No. 1 export business.

Corbin is president and CEO at the modest headquarters on Glendale Avenue. There, she and about 30 colleagues build a machine that keeps winning new buyers in the cost-conscious, productivity-minded manufacturing world.

The Sierra U.S.A. Skiving Roller Burnishing Machine—that's a mouthful. Put simply, this big dude is a state-of-the-art machine. It shaves and polishes the insides of metal cylinders used in hydraulic lifts.

The 50,000-pounder is an increasing hit with the makers of fork and marine lifts, dump trucks, bucketloaders and other construction equipment.

Sierra U.S.A. models range in price, with the crème de la crème as high as $500,000. Annual sales volume is in the millions.

On a recent day as I visited Corbin and team, I saw their typical energy. CEO Corbin glided around with the brisk step that is her trademark, tending to various tasks, like fielding a phone call from London, then one from Dublin.

Inventor Ron Porter, Sierra Machinery's veteran of some 30 years, showed me sophisticated equipment and, modestly, didn't say he has several patents pending. Nearby, electrical chief Larry Yount toyed with high-tech gadgetry.

Amid the swirl of productivity, office manager Mickey Jones shared insight into boss Corbin:

"Krestine has overcome any notion that a woman can't operate in such a specialized, traditionally male world."

Corbin has no female CEO counterpart in her field in the United States or in the world, and if being a woman in a man's world had any early drawbacks, she quickly thrashed them.

A family tragedy led Krestine Corbin, who is single and the mother of two daughters, into this phase of her life. Her brother, Larry Dickinson, just 44 when he died unexpectedly of natural causes in 1984, was a genius inventor and CEO of Sierra Machinery.

Corbin was a leading fashion expert and writer living in Manhattan and flying regularly to Europe. The only surviving sibling of a Nevada family that dates to 1864, the year we became a state, Corbin rushed home to a horrendous challenge— learning a complicated business on a crash basis.

Brother Larry had developed the big burnisher, but did not live to field-test it. It took his sister's vision, marketing savvy and courage to take Sierra to the world.

Corbin's organizational and marketing leadership, and her team's extraordinary production and maintenance reliability, have pushed Sierra's chief product to No. 1 in world market share.

By the mid 1980s, with America's manufacturing base dwindling, Corbin sensed "we had to sell overseas to survive." Now, more than 50 percent of Sierra Machinery sales are international.

Corbin wrote a tightly composed, effective script to back up a video promotion that was a major hit last month at a Chicago trade show. When John Deere Plow and Planter works of Moline, Ill., bought its second machine from the Nevadans, the acquisition instantly replaced 26 traditional honing machines.

From her office or her southwest Reno home, she speaks to the world by phone or fax.

"Always," office manager Jones declares, "Krestine is excited about her colleagues, their product and her customers."

As a student at the University of California, Davis, where she got her home economics degree in 1958, Krestine Dickinson Corbin was a national winner in a make-it-yourself-with-wool contest. It is clear that today she is honing a niche as No. 1 in a world that once was exclusive male territory.

Oct. 14, 1990

Nevada Star Wins Role on Broadway

NEVADA'S GIFTED singer-actress, Rebecca Judd, is thrilled by the kind of Christmastime news a star wishes for, but rarely hears.

The University of Nevada's best-known speech and drama graduate (1987) is returning to Broadway briefly, in a major role in the classic *Phantom of the Opera*.

Scores of stars have played the pivotal role of Madame Giry. Judd won the role on Broadway, with the blessing of Hal Prince, Tony Award-winning director of *Phantom*.

Judd appears Jan. 2-20, substituting for vacationing Leila Martin, who has performed the role on Broadway since 1988, when the show won eight Tonys.

Despite the brevity of Judd's appearance, this will be her most significant Broadway exposure. "I hope this will lead to fresh opportunities," she says.

Director Prince last saw the Nevada mezzo-soprano as Giry early this year at Orlando, Fla., in the show's third national touring production. He was pleased with her performance—and there's no more significant theater figure to impress than this influential man.

Judd is profoundly familiar with the Giry role: With the national company, she performed it more than 1,000 times, in 30 months. Giry wields a heavy staff in some scenes—the part is the most strenuous in the Andrew Lloyd Webber musical (next to that of the Phantom himself). Judd performed hurt many a time.

Undaunted, she signed two contract extensions with the company.

But finally, worn down by the demanding schedule, she left the show in mid 1995.

She later bought her first home in Red Bank, N.J., an easy train's commute to Manhattan. Now rested and in top shape, she was itching to get back into stage harness, when the Giry

258

call came.

Rebecca Judd first reached Broadway, understudying the beggar woman role in *Sweeney Todd*. Then she won a part in the Tony Award-winning *Secret Garden*, starring Mandy Patinkin. When she left the show in 1992, she had appeared as a dreamgirl 596 times, in 18 months.

Judd's unlikely Nevada-to-Broadway trail is the stuff prizewinning fiction is made of. Except this story is true.

Born in Fresno, Calif., in 1954, Judd moved with her family to Gardnerville when she was 12. As a girl, her singing was confined to church choirs.

Then came the miracle. She earned a role with Proscenium Players in Carson City, meeting the town's Ms. Showbiz, Maizie Jesse, who sensed Judd's potential.

Voice training began in 1980, and Judd's influential first coach, Susan Frank, helped Rebecca believe in herself. "If you're serious, you can become a professional," Frank said. Two years later, Judd heeded Frank's recommendation: Study voice with University of Nevada, Reno professor Ted Puffer.

At Nevada, she had challenging roles, blossoming rapidly under the excellent Nevada Rep directors, James Bernardi, Bob Dillard and David Anderson. Those who saw her as Miss Sara Brown in *Guys and Dolls* and Eva Peron in *Evita* still savor her exceptional performances.

Nevada speech and theater faculty veteran David Seibert, a longtime Judd mentor and fan, is thrilled by the latest *Phantom* news. "I couldn't be happier. They broke the mold when they made Becky Judd!" he beams.

Dec 24, 1995

Jefferson Lives again with Jenkinson ___

ON THURSDAY NIGHT, Clay Jenkinson will suit up in his breeches, colonial blouse and wig.

At 7:30, he will glide on stage at Nightingale hall at the University of Nevada, Reno campus, to present his Thomas Jefferson interpretation.

For those of us who cherish Jefferson lore, and the third president's genius, and his mystique, Jenkinson gives the ultimate gift. The University of Nevada professor has brought the famous American to Reno audiences many times. Awed listeners keep coming back for more.

Word of mouth attracts new fans. So does Jenkinson's monologue and question-answer sessions, heard Fridays on KOH-AM radio.

Unless I miss my guess, 615-seat Nightingale will be packed with adults who crave reaffirmation of Jeffersonian values; and with students who deserve intimacy with the man who wrote the nation's birth certificate—the Declaration of Independence.

Rhodes Scholar Jenkinson is electrifying in the Jefferson persona—I have seen this portrayal nine times, and always there are the fresh rewards and surprises, and a deepening appreciation of Jefferson's uniqueness. This is as entertaining as the best of Broadway. The ultimate American civics lesson without exam.

The Nevada Humanities Committee is presenting, "An Evening With Thomas Jefferson and Friends." It is a benefit for the Great Basin Chautauqua, the outdoor tent show at Rancho San Rafael Regional Park in July, featuring famous 19th century

260

visitors to Nevada. Jenkinson is founding director of the Chautauqua.

A scholar trained in literature and the classics, he speaks Jefferson's own words and the actual dialogue of Jefferson contemporaries. Audiences relate what is said to today's society.

Near the conclusion, Jenkinson, who has a photographic memory, moves out of character, giving a fascinating summarization.

Thursday's show may be the most significant Jenkinson has ever done—his Jefferson has appeared about 1,100 times, in more than 30 states. The big news is that this is a vital tune-up, before a lifetime dream comes true.

In 1989, in a first letter to me, Clay Jenkinson said, "My dream is one day to take Jefferson to the White House."

The dream comes true April 11, as the yearlong celebration of the 250th anniversary of Thomas Jefferson's birth comes to an end.

Jenkinson, as Jefferson, is to be the only presenter at the dinner gala for 250 guests, including Hillary and Bill Clinton; Tipper and Al Gore; 50 of the foremost Jefferson scholars; an expert in each Jefferson discipline—architecture, horticulture, education, civil liberties, press, religion, science, to name a few; also diplomats, cabinet members, leaders of Congress and the White House press corps.

A commemorative coin, struck by Congress to honor Thomas Jefferson's memory, will be unveiled.

The National Endowment for the Humanities is host.

Jenkinson will have 40 minutes to present Thomas Jefferson. He is certain to get a question or more from Bill Clinton, the 42nd president.

It could well be the third president replies to the 42nd, "My advice is to retire. Go read. Take up a farm in Arkansas."

March 21, 1994

261

Her Late Start Hasn't Slowed Reno Lawyer

NANCY LEE VARNUM has goals aplenty to sustain her through the new year, and over the long haul. But people who admire her and recognize her bright potential know she will measure up, as opportunities multiply.

The former corporate attorney for Harrah's has now struck out on her own, establishing a law practice in Reno. Earlier, she had done her clerkship with Washoe District Court Judge Brent Adams. Before she joined Harrah's in 1993, I asked Adams about her, and he gave a degree of praise he reserves for the best.

"Nancy (Varnum) is insightful, a scholar and wonderful personality," the jurist said. "She's a Mary Poppins, simply perfect in every way."

Varnum grew up in a hardworking blue-collar family. She didn't go to college until her two daughters were well into their own schooling. But since she unleashed her education commitment and formidable intellect, she's been unstoppable.

She graduated with high honors from Mercer University, Atlanta, in 1989. Next came a law education at highly regarded Emory University in Atlanta. She finished in 1992.

The Phi Kappa Phi scholar interned with the Internal Revenue Service, was a summer intern with Nevada Attorney General Frankie Sue Del Papa, then clerked for Adams.

Unexpectedly widowed in early 1994, she has carried on positively, with the can-do philosophy that's her hallmark.

The sensitive lawyer will focus on family practice. "There is a major need in our community for my specialty," she says. "I want to help people make a difference."

She reserves her deepest love and commitment for her daughters, who are in the high-achiever mold of mother.

Laura Arnold, 26, graduated from Cal-Western School of Law and, in October, passed the Nevada Bar examination. She also did a summer internship with Brent Adams. A mother-daughter law firm is rare. But don't be surprised if, one day, a Reno legal shingle says Varnum & Arnold. Or Arnold & Varnum.

Kristy Arnold, 23, is a University of Nevada mechanical engineering student, now doing her student work internship with Sierra Pacific Power Co. Mother chuckles and says, "Kristy just loves the hardhat and boots." She graduates this spring.

Nancy Lee Varnum began her higher education at an age once considered "too late." Her undergraduate studies were undertaken at 40; she was 44 when admitted to law school.

However, being a non-traditional student helped strengthen her determination.

She declares, "If you want it, you'll find a way. At first, I didn't have the financial resources. But I discovered that once you begin, resources are available." She took out loans to pay her way.

She will turn 50 on July 1 and is still whacking away at the high debt she had to assume.

Yet, the future is bright for the woman who has worked diligently to improve herself.

She is most cheerful about that big, wonderful, challenging world of today and tomorrow.

To her, there remain limitless avenues of learning, of professional expansion and of personal happiness.

The jurist, Brent Adams, said it so well of her in a letter of recommendation in 1993.

"Without exception, Nancy (Varnum) has been the finest law clerk I have ever employed."

Jan. 8, 1995

HEALTH AND OTHER HAZARDS OF LIVING

I'm Back in the Swing of Things _____

GOOD GRIEF, my dear friends! Just when lots of you were confident you'd gotten shed of me for good, I've forsaken my malingering. For 54 years, the newsroom has been my favorite workplace. Now I am back in here again. Happy days!

I last wrote you a personal note on Sept. 10. Three days later, I underwent open-heart surgery. Today's words will update you on why I've been missing in action this long.

This year, I was among the roughly 360,000 coronary bypass patients in America. In my life span, I busted many a health rule, believing that all I'd been hearing was applicable to the other guy. But to think, "Not me!" was a copout. Or as my sainted mother would put it, "Your excuses are a crock, Sonny boy."

Just in case you are prey to shaky lifestyle habits, as I was for too long, here is my advice. Following any or all could sharply reduce coronary surgeons' hefty workloads.

Advice: Avoid being overweight as one would the plague. Don't pig out. Exercise. Monitor your blood pressure. Work, yes. But savor playtime, too. It can help to avoid stress, of course. For God's sake, don't use tobacco. On Dec. 3 I reached my 20th anniversary as a non-smoker. A week ago, I asked my cardiologist, Dr. Stanley I. Thompson, what would have happened to me had I not given up tobacco. He instantly answered, "You'd be deader than a proverbial doornail."

My surgery occurred on Sept.13 at Sequoia Hospital in Redwood City, Calif. They put me to sleep with what a nurse told my wife, Marilyn, was the most potent dosage of "milk of amnesia." My two functioning coronary arteries were severely obstructed, reducing blood flow by some 80 percent.

Dr. Vincent Guadiani and his team sawed into my breastbone, pried open the rib cage with a steel retractor, and commenced the delicate follow-up. A foot-long incision was made on the inside of my right leg, below the knee a vein was "harvested" and used in two bypasses to reroute coronary blood flow. One coronary valve was replaced. A second was repaired.

The operation required nearly four hours and then they closed, sewing me up with my new foot-long "chest zipper."

They had me on some reluctant feet some 18 hours later, but the "milk of amnesia" so blanked me out that I barely recall the next three days. However, I do remember nurses repeatedly asking, "Rollie, tell us what city you're in." This is routinely done to assess whether you've been hit with a stroke. For the life of me, I couldn't remember "Redwood City." But I did shakily answer, "Some town about 30 miles south of San Francisco."

Total healing may require a full year. I've spent the past 16 weeks pretty much homebound. Now I feel energy anew and pledge to do my best for readers. And for myself, too.

Dr. Guadiani has operated on many northern Nevadans, more lately Tim Jones, director of arts at the University of Nevada, Reno. The doctor's humor matches his surgical brilliance.

A few years ago, after he performed open-heart surgery on Reno's Mrs. Harry (Ann) Parker, she asked details. He answered, "We've given you a pig valve." Shocked, she said, "This can't be. I am Jewish, you know!"

Not to fret," Guadiani, replied, backtracking. "We've given you a kosher valve."

Dec. 24, 2000

Poking Fun at Fear of Needles _____

IT IS SUMMER 1950. I've just turned 19. In another month, I'll drive to Reno to enroll as a freshman at the University of Nevada.

I have never had a physical examination and my mother feels I should affirm my good health before I leave. She makes an appointment for me at the new Fallon Clinic. I cheerfully check in and the new young doctor in town, A.J. Dingacci, finds me fit, then says, "Just one more thing. We'll draw some blood and check it out."

He hauls out this needle. I turn pale around the gills. I make the mistake of gazing at the needle as it slithers into my arm. Then it is over. He puts the billing statement in my quaky palm. I still remember his words, "You can pay the $5 up in the front office."

I shakily walk out of his exam room and into a hallway. There I faint. I am just regaining consciousness as they haul me into a chair. A nurse tries to suppress a giggle and I ask, "What's funny?" She says, "Sorry, but you just don't look like the type."

In the ensuing half-century, I have feared few men and even fewer beasts. But the blood-getters, as I call laboratory technicians, give me the chilly-willies.

I am afflicted with needle-phobia. As an undergrad, I check into the campus infirmary with a bad cough. They stick a needle in me and I faint. I visit my diabetic father in summertime and have to sprint from the room as he gives himself insulin shots.

While I'm serving in the U.S. Army in Kansas, the birth of our second son is imminent. The military hospital staffer tells me, "Your wife is RH-negative, so we'll have to check your blood type."

"No problem," I chirp. "It's right here on my dog tag. O-Positive." But the hospital staffer insists, "We must do our own blood work."

I put on the big stall, knowing my veins will again play hide-and-seek when the guy in the white jacket stalks me. I stall until

269

Marilyn is close to nine months pregnant. The unrelenting Army calls again. "If you get your blood checked, your total hospital bill will be only $7.50. Otherwise, your wife will have to give birth in the public hospital and it will cost you about $500."

I wobble into the Army lab.

"I'm a fainter," I tell the young tech. He pokes, jabs and prods. I am not aware of all his probes because I've fainted.

The baby is born in the Army hospital on a Friday the 13th, and it is our lucky day until Marilyn suggests we name him Lance. I shudder. It can't be Lance. That could always remind me of needles. We name the baby Wayne.

Even after all these years, my phobia taunts me. I have yet to meet a lab technician who looks happy. In London, where in January I am hospitalized, the techs have those mournful faces you see on the Easter Island statues.

It is in England that I tell my cardiologist it is nearly impossible to draw blood from my arms. His reply sounds sinister. "No problem. We can get it from veins in your groin." I hurriedly plead, "Keep using my arms."

One early morning on the other side of the Atlantic Ocean, I tell a visiting nurse from Australia what a pity it is that I suffer needle-phobia. She refuses me an ounce of sympathy. Instead, she orders, "Lad, don't get your knickers in a twist."

After my later release from Saint Mary's Regional Medical Center in Reno, my cardiologist, Dr. Stanley I. Thompson, apologizes and says, "I realize your anxiety, but we have to continue blood tests to determine whether the medications are doing their work. Just tell the lab techs to use the smallest needles."

So, in my most recent visit to the lab, I remain the natural-born coward. I advise the tech, "I sometimes faint. My doctor suggests you use the tiniest needle you have."

She replies, "Yes. The ones we use on big babies."

April 23, 2000

270

Reaching a New Summit _____

IF YOU HAD PREDICTED 18 months ago that I would climb Mount Rose on July 24, 1991, my 60th birthday, I'd have laughed and suggested you undergo analysis.

My reaction to such an improbable forecast would have made sense because, one-and-a-half years ago, my legs and lungs had taken early retirement, never to serve me rigorously

again. Or so I had convinced myself. I couldn't, or wouldn't, walk a slow mile without resting frequently.

A San Francisco visit was acceptable, provided I got to ride over those hills. I loathed stairs. Years before, as a high school and college athlete, I had been superbly conditioned. But later, I let poor nutrition and a sedentary life be my companions. Between their stealth and my growing sloth, I nearly got myself killed.

When we are young, we don't believe those good health messages are applicable to us. Sometimes we must be beaten to a pulp to get the message.

I was in my 50s when poor habits began to beat me up. Live on the dodge and eventually you can't dodge the big ones.

I had quit smoking for good in 1980, but remained overweight and inactive physically. Two years later, at 50, I had a heart attack. Then, in 1984, I was down with lymphatic cancer. But chemotherapy and radiation therapy saved me.

In my effort to be a bionic man, I also had two cataract sur-

271

geries, a hernia repair, a four-day hospital stay with coronary fibrillation (sorry you had to join the club, Mr. President) and a 28-day stay in Saint Mary's Regional Medical Center, isolation, when my white-cell count dived perilously low.

I'm not listing this health scorecard to get your sympathy. I brought most of this on myself. Be warned, however. Maybe you can learn from this. I finally did.

Eighteen months ago, after many failed diets, I at last signed up for Saint Mary's Optifast weight-management program. My weight fell away steadily, aided immeasurably by my now-daily walking ritual. I was down 80 pounds at one juncture. I have maintained my weight over the past year; my net loss is 72 pounds.

Three months ago, my cardiologist, Dr. Stanley I. Thompson, put me on a mechanized treadmill for my annual stress test. I stayed on just short of exhaustion. He said I did OK—at least better than expected for a man of 59.

I told him I hoped to get into good enough condition to do what I once believed impossible—climb Mount Rose, the queen of our territory, with the highest summit around Lake Tahoe.

"Go for it if you wish," he answered.

Before leaving, I asked, "What is likely to ultimately take me out for the final count?" He looked at me evenly and replied quickly. "It probably will be a heart attack."

But then Dr. Thompson grinned and said, "If you continue to take care of yourself, and have a little luck, we'll try to make sure that doesn't happen 'til you're 99."

I worked harder to get in condition for Mount Rose. To be in shape for hills, one must hike hills. Rollan Melton, who a few years ago never met an elevator he didn't like, lately has been tackling the hills, especially in the still-undeveloped ground above Caughlin Ranch.

The question was when to take on Mount Rose, which is 10,776 feet high.

My wife, Marilyn, settled matters. "Climb it on your birthday! That way, you'll always remember how you spent your 60th."

Before I could protest with an "I'm not ready yet," she had invited friends to join us on the hike.

Last Wednesday, at 8:30 a.m., we (wife, son Kevin, and nine

friends) began our climb about three-tenths of a mile west of the Mount Rose Highway summit.

The top of Mount Rose was ahead, 2,256 feet up. It took us four hours to reach our destination. The trip is not for those who are faint of heart or legs. Switchbacks helped immensely. I didn't go up there to baby myself. Yet I wasn't about to try a foolish footrace, either. Frequent pauses to see the gorgeous sights provided welcome rest.

Our little band strung out and I fell back, as I had expected. But even during the toughest final mile, above the tree line where the temperature is cooler and the air thinner, I felt the thrill of achieving what I once thought beyond my capacity.

I saw during the climb, and understand more clearly now, that it wasn't merely a physical achievement I had sought. Breaking down barriers is mental, too. To refuse to believe we can do something is to deny ourselves a banquet on the other side.

I was dead last to the top, but it was being there with family and friends that was the joy. I arrived at turtle's speed, but they cheered me in as though I was Edmund Hillary, putting down a flag atop Mount Everest.

The Mount Rose adventure reinforced a growing belief. The mountain, and climbing it, becomes a symbol. Indeed, we must work to extend the good years and their vitality.

I can't buy Seneca's line, "Old age is an incurable disease." I do embrace what my Mount Rose fellow hiker-friend, Robert Pearce, declares, "Never think of getting older. Age has nothing to do with numbers."

As to the future, let us contemplate the birthday greeting sent me by Debbie and Alan Squailia:

"Tomorrow is an unanswered question, a new challenge to face, a new adventure to explore."

July 30, 1991

If Only We Could Be Wise but Not Old

WEDNESDAY was the 149th anniversary of Brigham Young's arrival at the Great Salt Lake. Thus, Mormons forever celebrate July 24 as Pioneer Day.

Because I was born on it, it once seemed that I might be a logical recruit for the Church of Jesus Christ of Latter-day Saints.

When I was 17, a Fallon schoolmate, Lorna Jones Bowler, regularly invited me to church. I went steady for awhile—to church, but not with Miss Jones. However, being incorrigible or unrecruitable, or both, I didn't sign up. She married a Mormon boy and they had eight children.

As for me, I ultimately married Marilyn. My other unshakable bond has been to the newspaper field. Will people keep reading papers? Not if someday they give up their interest in life.

Anyway, Time Marches On, as Lowell Thomas used to say, and does anyone under 55 remember him? As of Wednesday, I turned 65. Wife Marilyn, peering at me for signs of new aging, asked, "How do you feel?" Lacking any fresh and original answer, I thought up this one: "Same as yesterday, but now a day older."

There are obvious advantages now. A 19-year-old colleague opened a door for me on Monday. On Tuesday, Richard Rowley, who is older, but more nimble, out-sprinted me for the luncheon check.

Now, I don't need to lie about my age to get the senior discount. Hey Mom, I made it! In observance of my three score and five, Don Dondero did a fly-over, dropped leaflets and took photographs as I lumbered after them. I had hoped for a money-drop.

Instead, I found only black-bordered "Geezerhood" paperwork. An advantage of column-writing is that I can share the truth. Honk if you know that Dondero was born on Jan. 31, 1920.

Gloria Luongo, the younger, sent a card, "Ya get a little older, ya get a little wiser and it's a lousy tradeoff." Fred Davis Jr., a few years my senior, says I may now prime the Social Security pump

274

any time I wish. "It's about time the government did something for you," Davis Jr. said.

Friends, taking note of my milestone, have reacted kindly. A thoughtful Pooh Bear's lovely care package contained a homemade muffin. A pal enlightened me with Furman "Brud" Arthur's column, composed back East, before he moved to Reno. Writing about the rewards of age, he declared, "I have decided that I no longer suffer fools, or bores, or false friends. There simply isn't time."

I have taken note of those who earlier reached milestone birthdays. Tom Brokaw, attaining 50, said, "An occasional octogenarian will say, 'Listen here, young man, when I was your age . . .' That's comforting if you spend all your waking hours with octogenarians."

Herb Caen did a piece when he turned 75 five years ago, and closed with, "The good news is that this is the last column I will ever write about my age. However, if I make it to 100, all bets are off."

My memories of the years it took to earn an occasional "Sir" salutation are coated with gold. Plus realism.

Long ago, I learned I wouldn't be an All-America center from Wolf Pack Land. Instead, I later coached a U.S. Army football team. After that infamous season (3 wins, 8 losses and 1 scruffy tie), I regularly invoked the excuse, "We suffered serious injuries and unfortunate bad hops." I don't remember ever admitting my team would have done great if only it had been blessed with a superior coach.

Speaking of blessings:

I have amassed a gorgeous family, and a batch of outstanding friends. I continue to rely on all for support, and the hard truth. People seem to figure I am now old enough to accept the hard stuff.

In another year, I'll reach my 50th year in journalism. Now, that's a milestone I look forward to. One of these years, I expect to really get the hang of what I'm supposed to be doing.

I can hardly wait to find out what those tomorrows bring.

July 25, 1996

275

Weigh-in: Where the Real Fight Is _____

WEIGHT LOSS is a fetish in our size-conscious society, but seldom more so than when a class reunion draws near.

It seems that the male is much less rabid about how he looks, as opposed to yesteryear; but females, assuming they've let excess weight hide their younger interiors, are more anxious about how classmates will view them. So pre-reunion shedding of girth can be close to an obsession.

But impending reunions don't give me the heebie-jeebies nearly as much as that other anxious time: weighing in at my physician's office, as the prelude to my semi-annual physical examination.

My moment of truth occurred last Monday.

The medicine man in charge of my life is Dr. Stanley I. Thompson, champion cardiologist of the Western World. We first met in the intensive care unit at Saint Mary's Regional Medical Center. The date was June 26, 1982. The doctor didn't pussyfoot around.

"You have had a heart attack," he declared. "You do have the prospects of a sound recovery, if you follow certain procedures." He put strong emphasis on weight loss, and in the ensuing 14 years, he has constantly reemphasized that need.

"It is really quite elementary," preaches the slim-trim Dr. Thompson, who has a body-fat percentage of maybe 2. "The less there is of you, the more efficient your heart will work for you."

Back to Monday.

The appointment was at 1:15 p.m., but my preparation began from the time my feet hit the floor. You'd of thought I was gearing for the weigh-in prior to a prizefight. Matter of fact, no patient I know of relishes a weight lecture from the physician.

Breakfast was slim and almost none, a Calcutta starve-in, you might call it. I gulped about enough liquid to quench a sparrow's thirst. I loitered around the bathroom but there really wasn't much reason to.

At the *Gazette-Journal* that morning, I was the epitome of a non-food saint. No decaf coffee, no journeys to the water trough, no furtive trips to the employee lunchroom, where myriad concessionaire goodies have too often won out over my good judgment.

To avoid keeling over from the absence of calories, I took my lunch at 11:30 a.m.: one itsy-bitsy apple, which I nibbled down to the core. Only the seeds escaped unharmed.

Instead of working on the following Thursday's column, I walked a few laps inside the newspaper building—maybe 1.5 miles—hoping to shrink away a few more ounces. Then, between stops at the men's room (I shouldn't have bothered), I systematically began stripping away anything of weight.

Before the drive to cardiologist Thompson's office on West Sixth Street, I stashed my wallet, retaining only my driver's license.

Off came my rings, my watch; and out of trousers came the pocket comb. While dressing for work earlier, I had thought of not wearing undershorts, but jettisoned that idea for fear I might have an accident en route to the doctor's office, giving ambulance drivers a hearty laugh.

I was into Thompson's waiting room early enough to make two bathroom runs—nothing doing, though. Confucius say, "Man who doesn't drink finds no need to tinkle."

Nurse Betty Jo McIntosh summoned me from waiting area to scales. "They want you weighed with shoes on." I marched in barefoot, put my shoes aside, and she seemed not to notice. I gingerly stepped on the upright scales, which shuddered a bit, then revealed my weight. (Sorry, dear reader, this is a privileged statistic, known only to my trusted doctor and me.)

I was hoping that Dr. Stanley I. Thompson, cardiologist extraordinaire, would praise my freshly recorded weight. Instead, he said, "Rollan, you're down five pounds since your last visit. You'll have to concentrate on doing better."

Oct. 21, 1996

He's Youthful in His Looks and State of Mind

RICHARD B. ROWLEY, the Reno developer, Realtor and ever-youthful slip of a lad, last January lumbered into his doctor's office for an annual physical exam.

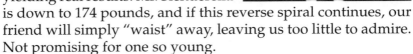

"As the nurse weighed me, I glanced down to see if she had her foot on the scale," he says with a laugh. "She didn't. I had hit my all-time high of 195 pounds."

Rowley has since denied himself ice cream, topped with hot fudge, and has sworn off all other food vices. For exercise, he rattles through his neighborhood on a rickety bike that's only a smidgen younger than he.

His weight-management plan is yielding real results. Mr. Slenderella is down to 174 pounds, and if this reverse spiral continues, our friend will simply "waist" away, leaving us too little to admire. Not promising for one so young.

Dick Rowley and I have long talked about his age, this subject having sprung eternal years ago when I wrote that, "Dick is youthful."

Most people don't save a Melton column clipping more than a second, let alone a day. However, Rowley, unlike the average young person, is an incurable saver, especially of written testimonies about his young looks.

He has clung to the "he is youthful" allegations as though they were chiseled on a biblical tablet. Reno's answer to Dick Clark still hauls around the tattered, yellowing piece of newsprint. Since its publication, he has worn out four wallets, and retains the clipping in the fifth.

278

Given the slightest excuse, he produces the faded column item, showing it to friends who wonder about his age. "See here," he appeals. "This affirms I am young!"

As another of his multiplying birthdays approaches (Aug. 5), this bachelor youth now begs me, "Don't publish my age. My girlfriends think I'm younger."

Of course, I am a kinder, gentler columnist than old Cory Farley. Thus, I shan't reveal how many calendars have collected moss since Rowley's birth year, it being the same year that Lindbergh flew to Paris, Babe Ruth rocketed 60 homers into orbit, and Dempsey again lost to Tunney.

The youthful Rowley picture seen here was taken when he ran for the state Senate. I forget the exact year, but I am advised by historians that the race occurred after Grant captured Richmond, and before Bill Raggio won his second term as district attorney. Fortunately, Rowley lost his Senate campaign, thus adding many happy years to his still young life.

Incidentally, this Aug. 5 also will be the 31st anniversary of the day our still-young photographer, Marilyn Newton, finally found permanent work at Reno's leading morning newspaper.

Aug. 5 also is the birthday of Reno's Elaine Bell, a former Miss Maine, who is chronologically younger, verily, I say, much, much younger than Dick Rowley.

But on the matter of age, Rowley, the philosopher, quotes a wise man: "Don't regret growing older. It's a privilege denied to many."

With that, one of Nevada's foremost raconteurs tells me a story, a dandy rib-splitter, and one that he will be pleased to share in certain unmixed company. It's called the "Moral of the story."

July 17, 1994

279

Too Many Memories to Remember _____

TODAY IS THE 125th anniversary of the *Reno Gazette-Journal*. I've been aboard nearly 38 of those years. So here is my personal

Murray

waltz down our newspaper lane, recalling stories and episodes, major and mostly minor, and remembering some past and present colleagues.

Most memorable visitor: I was *Gazette* editor in 1965 when a bearded man, wearing only a bathrobe and sandals, burst into my office, shook hands and declared, "I am Jesus Christ. Get out your big type."

Best nickname invented by a reporter: Thirty years ago, a nude man was stealing gaming chips from casinos night after night. Public interest zoomed after reporter Dewey Berscheid nicknamed the suspect, "Running Bare."

Most noted reporter free-fall: Ed Martinez won a major state press prize for the first story he ever wrote for us. He faded afterward but escaped obscurity by becoming a noted artist and University of Nevada art professor.

Most fierce butt-chewing: Reno was drenched by a spectacular mid '60s lightning storm. But we got not a single picture. Our chief photographer told publisher Charles G. Murray he had not gone outside, fearing his camera would get wet. My fear was that Murray would kill him.

Most traumatic time in newsroom: On my third day as the paper's managing editor, Nov. 22, 1963, when John F.

Kennedy was assassinated in Dallas.

Most shy eccentric: We were never able to get a decent picture of bizarre Reno multimillionaire LaVere Redfield. We tried, but he was all elbows and back. He once phoned and asked to come see me. But he made me promise to keep our photographers at bay. He pleaded that we give up trying for his picture. I turned down his request. We never did photograph him.

Toughest era: the Vietnam War before public sentiment turned against American involvement. Many people blamed the messenger press. One day, speaking to a Nevada journalism class, students hounded me into retreat. My wife, Marilyn, quit her bridge club in tears after other players violently denounced the newspaper and its "rogue editor, Melton."

Most lost soul: Marilyn Monroe, whom I encountered when she was in Reno, filming *The Misfits*. She was in tough shape and not in 1,000 years would I have recognized her on my own.

Most photogenic person: Marilyn Monroe. Reno photographer Don Dondero has said it was impossible to get a bad picture of her.

Few people I've met have been as fascinating as the Reno colleagues I've had since 1957, including:

The late editors:

• Paul A. Leonard—his constructive approach made the town feel good about itself.

• John Sanford—his voice was a cross between Andy Devine's and fingernails on a blackboard. Sanford had a rough exterior but was a pussycat within.

• Joseph R. Jackson was the tireless Iron Horse of Reno news executives. Joe was a great man, and so was Charlie Murray, fantastic editor-teacher. He was my foremost benefactor.

• Ty Cobb, now 80: I still see him hunched at his typewriter, sprinting to make a deadline.

• Bill Eaton: The late police reporter always suspected the "prime suspect was innocent."

Today's senior colleagues:

• Sharon Genung has been holding our clerical corps together since Aug. 12, 1963.

281

• Tim Anderson, versatile reporter, is in his 28th year. Has done every task in the newsroom except clean his desk.

• Phil Barber, in his 25th year on the police beat; no law-enforcement reporter has served with more distinction.

• Bruce Bledsoe: The erudite editor of Opinion, in his 25th year. The eloquent writer takes noontime hikes to rev up his journalism lung power.

• Marilyn Newton: In her 33rd year, mostly as a photographer. A sweetheart, with a brave heart.

• Steve Sneddon: A son of Kansas who stopped off in Idaho before starting his distinguished Reno sportswriter career 25 years ago.

Nov. 23, 1995

INDEX

List, Robert, 186
Little Waldorf, 223-24
Lombardi, Dr. Louis, 85
Lummus, Nola Kobler, 162-63
Manoukian, Don, 79
Mapes, Charles Jr., 228-29, 231, 234
Mapes Hotel, xxii, 47, 210, 222, 224-25, 228-30, 231-33, 235;
    Coach Room, 231-33; Sky Room, 224, 229, 235
Martin, Aileen, xxii, 243-45
Martin, Bernice, 243
Mason Valley News, 205-06
McCarran, Patrick, 200
McCloskey, Jack, 206, 215
McCulloch, Frank, 47, 249-50
McQueen, Robert, 188-89
Melton, Beulah ("Rusty"), 71-72, 267
Melton, Bronna ("Brownie"), 69-72
Melton, Marilyn, 12, 22-23, 99-100, 267, 270, 272, 274, 281
Melton, Rollan Sr., 67, 236-37
Miller, Robert, 51, 93
Misfits, The, 234-35, 281
Monroe, Marilyn, 234-35, 281
Moore, Archie, 202, 236-37
Motley, Marion, 193-94
Murray, Charles, 280
National Association for the Advancement of Colored People, 185
Nelson, Agnes, 88
Nevada State Museum, 94
Newton, Marilyn, 279, 282
O'Callaghan, Mike, 186
Piscevich, Margo, 77-78
Powers, Roy, 79, 198
Quinn, David and Sharon, 232
Raggio, Bill, 11, 93, 106-07, 221, 279
Raggio, Dorothy, 106-07
Randall, William, 164-65
Reagan, Nancy and Ronald, 49-50
Redfield, LaVere, 222-23, 227, 281
Reid, Harry, 56
Reno Arch, 222
Reno Little Theater, 56, 246
Reno-Sparks Convention & Visitors Authority, 57
Riverside Hotel, 47, 222, 229, 239
Roosevelt, Franklin D., 40

285